Constructing an Incarnational Theology

Why did Jesus come? The traditional argument is that he came to redeem us from sin and destroy death, and thus reverse the fall. Many have long found this unsatisfactory, because it centres human deficit, rather than divine abundance. In this study, Samuel Wells traces his notion of 'being with' right into the Trinity itself, and in dialogue with Maximus the Confessor, Duns Scotus and Karl Barth, among others, articulates a truly Christocentric theology in which God's means and God's ends are identical. In the process, Wells not only greatly expands the compass of 'being with', showing its scriptural and doctrinal significance, but also offers a constructive account of the incarnation, cross and resurrection of Jesus that out-narrates conventional atonement theories. Wells correspondingly proposes an account of sin, evil, suffering and death that accords with this revised understanding. The result is a compelling and transformational proposal in incarnational theology.

SAMUEL WELLS is Vicar of St Martin-in-the-Fields and Visiting Professor of Christian Ethics at King's College London. A regular contributor to 'Thought for the Day' on BBC Radio 4's *Today* programme, he has published forty-six books, including works on Christian ethics, mission, ministry, scripture, liturgy and preaching.

Constructing an Incarnational Theology

A Christocentric View of God's Purpose

SAMUEL WELLS
King's College London

CAMBRIDGE
UNIVERSITY PRESS

CAMBRIDGE
UNIVERSITY PRESS

Shaftesbury Road, Cambridge CB2 8EA, United Kingdom

One Liberty Plaza, 20th Floor, New York, NY 10006, USA

477 Williamstown Road, Port Melbourne, VIC 3207, Australia

314–321, 3rd Floor, Plot 3, Splendor Forum, Jasola District Centre,
New Delhi – 110025, India

103 Penang Road, #05-06/07, Visioncrest Commercial, Singapore 238467

Cambridge University Press is part of Cambridge University Press & Assessment, a department of the University of Cambridge.

We share the University's mission to contribute to society through the pursuit of education, learning and research at the highest international levels of excellence.

www.cambridge.org
Information on this title: www.cambridge.org/9781009492706

DOI: 10.1017/9781009492669

When citing this work, please include a reference to the DOI 10.1017/9781009492669

First published 2024

A catalogue record for this publication is available from the British Library.

A Cataloging-in-Publication data record for this book is available from the Library of Congress

ISBN 978-1-009-49270-6 Hardback

For my grandparents

Israel Morogowsky 1899–1963

and Eugenia Morogowsky 1901–67

Born in Kyiv; died in Kent.

Contents

Preface

I am most grateful to Peter McDonald and the McDonald Agape Foundation for offering me the opportunity of a research fellowship. I am very much indebted to +Sarah Mullally, Bishop of London, for persuading me to accept this offer, and for her generous encouragement. I am beyond thankful to my clergy colleagues, lay leaders, staff and congregation at St Martin-in-the-Fields for shaping their lives so as to invest in this project and take on the responsibilities I vacated to enable me to concentrate on it with my whole heart and mind.

Two people have shaped this study profoundly. Edwin van Driel's book *Incarnation Anyway* was vital in helping me conceive the project, and his kind interest, critical interaction and companionship have been a source of inspiration throughout. Geoffrey Ready engaged with my work from afar for a long period, and wrote to me to point out that I had neglected the Orthodox tradition in ways he made explicit. His support and insight have been hugely appreciated.

Farley Lord and Rebecca Bridges kindly studied the chapters closely as they were written and provided thoughtful, engaging and imaginative responses and suggestions. I am very much in their debt. Farley also provided the index. Robert Pfeiffer also engaged in stimulating ways with the project once it was largely complete.

I am very glad for those who made my study period in Durham, North Carolina, such a rewarding one. Meghan Benson, Rick Wilfong, Ira Mueller, Paige Fisher, Patti Paine, Norman Wirzba, Gretchen Ziegenhals, Kavin Rowe and Stanley Hauerwas, together with Katie Benjamin and her team at Duke Divinity School Library, each, in generous ways, shared resources, hospitality and ideas. I am also grateful to Zoe Lord, who kindly chased up sources I did not have close at hand.

My thanks to Jo, Laurence and Stephanie are never-ending; especially for their encouragement to take some time away to ponder and reflect, and their enthusiasm at every subsequent stage.

The book is dedicated to my maternal grandparents, whose courage, endurance and devotion to Christ knew no bounds. Their lives show me that there is no church without Israel, that faith is for sharing and that there is nothing that refines discipleship like persecution.

I refer in the text to a large number of historical sources, many of which use language that sits uncomfortably today. I have thus sought in the text to address linguistic imbalances. For example, I avoid male pronouns when referring to the Trinity as a whole, and have adjusted quotations where this is possible without revising the sentence structure. I prefer the term 'realm of God' to the implicitly masculine 'kingdom of God': I find 'realm' a more suitable rendering than 'reign', since it retains the hint of territory as well as authority. I have generally avoided the capitalisation of divine pronouns found in the more traditional sources. I spell 'church' in lower-case letters as penance for its many failings. I often use 'humankind' as a synonym for the more traditional 'man'; where 'men' means individual persons, I use the term 'human beings'. Except where otherwise specified, scriptural quotations are taken from the New Revised Standard Version.

Introduction: Making the Story New

Three times in the New Testament we hear the phrase 'before the foundation of the world'. We find it at John 17:24, Ephesians 1:4 and 1 Peter 1:20.[1] In each case it means the same thing: God chose to be incarnate in Jesus before there was any creation, because in Christ, God willed to be in relationship with us. Which means God's intention to become incarnate in Jesus was the reason for creation. All of which sounds fittingly Christocentric, until one realises what else it means, but does not actually say. And that is that Jesus could not have come to fix the results of the fall – because God's decision to become incarnate in Jesus was made before there ever was a fall.[2] So every theory that elaborates upon the conviction that Jesus had to die to fix the problem of evil, sin and death misses the crucial revelation made three times in the New Testament itself: that was not why Jesus came. Jesus came to be with us in time so that we could be with him forever.

This study seeks to work out the implications of this realisation. In doing so, it aims to overturn the anthropocentrism of so much theology and preaching. Popular Christianity often focuses almost

[1] John 17:24: 'Father, I desire that those also, whom you have given me, may be with me where I am, to see my glory, which you have given me because you loved me before the foundation of the world.' Ephesians 1:4: 'Just as he chose us in Christ before the foundation of the world.' 1 Peter 1:20: 'He was destined before the foundation of the world, but was revealed at the end of the ages for your sake.' See also John 17:5: 'Father, glorify me in your own presence with the glory that I had in your presence before the world existed.'

[2] It will be clear that this way of phrasing the matter imitates the language of Karl Barth – hence the use of the term 'decision', which is his terminology rather than mine. A consistent theme of the book is the degree to which I follow a number of Barth's distinctive theological moves, yet seek to make major revisions in his characterisation of reconciliation and eschatology. I do that in conversation with theologians of different eras and in developing constructive alternatives.

exclusively on human problems – mortality and guilt – that it looks to Jesus to fix. In this book I offer a theocentric account, based on God's purpose, and a Christocentric story, centred in God's purpose to be with us incarnationally in Christ and eschatologically forever. It is not that sin is underestimated – it is that overcoming sin is too short a story, and one that insufficiently attends to God's original and ultimate purpose.

There is an ecclesiology and a politics assumed in both the conventional account and my own. A church that claims to be able to determine who finds eternal life, by developing a particular theory of the atonement and by identifying what convictions and behaviours dovetail with that theory, is making an unwarranted bid for control – not just of human beings, but of divine purpose. By contrast a church that perceives God's original, unfolding and ultimate purpose as being with us in Christ redirects its attention to fostering relationships of being with God, one another and the creation as its principal form of ministry and mission. Meanwhile a church that perceives a narrow aperture to a specific understanding of salvation will have its eyes focused on getting the maximum number of people through the neck of that bottle; whereas a church that understands its calling as living God's future now will concentrate on modelling relations of trust, dynamism and wisdom and catalysing such interactions across all aspects of society, whether explicitly Christian or not.

I understand that my judgements on the reason for and significance of the incarnation constitute a case that needs defending and asserting on a number of fronts. I do that as follows.

In Chapter 1 I set out a summary of a truly incarnational theology. In doing so I touch on all the themes that will subsequently arise, and put them in a logical sequence. The questions raised by this summary are the ones I seek to address in the subsequent chapters: the summary is thus a taster for my whole argument. In addition, in the first chapter I elucidate seven principles that are derived from the summary and that guide my investigations and proposals in the rest of the book. This is a theocentric story that centres God's abundance, in contrast to the anthropocentric tendency of much theology, which introduces and comes to define God largely as the provider of the solution to human problems. It is a story whose beginning, middle and end are about Jesus, rather than one in which Jesus has a specific role to fix the human predicament. It is a story of God's sovereignty and freedom, not one in which God has to obey absolute laws around honour or justice. And it is a story in which God's means and ends are identical: there is no detour by which God achieves good things in a dubious way: God's who is characterised by how as much as by what and why. The first chapter is thus a challenge to which the subsequent chapters seek to rise.

Then I make a scriptural case for my proposal. Almost every theological account has to set different emphases and pronouncements of scripture alongside each other, and acknowledge that there are very few questions on which the Bible speaks with a single voice. Part of the task of the theologian is to pull strands together and highlight trajectories of thought, noticing correspondences and resonances and drawing inferences and interpretations – and then to set out thoughts in an ordered sequence that attends to the whole. This is what Chapters 2 and 3 seek to do. In Chapter 2 I consider what God truly wants for humankind and creation, and the ways Jesus' incarnation both embodies and advances that purpose. I discern three forms that purpose takes: covenant, community and communion. I then explore the scriptural and incarnational grounding of these three themes. What these themes have in common is that they are both means and ends: they model in temporal existence the character of eternal essence, being with God forever. While it would be oversimplifying to ascribe the three terms respectively to Israel, church and eschaton, because they overlap so greatly, nonetheless such an ascription highlights the comprehensiveness of the three terms in their rendering of God's unfolding purpose for how people are to respond to divine initiative. This also entails an account of where and how evil, sin, suffering and death are addressed, if dismantling them is not perceived as what the incarnation is principally about.

The scriptural story is oriented towards God being with us so that we in turn might be with God, one another and the wider creation. Creation comes about because of God's desire to be with us in Christ. The notion of being with is pervasive in the Bible from God creating Adam and Eve as companions (Gen 2:22) and seeking to walk with them at the time of the evening breeze (Gen 3:8) to the moment the loud voice from the throne says that the home of God is among mortals, that God will dwell with them and that God will be with them (Rev 21:3). But the potential of being with has not always been fully appreciated. So in Chapter 3 I revisit the eight dimensions of being with articulated in my earlier work, and highlight the scriptural and incarnational significance and resonance of these eight dimensions. This establishes that being with is not a sweeping label or slogan but a textured, nuanced, scripturally founded and incarnationally rich notion describing not just the destiny of God's purpose but the great part of the way God – and we – realise that purpose. Presence, attention, mystery, delight, participation, partnership, enjoyment and glory are all profoundly scriptural notions, found throughout the Bible, and constitute a fair portrayal of the ministry of Jesus. These dimensions ensure that being with is no abstract concept but a rich account of God's inner-Trinitarian life and God's life with us now and always. This chapter completes Part I.

In Part II I engage with those who have trod this path before.[3] I am seeking here not to tell a historical tale of theologians and their cultural and political circumstances, but to take the opportunity to glean from them transferable themes and insights that can assist with my argument. I treat such theologians in three groups. The first,

[3] Karl Barth explains this transition adeptly:

> Exegetical theology investigates biblical teaching as the basis of our talk about God. Dogmatics, too, must constantly keep it in view. But only in God and not for us is the true basis of Christian utterance identical with its true content. Hence dogmatics as such does not ask what the apostles and prophets said but what we must say on the basis of the apostles and prophets.
>
> Church Dogmatics, *vol. I/1, trans. G. W. Bromiley, ed. G. W. Bromiley and T. F. Torrance, 2nd ed. (Edinburgh: T & T Clark, 1975), 16*

stretching back to the earliest theologians such as Irenaeus but beginning in earnest with the seventh-century monk Maximus the Confessor, shares the conviction that Christ's coming was not a reaction to the fall, but is generally much more focused on the eschatological aspects of the story, notably our deification by the Holy Spirit, and the insight into eternal life offered by Christ's transfiguration. This is the subject of Chapter 4. The second, most fully represented by the late thirteenth- and early fourteenth-century Franciscan John Duns Scotus, asserts that the incarnation of Christ has primacy among all God's purposes, and insists that Christ's coming was not dependent on the fall. The third, clustering around the twentieth-century work of Karl Barth, especially his *Church Dogmatics*, recalibrates the old debates about election (that some are predestined for salvation, others for damnation), to suggest that election refers to Jesus Christ. Christ is not just the object of election (chosen by God); he is also, as a person of the Trinity, the subject of election (the God who chooses). Almost without exception, despite their shared emphasis on incarnation, all the authors examined revert to a fairly conventional account of salvation hinged around Christ's passion, death and resurrection; which puts my rendering of Christ's cross in tension with all of them, and leaves me wondering if they truly uphold my key principle, the consistency of God's means and ends. Nonetheless these three investigations significantly enrich the notion of being with and its implications for theology.

Once I have garnered key themes from these theologians, I move to Part III, in which I match together these gleanings with the theological principles, scriptural themes and dimensions of being with articulated above. I elucidate a brief theological conspectus in four chapters, expanding on the story of God outlined in Chapter 1. In the spirit of offering a truly incarnational theology, I cover several of the traditional topoi of systematic treatments, but within an incarnational narrative that affirms the theocentric rather than anthropocentric emphasis of theology. I first look, in Chapter 7, at the Trinity, and perceive the ways it embodies being with in its ultimate and definitive form. The persons of the Trinity are utterly occupied with one another's attention, delight, mystery and enjoyment. While the church came to understand the significance of Christ before articulating the doctrine of the Trinity, I assume that in presenting God's purpose we must explore who God is ahead of describing how God acts. I then move in Chapter 8 to God's purpose, understood first as expressed in the incarnation, which entails creation and finally yields eschatology. Here I am concerned to examine how scripture grounds both creation and eschatology incarnationally in the narrative of Jesus. Next in Chapter 9 I take up God's unfolding purpose. Here I explore the Holy Spirit, narrated through Israel, church and God's realm. I understand the work of the Holy Spirit as making Christ present in these different spheres of God's story. Finally in Chapter 10 I address God's unbreakable purpose, where Christ's cross, resurrection and ascension are explored, and evil, sin, suffering and death are revisited; meanwhile the notion of the fall is renarrated. In my conclusion I indicate where the argument lands and which areas invite further exploration.

The project is one of relocation – from anthropocentrism to theocentrism, from a concentration on reversing the results of the fall to a focus on the coherence of God's original purpose with incarnation, creation and eschatology. En route I make a case for a corresponding reading of scripture and reception of tradition. I also argue for the scriptural and incarnational potential of the dimensions of being with, and for a constructive theology built around God's desire to be with us in Christ incarnationally and eschatologically – a desire that governs our reading of Christ's death and resurrection. The book is designed as nine chapters assembling all the resources to ensure that the claims put forth in Chapter 10 make sense.

PART I The Story of God

1 An Incarnational Theology

THE STORY OF GOD

There are two realms: essence and existence. Essence names that which is forever; existence names that which abides for a limited time. There need have been no existence. Essence is sufficient unto itself. Essence is constituted by three persons, so in one another that we call them one, so with one another that we call them three. When we consider their relations with one another, we call them Trinity; when we consider their purpose beyond themselves, we call them God.

God is characterised by these three persons being with one another in utter and mutual relationship. 'Utter' means they have no need or urge to look beyond themselves; these relationships are completely absorbing and rewarding, creative and fruitful. 'Mutual' means these relationships are entirely complementary, and there is no sense in which one party is more important, powerful or directive than the others. They are relationships of joy and delight.

Yet in the mystery of these utter and mutual relationships, God chooses to be with another beyond these relationships, not because these relationships in any way fall short, but because God is characterised by effervescent abundance.[1] This abundance emerges initially

[1] Robert Jenson provides perhaps the best way around the infelicitous language of 'choosing' here, although he cannot avoid it altogether. '

According to Barth, the event of God's choice to be one with us in Jesus Christ must itself be a prevenient reality of Jesus Christ in God's eternity. This is so because God's choice to be one with us is in itself a self-determination of God to unity with us, and just so is itself the chosen state of affairs; and Jesus Christ *is* the chosen state of affairs. Thus, Jesus Christ, the God-*man*, happens in eternity before all time, as the reality of the choice by God to be God with this man. ... We must acknowledge God's being as itself *event and action*. For Barth, this is the same as to say that God is

and principally in the Son, who in Jesus Christ is primed to participate in something beyond God: something called existence. Jesus Christ is to be the way the relationship between essence and existence is embodied. Only in the realm of existence, when the persons of the Trinity are given narrative display, can we begin to consider the story of God, and distinguish God from all there is. The Holy Spirit fosters the relationship between Jesus and creation.

In order for embodiment to take place, existence needs to come into being. The creation of existence comes about because of God's effervescent abundance. The purpose of existence is first of all to provide the theatre for the encounter between Jesus Christ and his companions. Those companions are known as human beings. But Jesus Christ's encounter, while definitively an encounter with human beings, is truly an encounter with the whole of existence, with, through and beyond human beings: that whole is called creation.

While all things in creation find their animation and apogee in Jesus Christ, creation itself has an integrity and abundance of its own. The detail and exquisite artistry of the living world is indescribable, and exceeded only by the extent and diversity of the universe beyond this planet. The billions of years before humankind began to dwell on earth and the elaborate process by which it came into existence likewise indicate the boundless imagination and abiding patience of the creator.

For all its detail and extent, existence is not essence. It does not last forever. It is the object of the Father's attention, the scene of Christ's incarnation, the sphere of the Holy Spirit's activity: but it will one day come to an end. Essence does not come to an end. The astonishing mystery of Jesus Christ's embodiment is not just that God

> perfectly *person*. The perfection of his personhood must mean that he himself chooses what he is; thus we must even say that God is his own *decision*.
>
> *Robert Jenson,* God after God: The God of the Past and the God of the Future, Seen in the Work of Karl Barth *(Indianapolis: Bobbs-Merrill, 1969), 31, italics original*

Interestingly, in the light of my language of eternity and essence, Jenson goes on to say, 'the history of Jesus has taken over the place in the structure of reality which "eternity" had in religious Christianity' (70, italics original).

willed to dwell among us and experience our life and share our griefs and consolations; it is that in due course, God wills to elevate our life from existence to essence – to draw humankind and all creation into the forever that is the realm of God. This forever will not be entirely foreign to humankind, that is, so swathed in the utter and mutual relationship of God that no persons shaped by existence could recognise themselves in it; it will instead be a realm, for humans, of so being with God, themselves, one another and the renewed creation that it epitomises and transfigures the highest experiences of created existence. It will thus not be new, but largely composed of reincorporated elements of the old. In this realm the utter and mutual relationship in which the persons of the Trinity experience one another will be the pervading experience of the elevated creatures. Every moment of true and genuine being with in existence is inspired by the Holy Spirit and transfigured in God's ultimate realm. The language of the realm (or 'kingdom') of God identifies those moments when God's original purpose in becoming incarnate, and God's final purpose in transfiguring existence, become visible in social relations of trust, dynamism and transformation on earth.

The intersection between God's original and final purposes is the incarnation of Jesus Christ – at a moment in time, at a place on earth, in particular circumstances and within the context of contingent events. It is of immense significance that Jesus spent the great majority – 90 per cent – of his life in obscurity, being with the people of Nazareth (besides such time as was spent in Bethlehem and Egypt, according to the scriptural account). On this profound underpinning of being utterly with the people of Israel, and humankind in general, rests his subsequent ministry. While he transitions following his baptism into more of a working-with approach – training and equipping his disciples, dialoguing with and confronting the crowd and the authorities, performing symbolic actions and offering wisdom, counsel and guidance – every aspect of this working with is directed at demonstrating, advocating and encouraging people towards profound relationships of being with God, themselves, one another and the creation. His commitment to being with is put to the ultimate test as he faces execution. But in his agonising death, facing the choice whether to be with humankind and creation or to be with God, he yet remains faithful to his commitment – God's original and final purpose – to be with us, even at the cost of jeopardising the utter and mutual relationships of the Trinity. And in his resurrection we behold the fundamental and ultimate inseparability of the Trinity and the unbreakable character of God's commitment to be with us. In Christ's ascension, we see for the first time the destiny God has for each one of us, that we shall enter the utter and mutual relationship of being with God, ourselves, one another and the renewed creation in the realm of essence: the prospect that constitutes God's final purpose. The name for this final purpose is communion.

Besides its definitive and focal embodiment in the incarnation of Jesus Christ, God's original and final purpose is disclosed in several ways. Perhaps the first is through covenant. The covenants with Adam, Noah, Abraham, Jacob, Moses and David described in the Old Testament each, to different degrees and in diverse dimensions, anticipate the embodiment of God's purpose in Christ by setting out what it means for God's people to be with one another and be a blessing to the whole world. When that covenant is inscribed in the Ten Commandments, there emerge a set of expectations and guidelines for how Israel is to live sustainably with God and with one another. A covenant is fundamentally a commitment to be with one another through sunshine and rain, and an indication of what practices will uphold, foster and enrich that togetherness. In this it differs from a contract, which is a set of undertakings between parties who are seeking not to be with each other or 'enjoy' one another, but instead to 'use' one another in legitimate, appropriate, non-exploitative and enforceable ways. The story of Israel is one in which God continues to cherish the covenant, while Israel sometimes lets it lapse into a contract and sometimes fails to honour it. When Israel has not lived sustainably and has fallen into exile, God renews the covenant by being made known to Israel definitively as a God of with, not of for – as a God who shares Israel's sufferings rather than simply conspiring to fix them. Such is the pattern of incarnational logic.

The name for the manner in which God's original and final purpose is understood by human beings is revelation. Revelation encompasses all the ways individuals and communities have witnessed, experienced and reflected upon God's desire to be with them, and the pattern by which such testimony has been distilled, refined and compiled by those given authority. While there may be many questions about how the scriptures reflect and embody some of the inadequate and unworthy social structures and communal expectations of the milieux within which they were recorded – one thinks for example of the dominance of men in public roles and the routine suppression of women's voices – there is no question that the Holy Spirit continues to speak through the text we have today. Revelation fundamentally proclaims God's purpose to be with us in Christ and our destiny to be with Christ forever. It does not and cannot examine every complex issue in succeeding generations, which can be addressed by exploring what forms of life most fully anticipate God's coming realm and equip God's people to be with God, themselves, one another and the creation. The scriptures continue to bring inspiration and revelation to this discernment, as does the tradition of God's people and the reflection on scripture, tradition and manner in which the Holy Spirit yields wisdom in the world at large.

Indeed that activity of the Holy Spirit is another way in which God's original and final purpose is disclosed and discerned. The Holy Spirit's definitive activity is to make Christ present in the human world and creation more generally. While celebrated moments may be those when glimpses of God's realm are most explicit – when a political dictator is unseated, when a major breakthrough is made to enhance humanity's relationship with the creation it has so depleted, when two parties are reconciled after a painful story of hurt and damage, when a community embraces and is enriched by the diverse identities and talents of people who have elsewhere experienced exclusion and rejection – the Holy Spirit is by no means active only in celebrated moments. The Holy Spirit is active in every instant of every life of every kind. Its activity is to enhance the utter and mutual relationship of being with and to draw all creation towards its destiny of being with God in Christ forever. The scriptures are accounts and perceptions of definitive ways the Holy Spirit has been active; but they are indescribably far from being comprehensive, because the Holy Spirit's work of catalysing and brokering being-with relationships is constant and ceaseless. The name for these relationships is community.

The abundance of God's imagination and the wideness of God's mercy are such that, while relationships characterised by being with are the icon and goal of the Holy Spirit's activity, the creativity and vibrancy of God's realm is experienced and cultivated in myriad ways. The arts imitate and echo the artistry and playfulness of God; universities seek to expand knowledge and by training and reflection to turn that knowledge into wisdom; sports exult in the agility of the body, the adaptability of the mind and the collaboration of a team to go beyond the sedentariness of conversation and personal endeavour alone. Labour preserves us from idleness, and can offer glimpses of a rewarding working with that makes evident how in organisations and institutions we can each be more than the sum of our parts. Opportunities to exercise gifts, acquire skills, develop habits, foster practices and form relationships of mutual upbuilding and respect create energy and give substance to the otherwise empty quest for independence or autonomy. Politics and struggle identify places where power and flourishing are unequally distributed and constantly evaluate whether conditions or commitments reflect or further the relationships that herald God's realm. Because of the Holy Spirit's ubiquitous activity, one can never say one is engaging in something other than the business of God. And the wider creation conducts its own drama of existence and symphony of praise, whether or not inhibited by the activity of humankind. All this – particularly that which is unjustly misused or cruelly discarded – is material ripe for reincorporation into God's ultimate realm.

From the moment Jesus embarks upon his ministry, he is surrounded by followers and thronged by the crowd. These near and distant disciples experience and embody the devotion, confusion and pathologies that his followers have replicated ever since. Jesus commissions Peter as the rock on which to found this community, breathes his Holy Spirit on his disciples at Easter and sends them forth them on the mount of Ascension. At Pentecost the Holy Spirit inspires and empowers a dozen fragile followers to turn the world upside down and do unbelievable things. Henceforth the community of people dedicated to modelling in its life the utter and mutual relationship of being with God, oneself, one another and the creation, and heralding this relationship as embodied in Jesus Christ and fostered by the Holy Spirit, is called church.

Like any human activity, church cannot simply practise being with to the exclusion of other ways of relating.[2] There is a great deal of working with, for example in church administration and decision-making, and some degree of working for, although on closer inspection preachers for example are working with when they dovetail their words with the activity of singers, accompanists, intercessors and presiders, let alone reviewers of draft sermons and participants in theological reflection and reading groups. Likewise voluntary congregational monetary giving looks like a form of working for but becomes an action of working with when seen as a common practice shared by all participants. Whatever the elements of working for and working

[2] The distinctions between the four categories of working for, working with, being with and being for are foundational for all my work about being with. Working for is where I have skills and knowledge and configure a relationship in terms of my assets, which I exercise, and your deficits, which I alleviate. Working with is a collaboration in which I join a group of agents who each bring their assets to the table to overcome a problem together. Being with is where I relate to you for your own sake, not for any ulterior goal. Being for is where I do not directly interact with you but nonetheless advocate for you or consider myself to address your problem without engaging you in that pursuit. For a succinct summary of the four categories see my *Incarnational Ministry: Being with the Church* (Grand Rapids, MI: Eerdmans, and Norwich: Canterbury, 2017), 8–13.

with, the telos of every activity is being with God, oneself, one another and the creation in truthful, reconciled and sustainable relationships of dignity, dynamism and mutual cherishing. The calibre of the church is the degree to which these communities exist – more than the number of communities seeking to claim the name 'church', or the number of individuals identifying with Jesus, or the influence those claiming to represent Jesus or church have over politics or society. The fact that the church in every age throws up egregious examples of communities far from this model and leaders using what should be enjoyed, including using people particularly vulnerable to exploitation, is a matter for prolonged repentance, and an indication of the difference between church and God's realm.

Within the church there are particular practices that offer opportunities to perceive that utter and mutual relationship of being with. Notable among those are sacraments. In baptism believers are with Israel as it crossed the Red Sea from slavery to freedom, and as it received the commandments on Mount Sinai showing it how to keep its freedom. Believers are also with Christ in going down into the waters and being raised back up again, both in his own baptism by John and in his death and resurrection. Believers become disciples as they are anointed in the tradition of Israel's prophets, priests and kings and take a candle to become lights in the world: thus again they share with Israel and walk with Jesus. Meanwhile in the Eucharist the community models what it means to live sustainably with God. Praise and scripture-reading align worshippers with God's original and final purpose; preaching locates that purpose in the present day; confession and peace restore worshippers in being with God, themselves, one another and the creation; then human labour and God's abundance are brought to the table, whereupon the retelling of God's original and final purpose, embodied in Christ, transforms them from the limitations of existence to the effervescence of essence, and the congregation becomes what it eats, the body of Christ, ready to be sent out to celebrate, foster and advance the utter and mutual relationships it has experienced together, thus making the whole world a

Eucharist. The sacraments of baptism and Eucharist, together with the life of prayer and the timely presentation of God's original and final purpose in preaching, are so important that the church sets aside and equips particular individuals to convene and prepare and offer them well; this is ordination. Such people invariably play important roles in governing and organising the community – but their key function is to trust and practise the time-honoured ways the Holy Spirit has proved to be with God's people.

While Christians long to be fully with God, and for their relationship with themselves, one another and the creation to be unsullied by the distortions, subversions and distresses of life in the world, they cannot assume that God's final purpose will immediately be realised – either upon their own death or upon the conclusion of the earth's story. For God may have many other stories to tell; the incarnation may be just one of God's several ways of interacting with something beyond; and there may be some things beyond yet to appear: we are, after all, talking about eternity, in which this might be one of many universes and the wonder of the Christian gospel may be exceeded by yet more exhilarating manifestations of God's glory. The one thing of which Christians may be confident is that the character of God, explicitly and definitively set forth in the incarnate Jesus, will not change. Christianity is, in the end, about a faithful God in whom we may place our utter trust. It is that, rather than any particular doctrine, that is the touchstone of all things.

A DIFFERENT STORY

This way of portraying the Christian faith highlights abundance, relationship, transfiguration and blessing. It differs significantly from other portrayals of the faith in a number of respects, which I shall now outline.

First, this is a story about God. That might sound obvious; but many renderings of Christian faith are really stories about us. '"God with us" is the centre of the Christian message – and always in such a way that it is primarily a statement about God and only then and for that reason a statement about us.'[3] The anthropocentric story of the need to address the panic about the past (guilt and bitterness), and to dismantle the fear of the future (death and the unknown), unduly shapes, if not overshadows, the Christocentric story described above. Theology is consistently displaced by anthropology. The story above is from beginning to end about God; even at the end it opens the door to future initiatives on God's part that might have little or nothing to do with us or the creation we know, but might be above and beyond our existence. They could be in another existence entirely, to which, in all likelihood, the second person of the Trinity will relate (or perhaps is currently relating) in Christoform ways.

Second, this is a story about Jesus. Again, that might seem to go without saying. But alternative versions of Christianity tend not to focus on Jesus, for diverse reasons. Most often, they instead centre on sin. Sin and mortality become the key players in the story, and Jesus is introduced some while after the story has begun (around three-quarters of the way through, if one calculates by a scripture page-count). In such narratives, Jesus is not the centre of the story; instead, he has a clear job to do, a role whose responsibilities are not set by him: he turns out to be not the shepherd but a hired hand, brought in to fix the sin and mortality problem. But there are other common ways of decentring Jesus. One is to highlight the eschaton, for example by portraying a rapture in which the faithful are taken up to heaven. The cost of overemphasising what lies ahead is to under-emphasise what lies behind: the more dramatic and decisive is the climax, the less significant and definitive becomes the incarnation. One subtler way to decentre Jesus is to employ theological language, yet to offer no account of ways in which Jesus' incarnation, passion or

[3] Karl Barth, *Church Dogmatics*, vol. IV/1, trans. G. W. Bromiley, ed. G. W. Bromiley and T. F. Torrance (Edinburgh: T & T Clark, 1956), 3, 5. I shall detail in Chapter 6 my concerns that Barth does not successfully disentangle his notion of with from his deeper assumption of for. But his insistence that this is a story about God is consistent and distinctive.

resurrection provide a template for discipleship and church today. Jesus quickly becomes a source of endorsement for whatever cause or initiative one planned to advance anyway. In contrast with each of these accounts, the story above is about Jesus from beginning to end. Creation is because of and through Jesus, all in scripture that precedes or follows him is anticipating or reflecting him, and all else is the activity of the Holy Spirit, which becomes recognisable when it looks like Jesus.

Third, this is a story of abundance. It is not dominated by deficit, either transactional (some kind of affront to honour) or relational (guilt at what we have done and bitterness at what has been done to us). It is not shaped around resolving a problem: there are undoubted obstacles, resistances and sabotage, as well as grotesque parodies of what God offers in Christ; but these do not get the prerogative of determining the narrative. The story begins, continues, is definitively characterised by and concludes in abundance. Fundamentally the story is one of the prevailing quality of more. There is at the beginning no shortfall in God; yet the Trinity's plenitude still finds it yields something beyond, and a relationship with that something beyond, known as creation. The incarnation is not an addition to God, being inherent in the configuration of the Trinity: and yet it still resembles more. Even in the mystery of cross and resurrection, there abides an inextinguishable surplus: when death has done its worst, God still has more. Should existence ever seem boundless and breathtaking, essence presents infinitely more. When creation has run its course, there is with God forever indescribably more. Even the incidentals are about abundance, not scarcity: there is far more of creation, in extent and detail, than anyone could possibly assess. There are myriad forms of social existence; even the variety of religious expression, rather than be perceived as heretical, schismatic, barbarous or alien, may be taken as a sign of effervescence. The life of God's realm is not so much about learning to be right not wrong, or better not worse, but more about finding ways to accommodate, enjoy and embrace endless dimensions, difference and diversity, and bring to the surface a variety of skills, gifts and identities. The life of being with always trusts that God has given enough and to spare.

Fourth, this is a story of God's sovereignty and freedom. There is here no extraneous justice to which God must pay respect, no honour to which God owes dues, still less an authoritative adversary that God must trick, surprise, bargain with or defeat.[4] God has no rescue to perform in Christ, and humanity is in no prison to which some formula or activity unlocks the key; there is no necessity governing every actor including God to which God and all others are subject, or obligation that Christ must uphold, or debt the Trinity must scramble about in its pockets to repay.[5] Such strictures are absurd: we are talking about the one whose glory fills the entirety of essence, and who initiated and choreographed the entirety of existence. How could the Trinity, whose life exudes generosity, mercy and creativity, be subject to some sinister, incorrigible, unyielding abstract compulsion? That is not to say the story does not need to reckon with sin, evil, suffering and death; but not as truculent landlords requiring back payment or desultory tyrants threatening obliteration. This is a narrative of God and God's glory and God's grace and God's generosity –

[4] Gustav Aulén refers to God's love as spontaneous – by which he means it is always prior to human action and never a response to the human predicament. See his *The Faith of the Christian Church*, trans. Eric H. Wahlstrom (Philadelphia: Fortress, 1960), 113–15. He also rejects the tension between divine love and divine justice described by Anselm. Instead, he understands that God's love *is* God's justice. He perceives the answer to evil as reconciliation rather than judgement (120, 147). The process by which God forgives is not one in which, by some transaction, Jesus satisfies divine justice. Jesus' life and death express God's love. Forgiveness is unconditional – there is no question of substitution (182–83). See also William G. Witt and Joel Scandrett, *Mapping Atonement: The Doctrine of Reconciliation in Christian History and Theology* (Grand Rapids, MI: Baker, 2022), 49–60.

[5] Here I refer to Anselm of Canterbury and his scholastic successors, who shift the basic metaphor of atonement from victory to punishment, honour and retribution, and the penal substitution model from John Calvin onwards. Anselm's work is a cause of controversy because he begins with notions that accord with Irenaeus and Athanasius: thus he sees humankind as created to enjoy God, and sin as disrupting the divine beauty and order of creation. However, he then switches to notions of sin as debt, divine justice as demanding punishment or satisfaction, and salvation as restoration of divine honour.

not about a kindly uncle agreeing to pay off an overdraft before getting in over his head and finally escaping.

Fifth, this is a story about an ongoing role for Jesus from beginning to end. In some prominent versions of the story, there is no particular role for Jesus before Gabriel announces to Mary that she is with child of the Holy Spirit: Jesus' function is to suffer and die – and in some cases to rise, although there are accounts in which even that is supernumerary. Likewise, thereafter Jesus is perceived as sitting at the right hand of the Father, a role that sometimes appears to be a reward for a mission accomplished – but not necessarily having any further part to play. Thus Jesus becomes an instrumental figure, more or less discarded once his work is done, although sometimes he returns on the clouds at the last day. In the story above, Jesus is foundational to the creation of the world, being indeed its raison d'être, is the embodiment of God and humanity's shared future, and sets forth in his life a template for all social existence in the light of God's mercy and grace. Jesus is made present by the Holy Spirit in constant and countless, almost continuous ways, though seldom recognised or credited, even by those who seek his face at every turn. It is an utterly Christocentric story: a story all about Jesus.

Sixth, this is a story of humanity and the creation's genuine flourishing. God wants all human life to be characterised by non-instrumental relationships of mutuality and utter offering to one another. This is not about a version of faithfulness that stunts development, stifles expression, silences energy or trammels all into one style of life. Created existence is one enormous offertory procession, in which human beings and diverse forms of life bring forward, consciously or not, amazing gifts of beauty and endeavour, patience and inspiration, kindness and endurance, creativity and hope, love and laughter. On some accounts, there is no explicit explanation of why God created the universe at all; nor any particular reason why God would want in Christ to release it from the vice in which it is held. In the story above, there are constant analogies of grace, gestures of solidarity, living patterns of love scattered throughout the world; God is not checking to discern if these are genuine forms of worship or intentional acts of discipleship – they are part of the human impulse to rejoice in God's glory, whether named, acknowledged, understood, revered or not. Relationships of utter mutuality can surface in any community or neighbourhood, among the most affluent or deprived, among the ardent atheist or humble believer. The Holy Spirit's work is relentless, and will never be suppressed. God is an artist, assembling and bringing to fruition every aspect of creation on the canvas of life – not an internet hacker, investigating our secret follies, or a bailiff come to make reckoning for our unpaid debts. Worship is humankind and creation's recognition of and response to God's original and final purpose; but that worship is a celebration of all that God is, not a grovelling statement of gratitude that implies that God in all justice should not have bothered. Likewise, discipleship is glad engagement in the ways of personal and social existence that lead to life, not a tight-lipped resistance to the world, the flesh and the devil, casting suspicious glances at any influence that might lead one from the narrow path.

Seventh and last, this is a story in which God's means and ends are identical. There is no detour via which God must adopt tactics or strategies inimical to the ways the persons of the Trinity mutually indwell and embrace each other. Throughout the story, the incarnate Christ – the reason for creation, anticipated in covenant, embodied in Jesus, made present by the Spirit, dwelling with us in glory – exercises entire congruence between who he is and what he does, why he does it and how he does it. He comes as a tiny child – utterly with, to the point, remarkably, of almost complete dependence. He grows as a youth, still with, known chiefly by his dialogue with the teachers in the temple (Lk 2:46, a moment that discloses who he is, what he embodies and whom he is called to be with), he lives with his disciples, still with, there being no place to lay his head (Mt 8:20), he is with the curious and the desperate, the sex worker and the collaborator, until he is arrested and forced into a crisis where it seems he cannot continue to be with both the Trinity and humankind

(Mk 15:34). Beyond this moment, in his resurrection he is once again with both the Trinity and all creation, and in his ascension he goes to be with the Trinity, promising to be with his disciples always (Mt 28:20), an undertaking fulfilled by the events of Pentecost. It is, throughout, a continuous story of with. There is utter, undeviating consistency of purpose and conduct. God does not change character to pull off some necessary activity to secure or guarantee something other than God. God is with; creates to be with; is with in Christ; is with despite all challenges; is with in Christ through the Holy Spirit; and will be with us and the renewed creation in Christ and the Holy Spirit forever.

In short, the whole story is about God's abundance, not our scarcity.

2 The Scriptural Story

In this chapter I explore three themes, identified in Chapter 1, each of which has a good claim to embody the purpose of God, the nature of incarnation and the character of everlasting life with God. The point is not to identify which is the principal theme: it is to conceive of the scriptural story as the weaving together of the three themes. The themes are covenant, community and communion. These three are in a sequential order: covenant exists to create community; community is fulfilled in communion. But they also interact as a circle – each clarifies and enriches the other. Together they constitute what it means for God to be with us, and what that being with entails in practical and loftier terms. They also involve what it means for us to be with each other, the stranger and the wider creation.

Covenant, community and communion adhere to the seventh principle articulated in Chapter 1 above: they are ways in which God's means and God's ends are identical. They render how being with is manifested between God, humankind and the wider creation now; but they are just as much descriptions of what it means for humankind and the wider creation to be with God forever. They are not mechanisms for getting humankind from creation to heaven intact; they are the very best that existence can offer in its own right. Yet they are not simply time-bound features of existence: they are ways in which participants can experience today what God promises to express forever. Covenant, community and communion are the qualities the incarnation embodies: Jesus is the covenant between God and creation; Jesus is the broker of the community that is both together with God and united with God; and Jesus is himself the communion that his life extends to all humankind. Covenant, community and communion are the way, the truth and the life. In the final section of this chapter, I reimagine evil, sin and death as those factors and forces that inhibit the three paths to everlasting life with God, and renarrate the scriptural story along the lines envisaged herein.

The argument of this chapter is this: once one recognises that the shape of the scriptural story is to cultivate covenant, community and communion, rather than simply abolish suffering and death, a richer notion of what it means for Christ to gather all things together emerges. It is a story of God's abundance rather than our scarcity. To grasp that, we need first to establish the three key themes of covenant, community and communion as ones that pervade scripture and are embodied in Christ.

COVENANT

The fact that Christians traditionally divide the Bible into Old and New Testaments makes the strongest case that the theme of covenant unites the entire scriptural witness.[1] While covenant finds its epitome, fulfilment and embodiment in Jesus, it pervades the Old Testament and characterises how God elects to be with Israel. Covenant is God's commitment to be with Israel – not to achieve some further goal, although Israel's flourishing and the blessing of the nations are certainly anticipated, but because being with, not in general but in particular, not as a means but as an end, not temporarily but permanently, is the reason for creation. Covenant is not the 'Plan B' after the failure of creation in the fall; it is the fulfilment of the reason for creation, and the anticipation of the true covenant, the incarnation itself.

Likewise liberation is for covenant. The exodus is not freedom from Egypt so much as liberty to be with God. The stipulations of

[1] Gary Herion explains the nature of a covenant, which, unlike a contract, depends entirely on the integrity of the parties making promises under oath. There is no recourse to judicial arbitration if partners are insincere in making promises or unreliable in keeping them. Only repentance and forgiveness can sustain them. They therefore depend on qualities such as honesty, integrity, loyalty, trust, selflessness and love. See his 'Covenant', in David Noel Freedman, ed., *Eerdmans Dictionary of the Bible* (Grand Rapids, MI: Eerdmans, 2000), 288–92.

Sinai are not constraints on God's wilful people – they are ways to live sustainably in order to continue to be with God perpetually; and being with God means being with one another and the wider creation.[2] In due course covenant also comes to incorporate being with the enemy. Israel being with the enemy means, in part, coming to appreciate that the enemy cannot define the meaning of its suffering; and that Israel will outlast any attempt to obliterate or nullify it. In Babylon this comes to mean Israel gaining a different notion of covenant from what it had previously. Israel discovers that covenant means God being with Israel. God appearing as a fourth figure alongside Shadrach, Meshach and Abednego in the fiery furnace transforms how Israel had understood the covenant: God does not quench the fire, nor rescue the three men from the fire; God is with them in the fire (Dan 3:1–30). Correspondingly God does not lift Israel out of Babylon: God is with Israel in Babylon. The covenant is not something that comes into play once Israel has land, king and temple: the covenant is at work even in the absence of such guarantees and blessings. The covenant is not simply a form of promise: the promise is a pledge that the covenant is God's permanent way of relating, not a step on the way to something beyond. The covenant is not rooted in God

[2] Ellen F. Davis makes this the theme of her *Scripture, Culture and Agriculture: An Agrarian Reading of the Bible* (Cambridge: Cambridge University Press, 2009). On pp. 19–20 she says,

> Creation is bound into a single, covenanted unity. Each of us is connected to every other creature by the great web of life that Isaiah and other biblical writers call *bĕrit 'ôlām*, a reality that is comprehensive in space and time (the word *ôlām* designates something infinitely extended in either direction). ... Like every other member of this covenanted unity, we humans occupy a place that is delimited by *tôrōt*, divine teachings, and when we violate the prescribed limits, the consequences are inevitably disastrous, for ourselves, for 'all flesh'" and for the earth, the fertile soil itself.

In his *Old Testament Theology: An Introduction* (Nashville, TN: Abingdon, 2007) Walter Brueggemann maintains that God's vision for Israel and for creation are twinned – bound together – because the one future-creating God is the sovereign of both. He highlights the flood narrative of Genesis 6–9 'at the centre of creation faith, a narrative account of the radical deathly undoing of creation' (374). He points out that the everlasting covenant with all flesh after the flood speaks of 'the wild animals, the birds of the air, and the creeping things of the ground' (Gen 9:16). And he pinpoints Hosea 2:18–23 as a key passage that unites Israel and creation in covenant.

being for Israel, but in God being with Israel: that is its origin, purpose and meaning.

And this covenant is not just an ideal. It is lived, inhabited and experienced. 'Oh, how I love your law! It is my meditation all day long. Your commandment makes me wiser than my enemies, for it is always with me' (Ps 119:97–98). The psalmist's love of the law is the love of the covenant; saying that the commandment is with me always is a way of saying God is with me always. Abraham trusts God, setting out as soon as God's commission has been uttered (Gen 12:5). Moses talks face to face with God, as with a friend (Ex 33:11). David dances before the Lord with all his might as the ark of the covenant is brought up from the house of Obed-edom (2 Sam 6:12–14). Josiah stands out as one who was with God in an exemplary way: 'Before him there was no king like him, who turned to the Lord with all his heart, with all his soul, and with all his might, according to all the law of Moses; nor did any like him arise after him' (2 Kings 23:25). And before the first covenant we find Enoch walking with God for 300 years (Gen 5:22). These are moments when the covenant is not given, bestowed, laid down, but profoundly lived, breathed, enjoyed.

To insist that the covenant is for its own sake is not to downplay the degree to which God is invested in it. Quite the contrary: if it were a means to an end, God could find an alternative means to that end. But if it is an end in itself, there is no way of assuaging the pain of faithlessness. Hosea 11:1–11 describes a relationship that is shaped around parental love and longing. 'When Israel was a child, I loved him.' It is hard not to identify with the pride and satisfaction of these words: 'It was I who taught Ephraim to walk. I took them up in my arms.' The memory interplays with the sense of fittingness. 'I led them with cords of human kindness, with bands of love. I was to them like those who lift infants to their cheeks. I bent down to them and fed them.' God teaches Israel to walk, surrounds it with tenderness and gives it solid food for the first time. Memory of the past then turns to grief in the present. 'The more I called them, the more they went from me … they kept offering incense to idols … they have refused to return to me. ... My people are bent on turning away from me.' This is not the setting right of guilt or the fixing of mortality: it is the restoration of a relationship. And at great cost: God struggles between sober pragmatism, passionate fury and tender compassion. 'How can I give you up, Ephraim?' says God. 'How can I hand you over, O Israel? ... My heart recoils within me; my compassion grows warm and tender.' God emerges with firm conviction: 'I will not execute my fierce anger; I will not again destroy Ephraim; for I am God and no mortal, the Holy One in your midst, and I will not come in wrath.' Finally Hosea offers us a glimpse of the future. God will be like a lion, who will roar, and God's children, Israel, will come trembling from the four corners to which they had dispersed, and be reunited with one another, with their homes and with God. Israel will be as timid and tentative as cooing doves in the face of the mighty roar of God. This is the cost and the promise of God being with Israel.[3] God has no ulterior purpose to fall back on; there is no mitigation for the moments when God's faithfulness is not reciprocated. God's decision to remain with Israel is not one that Israel can persuade God to uphold: in the end, God faces the poignant recognition that there is no alternative: the decision has already been made.[4]

[3] In Isaiah 46: 3–4 we read, 'Listen to me, O house of Jacob, all the remnants of the house of Israel, who have been borne by me from birth, carried from the womb; even to your old age I am he, even when you turn grey I will carry you. I have made you, and I will bear; I will carry and will save.'

[4] In his 'Image of God and Incarnation', *Interpretation*, 24/3 (July 1970), 336–56, Ulrich Mauser describes how God's anthropomorphism and humankind's theomorphism converge in Hosea:

> The anthropomorphic mode of speech about Yahweh aims at portraying God's condescension to human history, to his participation in that history, and to his sharing of the human condition. At the same time, the prophet of Israel is depicted in a remarkably theomorphic fashion in that his life story as a man becomes, at least partially, a representation of God by participation in God's condition. Human life is consequently understood as an image of God which in turn presupposes a concept of the divine in which Yahweh is so essentially God for and *with* Israel that the human is lodged in him.
>
> *(355, italics added)*

This is not an instrumental relationship, in which God chooses Israel as the best vehicle for the divine plan. Just as Israel is described as God's child, so it is portrayed as God's spouse. 'For your maker is your husband, the Lord of hosts is his name; the holy one of Israel is your redeemer, the God of the whole earth he is called' (Isa 54:5). The call to holiness is a call to be with God rather than any method to achieve some further aim: 'You shall be holy, for I the Lord your God am holy' (Lev 19:2). And that call is not provisional, but unlimited in duration: 'with everlasting love I will have compassion on you', says God (Isa 54:8).[5] If Israel had a role to perform, such as being the means through which the nations found salvation, then after that role had been performed, there would be no purpose for Israel; neither would there be any love for Israel other than regard for a former business partner.[6] But God's love for Israel goes far beyond any instrumental goodwill: Israel is God's child, God's spouse, God's companion forever.[7]

5 Kendall Soulen points out that nothing in the call story of Abraham in Genesis 12 'suggests that God's primary motive in calling Abraham is any special concern with the problem of sin, evil, or wickedness. To the contrary, God's motive seems chiefly to be the sheer fecundity and capaciousness of the divine good pleasure.' R. Kendall Soulen, *The God of Israel and Christian Theology* (Minneapolis, MN: Fortress, 1996), 120, quoted in Edwin Chr. van Driel, 'Incarnation and Israel: A Supralapsarian Account of Israel's Chosenness', *Modern Theology*, 39/1 (January 2023), 3–18 at 15 n. 47.

6 There is an almost unavoidable connection between a functional notion of God's relationship with Israel and the tendency towards supersessionism. 'If the relationship between God and Israel is purely functional, then once the purpose of Israel's election is fulfilled, there is no function left for this people and Israel could easily be replaced.' Edwin Chr. van Driel, 'Climax of the Covenant vs Apocalyptic Invasion: A Theological Analysis of a Contemporary Debate in Pauline Exegesis', *International Journal of Systematic Theology*, 17/1 (January 2015), 6–25 at 20.

7 Edwin Chr. van Driel, in his 'Incarnation and Israel', 5–6, characterises N. T. Wright as just such an instrumentaliser, because Wright describes Israel's role as to bring blessing to the world in a corresponding way to that by which Adam and Eve had brought a curse. Wright says,

> The point of 'election' was not to choose or call a people who would somehow mysteriously escape either the grim entail of Adam's sin or the results it brought in its train. It was not – as in some low-grade proposals! – about God simply choosing a people to be his close friends. The point was to choose and call a people through whom the sin of humankind, and its results for the whole creation, might be brought

We could call Moses' encounter at the burning bush (Ex 3:1–15) a definitive depiction, or prefigurement, of the covenant. God *sees* – God sees Israel's misery. God *hears* – God hears Israel's cries. God *knows* – God knows Israel's sufferings. Nothing the slightest bit distant, inscrutable, controlling or vengeful here. This is profound *attention*, real relationship, where God does not just look but sees and perceives, God does not just hear but listens and appreciates, God does not just know but learns and understands. The blazing fire of God's love is not just about doing and ordering – it is about perceiving, appreciating, understanding. But the final two verbal phrases offer a remarkable extra dimension. The first is 'I have *come down*.' Christians can only see in these words not a geographical reference but a theological one: Jesus is God come down. Jesus is God who sees, hears, knows. Jesus is the blazing fire of God's love. The second is 'bring them up'. Again, to a Christian reader, these words more than hint at a more explicit formulation: *'I will raise up.'* If 'I have come down' means incarnation, 'I will raise up' means resurrection. Jesus 'came down' to be in relationship with humankind and share its plight. Jesus 'rose up' to raise humankind and the creation to life in relationship with Father, Son and Spirit forever.

Likewise Moses has two complaints to God: 'I can't do this' and 'I don't even know your name.' God's name is 'I am who I am.' It is the essence of existence. It is that thread that links earthly existence to eternal essence. It is being itself. But then when God transforms Moses' inadequacy and isolation, God says, 'I will be with you.' Thus the vocabulary for God's identity, 'I am what I am', and for

> to the point where that sin, and those results, could at last be defeated, condemned, overcome.
>
> N. T. Wright, *Paul and the Righteousness of God (London: SPCK, 2013), 1208*

Van Driel also notes that the missiologist Christopher J. H. Wright takes a similar view in remarks like these: 'The election of Israel is instrumental, not an end in itself. God did not choose Israel that they alone should be saved, as if the purpose of election terminated with them. They were chosen rather as the means by which salvation could be extended to others throughout the earth.' Christopher J. H. Wright, *The Mission of God: Unlocking the Bible's Grand Narrative* (Downers Grove, IL: IVP Academic, 2006), 263.

God's action, 'I am with you'' is the same. Thus to say 'being' and to say 'with' and to say 'God' is to utter words that in this story mean largely the same thing. God discloses God's identity in the word 'being' and God's purpose in the word 'with'. Thus is the burning bush story the disclosure of God's identity, and the revelation that covenant is inherent in God's identity. God is fundamentally a God of with. And with entails covenant.

Holiness connotes distinctiveness and difference. But it is fundamentally a statement of whom Israel is called to be with. That means fundamentally God; but it has implications for every aspect of Israel's life. Leviticus 19, which calls Israel to be holy, goes on to insist on generosity with the fruits of the soil, fair treatment of employees and a living wage, solidarity with people with disabilities, compassion for the aged, integrity in judicial proceedings, health and safety provisions, ecological awareness, equality before the law for minority ethnic citizens and honesty in business transactions.[8] This shows a remarkable expansiveness in the conception of those with whom Israel is called to dwell – and of what holiness entails. Holiness means sustainable living with God, one another, the stranger and creation: exactly what covenant means.[9] The quality of this covenant is best and most frequently expressed in the term *hesed*, meaning steadfast love or loving-kindness, which occurs 250 times in the Old Testament. More than half of these occurrences are in the Psalms.

[8] See Christopher J. H. Wright, 'Ethics', in Willem A. VanGemeren, ed., *New International Dictionary of Old Testament Theology and Exegesis* (Grand Rapids, MI: Zondervan, 1997), 585–95 at 591–92.

[9] Norman Wirzba comments, contrasting covenantal and contractual sensibilities,

> Covenantal ways of being are all about establishing sympathetic and nurturing relationships with others because people recognise their need of each other. Attention and attunement to others are hallmarks of a covenantal mind because one assumes that genuine flourishing is mutual and that the good of individuals is best realised in a community that nurtures them. . . . Scripture reveals God as the one who commits to be with people, fellow creatures and the whole of creation as a feeding, sustaining, healing, forgiving, reconciling and liberating presence *no matter what happens*.
>
> *Agrarian Spirit: Cultivating Faith, Community and the Land* (Notre Dame, IN: University of Notre Dame Press, 2022), 158–59, italics original

The use of the term in Lamentations 3:22 – 'The steadfast love of the Lord never ceases' – just as Judah is facing up to the destruction of Jerusalem, is a perfect example of how *hesed* means God's with rather than God's for.

If God's relationship to Israel is not an instrumental one, is it simply a being-with relationship? One significant passage would suggest so. In Deuteronomy 7:6–8, God speaks of Israel being the object of love for its own sake: 'For you are a people consecrated to the Lord your God: of all the peoples on earth the Lord your God chose you to be his treasured people. It is not because you are the most numerous of peoples that the Lord set his heart on you and chose you – indeed, you are the smallest of peoples; but it was because the Lord loved you and kept the oath he made to your fathers that the Lord freed you with a mighty hand and rescued you from the house of bondage, from the power of Pharaoh king of Egypt.' Here election is tied not to a specific role, and certainly not to admiration for Israel's excellence, but to love and loyalty. Is this all that matters?[10] Not quite. If we return to the principle 'creation is for covenant', we can perceive that Israel was not simply a wandering people God settled upon: creation was initiated so that there would be an Israel. There was no Israel before God loved it. God created all things in order for there be an Israel to love.

Why? Here the centrality of Christ provides a Christian answer. In loving Israel, God is loving the people through whom the incarnation would come about. Jesus is born to a particular people with its own history and context, a people in whom covenant has been

[10] Edwin Chr. van Driel, 'Incarnation and Israel', 7–8, argues that Michael Wyschogrod, Jon Levenson and Walter Moberly all overstress the degree to which God's love for Israel is inexplicable and (in van Driel's word) irrational. See Michael Wyschogrod, *The Body of Faith: God in the People Israel* (Lanham, MD: Rowman and Littlefield, 1983); Jon D. Levenson, 'The Universal Horizon of Biblical Particularism', in Mark G. Brett, ed., *The Bible and Ethnicity* (Leiden: E. J. Brill, 1996), 143–69; and R. W. L. Moberly, *Old Testament Theology: Reading the Hebrew Bible as Christian Scripture* (Grand Rapids, MI: Baker Academic, 2013), 43–52. Wyschogrod maintains that God loves Israel 'because he sees the face of his beloved Abraham in each and every one of his children as a man sees the face of his beloved in the children of his union with his beloved' (*The Body of Faith*, 64).

embodied for generations, centuries, even millennia: Jesus is the fulfilment and embodiment of that covenant. Without the incarnation, we could not know why God chooses and creates and loves Israel (in that order). But without Israel, we would not know who Jesus is. Jesus is born among a people facing occupation, persecution and internal conflict – a people with its back to the wall.[11] But Jesus is born among a people whom God has called from a far country, brought out of slavery, shared in covenant belonging, returned from exile, dwelt with in plenty and in pain and persisted with as a companion: intentions formed before the foundation of the world. In Paul's words, 'Those whom he foreknew he also predestined to be conformed to the image of his Son, in order that he might be the firstborn within a large family' (Rom 8:29). That family is Israel.[12] Jesus' narrative is in significant respects a recapitulation of Israel's narrative: he goes down to Egypt as Israel did, begins his ministry at the Jordan as Israel entered the Promised Land there, faces temptation in the wilderness as Israel did, calls twelve disciples as Israel had twelve tribes, preaches on the mount as Moses received the commandments on a mountain, assembles outcasts and restores the rejected as God reassembled Israel from exile, dies on a tree as Adam sinned at a tree and so on. In all these ways the incarnation is the assembling of Israel's whole experience before God. The incarnation of Jesus and the calling of Israel become

[11] Howard Thurman, *Jesus and the Disinherited* (Nashville, TN: Abingdon, 1949; repr. Boston: Beacon, 1996). Thurman takes the extra step of saying that, since Jesus came to an Israel under occupation and facing the constraints of being an oppressed people within its own country, those who share such circumstances – he is thinking of African Americans in the United States, particularly but not only before the Civil Rights movement – have a unique vantage point on reading the gospels.

[12] Edwin Chr. van Driel, 'Incarnation and Israel', 13, notes that both Abraham and the gentiles are brough forth *ex nihilo*, owing their existence to election:

> When the promise comes to Abraham he is one who, looking at himself, sees one who is 'as good as dead' (Rom. 4:19). His wife is barren and unable to produce offspring. But out of nothingness God calls forth a people to love. This movement repeats itself when the gates of Israel's covenant open and the gentiles are ushered in. They who 'once were dead' are now made alive as we are knitted into Christ and his covenantal family (Eph. 2:4–5). Election precedes creation. Love precedes the existence of a people.

logically and narratively inseparable. Jesus does not supersede the covenant: he embodies it, defines it, lives it in joy and agony, and invites the nations to join it.

Thus to say that the covenant unites the whole scriptural witness and to say that Christ is the focal point of God's purposes are to say the same thing: because Christ is the covenant. Christ doesn't come to bring the covenant or even, in the end, fulfil the covenant: he is the covenant. 'All things have been created through him and for him. He himself is before all things, and in him all things hold together' (Col 1:16–17). He both holds God and creation together and is the reason why things are together. He is the mystery of how all things will be gathered up to be with God, and he is the mystery of how that original intention was embodied as far back as God's words to Abraham. Covenant is thus not an injunction, arrangement, contract or bargain, but a prefigurement of how all will one day be with God in Christ.[13]

This is confirmed by a passage that one theologian calls 'the most crucial theological statement in the Old Testament'.[14] He is referring to 2 Samuel 7, which on the surface is about a powerful king trying to legitimise his regime by building a grand temple to the God who underwrites his authority. But a careful read discloses three questions at the heart of the covenant. The first question is, where is God? David sees his stable period of kingship in the newly conquered city of Jerusalem, uniting the northern and southern tribes, as

[13] This plays an important role in Karl Barth's account of reconciliation. Israel as a nation exists only in its history with God (*Church Dogmatics*, vol. IV/1, 23). The covenant of Jeremiah (Jer 31:32–33) reveals the purpose of the Mosaic covenant: 'I will be your God and you will be my people.' Paul describes a covenant of the Spirit rather than the letter. God's original purpose was to be humankind's covenant partner in Jesus. The purpose of the covenant becomes an event in him' (*Church Dogmatics*, vol. IV/1, 38). The covenant is fulfilled in the mediator, God incarnate. This is how God keeps the covenant. Barth affirms Israel: 'The Word did not simply become any "flesh" … It became Jewish flesh … The conclusion and sum of the history of God with the people of Israel, the One who fulfils the covenant made by God with his people' (*Church Dogmatics*, vol. IV/1, 166).

[14] Walter Brueggemann, *First and Second Samuel* (Louisville, KY: John Knox, 1990), 259.

the perfect moment to make a grand and permanent home for the ark of the covenant, enthroning God and at the same time enshrining his own leadership. But the prophet Nathan expresses ambivalence about the project. He points out that God is not a creature under our control, and God's purposes are not exhausted by our needs. Nathan goes to the heart of the anthropocentric tendency of faith – the attempt to control God, to limit truth, to put it in a building, make it our creature for our use and purpose. God is utterly other than us – and yet, as Nathan says to David, God is with us wherever we go.

The second question is, what does God want? David wants to build a temple for God. It is not clear that is what God wants. But David has a mindset that faithfulness is doing lots of things for God, and faithfulness for a rich and powerful king must mean doing very big things for God. This is a form of bribery. This kind of gesture is not about a real relationship: it is about offsetting damage, given that there is no real relationship. But Nathan does not utter the word 'if'. The covenant between God and Moses is dominated by the word 'if': if you keep my commandments, you will prosper. It is conditional. 'If' is the tiny word that echoes all through the Old Testament to this point. Nathan abolishes 'if'. There is no 'if' in what God says to David through Nathan: it is replaced by 'always'. The third question is, can we lose God? Second Samuel is the zenith of Israel's power and faithfulness: it is the high watermark of the Old Testament. And yet it is written in the knowledge that years later it all disintegrated. Here Nathan offers two responses. He says 'forever'. And he adds, 'I will raise.' This is where a Christian reading of the story perceives that Jesus did experience the alienation of God's people and Jesus did experience the alienation of God. Everything that might jeopardise the word 'forever' was embedded in his passion and death. But God raised Jesus. That raising demonstrates the fact that we cannot lose God. God and forever are not just two things it is nice to have: they are the same thing.

Here covenant discloses its three central questions: Where is God? What does God want? Can we ever lose God? The Christian answer to all three questions is one word: Jesus. God is with us in the one who expresses and embodies everything God means to us and everything we mean to God. God wants to be with us in Christ. God is not especially drawn to us offering gifts or making sacrifices, if such acts betray the suspicion that we are resorting to bribery. What God wants is our companionship in Christ. It sometimes seems we can lose God, and in the way humankind treated Jesus it went as far could be imagined towards doing so: but God raised Jesus, and showed us that nothing can finally separate us; so there can never be any further doubt.

COMMUNITY

Heaven is the end of painful separation. The hardest things in life are about painful separation: the separation of distance, discord and death. For those who seek relationship with God, separation from God is the hardest thing of all: the separation of despair. Heaven is about the end of painful separation, being close, even intimate: but not about losing identity, being the same as each other, with no separate being. Even passionate love finds the other's difference as thrilling as their sameness. In relation to God, salvation is not constituted by being absorbed into the divine essence. It is about retaining identity, a healthy separateness, albeit one whose identity is found in Christ, and one that loses all the negative associations of separateness.

This balance, between the togetherness that is like being utterly united, and the separateness that ensures this is relationship and not absorption, names the perfection of being we strive for on earth and long for in heaven. The togetherness is called union. The relationship is called 'with'; the Latin for 'with' is *com*. Thus we have communion. Communion is the centre of the Christian faith, because it names the experience we can glimpse on earth that we can know fully in heaven: being with but also being together. 'Communion' is also the word for the ceremony in which we tell our truthful story and infuse it with the story of God, 'with' and 'union' again, and the bread and wine are both ordinary foodstuffs and carriers of Jesus, who when we consume the elements is both in us and with us.

But being human is not just about 'soft' feelings and experiences. It is also about the 'hard' planning and preparing, paying for and making, organising and running, working and restoring. This is communion turned into practical action. There is a similar but different word for this – a word so similar to communion that it is almost the same, but still different enough that it is a separate word. That word is 'community'. Communion and community name the two aspirations of church. The one is about being in, and bringing others into, relationship with God; the other is about relating civilly, cordially and sacrificially with one another, and attending to the things that need doing to function humanly. When Jesus talks of the realm of God, he is talking about this communion and community becoming a reality for all people. Here I consider community before proceeding to communion.

Community can mean a gathering or group of people, for which the New Testament words are *ekkelsia* (assembly), *hagioi* (saints), *agapētoi* (beloved ones) and *allēlōn* (one another); or an experience of being with one another, for which the Greek word is *koinōnia* and the Hebrew *shalom*.[15] For covenant faithfulness, as we have seen, community is a form of recognising whom Israel is called to be with, notably the disadvantaged – the widow, the orphan, the stranger. Fostering community means offering protection to the alien while being mindful that not all the new gifts a foreigner can bring are

[15] Rebekah Eklund points out that *allēlōn* is in fact the most common New Testament word denoting community:

> There are approximately 40 'one another' commands in the epistles; bear one another's burdens, build up one another, and so on. The most common imperative is to love one another, appearing ten times. This Spirit-enabled love between believers is not limited to 'sympathetic disposition' but extends into acts of sharing and material assistance, a stance shared by James, who describes love as concrete acts of service.

'Community', in Robert L. Brawley, ed, The Oxford Encyclopedia of the Bible and Ethics, *vol. 1 (New York: Oxford University Press, 2014), 107–11 at 109*

beneficial to the community. Paul Hanson traces these social commitments to the exodus experience. He argues that by delivering Israel, God annulled religious and social systems tied to special privilege, and abolished the caste system as a social structure. Within this new community, every individual was equally precious to God, and the social structures of the covenant between God and people protected everyone from exploitation and oppression.[16] Hanson also links these transformed and transformative social practices to the primal quality of response to God's initiating, gracious activity – namely worship. Worship acknowledges the source and centre of life and of freedom, and orients other realities around that source and centre. It turns out that all other realities in the world are derivative, only finding their meaning in relation to the reality of God.[17] Hanson summarises the defining characteristics of Israel's community as a triad of righteousness, compassion and worship, themselves summarised in Micah by the epigram 'Do justice, love kindness, walk humbly with your God (Mic 6:8), and by Jesus as 'justice, mercy and faith' (Mt 23:23).[18] Thus the covenant enshrines the benefits of liberation from slavery.

The word that epitomises the aspirations of Israel for community is *shalom*. Shalom is a notion of cosmic harmony in which creation and all creatures are at peace with God: as depicted in the ubiquitous phrase 'I shall be your God and you shall be my people.' Peace includes prosperity and righteousness, but also reconciliation

[16] Paul D. Hanson, *The People Called: The Growth of Community in the Bible* (San Francisco: Harper and Row 1986), 22–23. Among social structures, Hanson includes systems of justice, land distribution, use of capital and treatment of vulnerable classes in society. He acknowledges (22) that 'this understanding of the exodus experience was more often neglected than preserved in ancient Israel, because of forgetfulness and the seduction of alternate ideologies'. He insists that 'Both in terms of the benefits enjoyed by members of the community and the responsibilities they bore toward others, the emphasis placed on equality and inclusiveness stands out within the ancient world' (469).

[17] Hanson, *The People Called*, 26.

[18] Hanson, *The People Called*, 70–78. Micah speaks in the context of what constitutes true worship. Jesus speaks in criticism of the scribes and Pharisees who tithe mint, dill and cumin.

with hostile neighbours and a healthy relationship with the non-human creation. This is an inherently future-oriented and inbreaking reality. It is identical to the blessing that Abraham was commissioned to bring to the nations; for it is not something Israel can experience in isolation. We may understand it in the language of being with God, ourselves, one another, the stranger and the new creation. It is the realm of God; it is the well-being of Eden; it is God's future that we are called to live now; it is the blessing that is received when we come face to face with God (Num 6: 24–26); it is the glory that the angels announced to the shepherds when they spoke of the wonder of Christ's birth (Lk 2:14); and it is precisely what Jesus embodies.

The New Testament portrays a more intimate version of community: 'Do not be afraid, little flock, for it is your Father's good pleasure to give you the kingdom' (Lk 12:32). Gerhard Lohfink sees this not as a narrowing of Jesus' vision, but as a concentration on his disciples in order to model the reign of God for Israel as a whole. The reign of God automatically implied the gathering of Israel. The sole meaning of the entire activity of Jesus is the gathering of God's eschatological people: this is what his exorcism of demons, his healing of the sick and his reception of sinners embodied.[19] Richard Hays, in making community the first of his three focal images found throughout the New Testament, draws these grand and humble dimensions together.[20] He describes the church as a countercultural community of discipleship, and the primary addressee of God's imperatives. He says he could equally well use the term 'church' in place of 'community', were the former term not subject to being misunderstood in terms of an institutional hierarchy. The point is that following Jesus is a corporate participatory activity, in which the

[19] Gerhard Lohfink, *Jesus and Community: The Social Dimension of Christian Faith*, trans John P. Galvin (Philadelphia: Fortress, 1984), 26–29. Lohfink is eager to dispel any notion that God's reign is a universal, interior reality in the souls of scattered believers.

[20] Richard Hays, *The Moral Vision of the New Testament: Community, Cross, New Creation, A Contemporary Introduction to New Testament Ethics* (San Francisco: Harper, 1996), 196–97.

question is not 'What should I do?' but 'What should we do?' He insists, 'By placing community first, we are constantly reminded that God's design of forming a covenant people long precedes the New Testament writings themselves, that the church stands in fundamental continuity with Israel.'[21] While 'covenant' epitomises Israel's sense of its relationship with God, and 'communion' identifies what Christian believers long to experience eschatologically and can fleetingly know today, 'community' names the day-to-day discovery of what faithfulness requires. Its ordinariness is part of its significance: constancy is not so much about grand individual gestures of sacrifice or example, but about a daily adherence to the practices that build up others.

The place where covenant and communion converge in community is baptism. In baptism the disciple is clothed in a new story – a story of covenant and communion. In baptism the candidates figuratively cross the sea from slavery to freedom, and graduate from wilderness to covenant, from recipients of ministry to ministers and missionaries themselves. They take their full place in community, inhabit covenant and share communion. Community is fundamentally constituted and shaped by story. Community is not necessarily or normally geographically detached; it does not always come from a unique place (all, after all, are created in God's image); but it inhabits a story about where it is going, and how God in Christ prepared that place from before the foundation of the world. If that community wants to understand its story, it looks to Jesus who embraces and reinterprets Israel's story. If it wants to know who Jesus is, it learns Israel's story. The most explicit reinterpretation of Israel's story in the light of Jesus comes in Luke 24:13–35 on the road to Emmaus – although such reinterpretations are scattered through Acts. Baptism is the moment disciples cease to try to create their own story, but gladly begin to inhabit Christ's story: one important but neglected feature is that to inhabit Christ's story means also to inhabit Israel's

[21] Hays, *The Moral Vision of the New Testament*, 199.

story. That story teaches it not just that God's covenant with Israel stipulates an honoured place for the outcast and stranger; it includes stories in which the outcast and stranger deliver and transform Israel. Thus the four lepers of Samaria enable Israel to withstand the Aramaeans (2 Kings 7:3–20).

When Jesus announces the realm or reign of God, he is saying that the aspirations for community embodied in the covenant and the truth of community to be experienced in the company of God forever are being restored and anticipated today. 'Today' is the resonant word he speaks in the synagogue in Nazareth (Lk 4:21) when he reads from Isaiah 61 of transformation for those experiencing poverty, imprisonment, discrimination and oppression. In his own life he inhabits all four dimensions: homeless in Bethlehem, in Egypt and around Galilee, he is poor. Arrested in Gethsemane, he is in prison. Cast out of Jerusalem, he is excluded. Nailed to a cross, he is oppressed. Jesus lives Isaiah 61; thus he inaugurates God's realm. Jesus' announcement of God's realm outlines the meaning of salvation. The fulfilment of covenant, community and communion means shedding impoverishment, imprisonment, discrimination and oppression. But more importantly it means embracing belonging, liberty, love and hope. Shedding chains is only half of this fulfilment. The other half is embracing restored relationships. Fighting injustice is half the story; modelling justice is the other half. The most radical and powerful word Jesus says in Nazareth is 'today'.

Community is not sentimental or cosy. In addition to the honesty and realism that life together requires, every community is in constant reflection about its boundaries, what constitutes upbuilding interaction and what is destructive, and how it relates to the individual outsider and the group outsider. In more subtle forms, a community needs to recognise when it has ignored, alienated, antagonised or oppressed an individual, a group or another community with which it should have been in fellowship. Ephesians 2:11–20 explains how a community that was made up of hopeless aliens and strangers has been brought near, and how Christ has created one new humanity out of two, making that community now citizens with the saints, members of God's household, and God's dwelling-place. This is a rousing yet challenging call to recognise what divisions on social, theological, economic, racial or political grounds demand and cost. The name for creating such a community out of division is 'peace'. This demonstrates the centrality of community for the scripture as a whole.

The transformation of social relationships envisaged in God's realm is always in dialogue with the practices of close community Jesus promotes amongst his disciples. To forgive a brother or sister seventy times seven (Mt 18:21–22), to part with all one's wealth (Mt 19:16–30), to relegate one's close family ties (Lk 14:26), to take up one's cross and follow (Mt 16:24–26), to take drastic action to dispel lust (Mt 5:27–30) – these are extraordinary injunctions that require devoted and communal adherence; alongside them come intimate practices of prayer (Mt 6:6), being invited to enter Jesus' own relationship with the Father (Mt 6:9–13), encouragements to settle disputes humanely (Mt 5:23–26) and common endeavours in mission (Mt 10:5–14). But calls to close community are constantly accompanied by gestures that open that community to those hitherto perceived not to belong – the notorious sinner, the collaborator, the unclean. And the unflinching portrayal of the disintegration of this close community through betrayal, denial and flight offers all the realism needed to demonstrate the challenge and cost of solidarity. Meanwhile in Acts there is the vision of the sharing of goods and mutual support (Acts 2:43–47, Acts 4:32–37), accompanied by a stark and uncompromising account of how demanding the policing of such practices can be (Acts 5:1–11). Once again community becomes the test of faithfulness and adherence to the way of Christ.

Perhaps the definitive articulation of the new community inaugurated by Jesus is found in the beatitudes (Mt 5:3–12). The first three – poor in spirit, meek and mournful – make clear that Christianity begins with the desperate. The middle beatitude of the nine – 'Blessed are the merciful, for they will receive mercy' –

implores disciples to treat others the way God has already treated them. The last three beatitudes – directed to the peacemakers, the persecuted for righteousness' sake and 'you when people revile you' – concern what happens to disciples when they follow the logic of Jesus' life and teaching, and thus seek to become a reconciling presence in the life of their neighbour. The gospel turns from words into community when it becomes apparent that the beatitudes are Jesus' autobiography: they are the story of Jesus. Each beatitude anticipates a moment on Jesus' journey to and death on the cross. He is poor in spirit when he shoulders the cross. He mourns when his heart is heavy in Gethsemane. He is meek when he is falsely accused and offers no reply. He thirsts on the cross. He is merciful when he says, 'Father, forgive them . . .'. He is pure in heart when he says, 'Not my will but your will.' He is a peacemaker when he tells Peter to put down his sword. He is persecuted and reviled by the priests, scribes, soldiers and bystanders at every moment in the passion story. The beatitudes are Jesus describing what it means to be his body in the world.

On closer inspection, each beatitude comes in three parts. The first part is a description of the cross. The final part is a description of the resurrection. Each beatitude has a resurrection promise. The beatitudes are a description of Jesus in his cross and in his resurrection. But between the cross and the resurrection lies a comma, which constitutes a valley between the horror of the cross and the wonder of the resurrection: a place where cross and resurrection meet. Jesus is the place where cross and resurrection meet. Christian community is the experience of that comma. The beatitudes are crucial because they draw together covenant, community and communion. In that they open the Sermon on the Mount, they are like a new decalogue, renewing the covenant. In that they speak of seeing God, being filled with righteousness and inheriting the realm of God, they promise communion. And in that they address those downtrodden and oppressed, the peacemakers, the persecuted and the reviled, they are a plea for a new community today to anticipate the true community God has in store.

COMMUNION

'There is no true being without communion. Nothing exists as an "individual", conceivable by itself. ... The person cannot exist without communion; but every form of communion which denies or suppresses the person is inadmissible.'[22] These words affirm the centrality of communion in scripture and theology, and identify the way communion is about being with to such an extent that it is almost a question of being united, but remaining so distinct that identity is never elided. This pattern is found on many levels; in what follows I explore six of them.

Communion fundamentally and definitively describes the relationship of the three persons of the Trinity. When Paul says farewell in the words, 'The grace of the Lord Jesus Christ, the love of God, and the communion of the Holy Spirit be with all of you' (2 Cor 13:13), he is not just describing the interaction of the Trinity with his readers: he is envisaging the relations of the persons of the Trinity with one another – a relationship that believers are invited to enter in prayer and to join in eschatological consummation. When at Jesus' baptism the Father speaks from the cloud, the Son enters the waters of the Jordan, and the Spirit descends as a dove, this is not just a demonstration of the Trinitarian activity of God in the coming of Christ; it is a window into that very interaction that is taking place constantly. The term *perichoresis*, though not coined in the Bible itself, refers to the mutual interpenetration or coinherence of the three divine persons whose every external action is infused by the energies of the other two. This offers a twofold notion of communion: as a characteristic of God both within the relations of the Trinity and in the shared external actions of the divine persons. What this is describing is the very epicentre of all things: the essence that precedes existence, in time as well as status. Communion is multidimensional, dynamic and ever

[22] John D. Zizioulas, *Being as Communion: Studies in Personhood and the Church* (Crestwood, NY: St Vladimir's Seminary Press, 1985), 18.

new; but it is simply the single word that sums up God's identity and purpose from the beginning, now and always.

Is there a second dimension of communion characterised by the hypostatic union through which Christ is one person with two natures, fully divine and fully human? This is a subtle question to which some would answer yes, but we must here answer no. The divine and human natures of Christ are certainly with one another, and the four Chalcedonian terms – without confusion, change, division or separation – clarify what the togetherness and the union entail when held delicately in one person. But is it appropriate to call this communion? John Zizioulas believes so. For him, communion with God, the aspiration for every human being, is patterned in relation to this communion within Christ.[23] What Christ is among humankind in the gospels, every disciple aspires to be forever: utterly with yet mutually in, a union that preserves the integrity and identity of the one being united and of God.

But there is a problem with perceiving the hypostatic union as communion. Chalcedon declared faith in two natures in one person: not in two persons in communion with one another. Human communion with Christ is a relationship of one person (or several persons) in close, interactive and profound connection with another person – in this case, Christ. This communion of human beings with Christ is not patterned after the communion that is within Christ. It is subtly but significantly different. Human relationship with Christ does not

[23] Christology, in the definitive form which the Fathers gave it, looks toward a single goal of purely existential significance, the goal of giving [humankind] the assurance that the quest for the person, not as 'mask' or as 'tragic figure', but as the authentic person, is not mythical or nostalgic but is a *historical reality*. Jesus Christ does not justify the title of Saviour because he brings the world a beautiful revelation, a sublime teaching about the person, but because he realises in history *the very reality of the person* and makes it the basis and 'hypostasis' of the person for every [human being]. ... Thanks to Christ [humankind] can henceforth himself 'subsist', can affirm [its] existence as personal not on the basis of immutable laws of [its] nature but on the basis of a relationship with God which is identified with what Christ in freedom and love possesses as Son of God with the Father.

Zizioulas, *Being as Communion*, *54, 56*, italics original

consist of an intimate connection (of two natures) *within* Christ's person; it is an external relationship, mediated by the Holy Spirit, between *separate* persons – who remain separate, even eschatologically.[24]

In a similar, but less complex, fashion disciples seek, in a manner comparable but not identical to communion, to be with themselves. This surely is what Nicodemus is looking for when he comes by night (Jn 3:2), what the rich young man still longs for despite his possessions (Mk 10:17) and what Peter knows he cannot find anywhere else when Jesus asks, 'Do you also wish to go away?' (Jn 6:67). All human beings are made in the image of God yet striving for God's likeness; both placed in a finite creation yet longing for eternal belonging; both seeking to establish their own integrity and generate their self-expression yet searching for commonality with others and creation. All persons are both in their context and distinct from their context, participants and bystanders. This is not communion with oneself, because communion is inherently about profound connection between separate selves; but we may still call it, in a looser way, being with oneself. This is not just an eschatological hope; it is a daily aspiration.

One undoubted further dimension of communion with God is the reason for and the destiny of creation.[25] Fully realised, conscious communion is the hope of humankind alone, but every creature and every dimension of the diverse creation will finally commune with God in its fitting way. Humankind's chief end is to glorify and enjoy God forever.[26] Communion with God is an entering into God's glory,

[24] I shall return to this theme in Chapter 4 in considering the Orthodox notion of communion.

[25] Barth, *Church Dogmatics*, vol. I/1, 107–08, describes being with God as the heart of revelation: 'The prophetic and apostolic word is the word, witness, proclamation and preaching of Jesus Christ … The promise of this word is this Immanuel, God with us … Holy Scripture is the word of [human beings] who yearned, waited and hoped for this Immanuel and who finally saw, hear, and handled it in Jesus Christ.'

[26] *The 1647 Westminster Shorter Catechism*, www.westminsterconfession.org/resources/confessional-standards/the-westminster-shorter-catechism. The scriptures cited are Romans 11:36, 1 Corinthians 10:31 and Psalm 73:25–28.

which denotes both God's character and God's reputation. God intends communion with humankind, embodies it in Jesus and through the Holy Spirit, and finally realises that communion eternally. Communion is what the notions of justification and sanctification are striving for. Justification is about our being able to *stand in the presence* of God, like a child being forgiven by a parent in spite of everything. Sanctification is about our being made holy and *being folded into* the character of God. Justification is the *com-* and sanctification is the *-union*. Communion is the everlasting fulfilment of everything justification and sanctification are seeking.

Communion involves being changed into God's likeness and being conformed to God's character. Human beings ultimately enjoy God: this is often depicted in relation to food. Humankind lives not by bread alone but 'by every word that comes from the mouth of the Lord' (Deut 8:3); God's words are sweet 'to my taste, sweeter than honey to my mouth!' (Ps 119:103); an invitation says, 'O taste and see that the Lord is good' (Ps 34:8); we hear of those who 'have tasted the goodness of the word of God and the powers of the age to come' (Heb 6:5); we are enjoined, like newborn babes, to 'Long for the pure, spiritual milk, so that by it you may grow into salvation – if indeed you have tasted that the Lord is good' (2 Pet 2:2–3).[27] Such experiences cluster in the principal scriptural image of heaven, a great banquet in which there is a seat for everybody (Lk 14:23) and no one shall go hungry (Jn 6:35).

Which leads to the fourth dimension of communion: worship, and, more specifically, the Eucharist. In baptism, catechumens are guided to the springs of the water of life and washed in the blood of the lamb. Their lives still have limitations, and they still sin; but henceforth they are in the presence of God and part of the body of Christ. *Com* and *union*: they are in communion. The Eucharist is a corporate

[27] See Geoffrey Wainwright, *Doxology: The Praise of God in Worship, Doctrine and Life; A Systematic Theology* (New York: Oxford University Press, 1980), 17–18.

enactment of the meal in which the community is promised it will never hunger or thirst again. It takes place in the presence of God, and, as participants eat and drink, in union with Christ – or, more exactly, the body of Christ becomes part of them. Communion again. Baptism and Eucharist are both forms of communion, in which we are united with God and yet remain in the presence of God, retaining our own identity.

Indeed, every moment of prayer is an enactment of this desire for and invitation to communion. The disciple seeks, for that moment, to be wholly embraced by the Holy Spirit, to be with the one who originates all things good and true. The collect for purity in the 1662 Book of Common Prayer articulates the aspiration to be with God in this way: 'Almighty God, unto whom all hearts are open, all desires known, and from whom no secrets are hid: cleanse the thoughts of our hearts by the inspiration of thy Holy Spirit, that we may perfectly love thee, and worthily magnify thy holy name.' Hearts, desires and secrets are laid bare, that the Spirit may cleanse the heart, bringing about perfect love and worthy worship. This is what human life should be like: this is what communion with God is.

Fifth, there is the communion of saints. This can refer to the diverse members of the body of Christ, all in touch and belonging to Christ and one another; or it can allude more specifically to the shared life of the departed with the church of today and tomorrow. Though the term was not coined until the fifth century, Paul gives thanks to the Father, 'who has enabled you to share in the inheritance of the saints in the light' (Col 1:12), and 1 John 1:3 declares 'what we have seen and heard so that you also may have fellowship with us; and truly our fellowship is with the Father and with his Son Jesus Christ'.[28] For Dietrich Bonhoeffer, the term means the restoration of the unbroken connection humankind enjoyed with God and one another before the

[28] The term is found in a sermon of Nicetas of Remesiana (in modern Serbia), who died in 414, and is thought by some to be the author of the Te Deum.

fall.[29] He describes eternal life as perfect community with God.[30] This the saints enjoy; but Bonhoeffer's chief concern is more with the church today than with the church eternal. In the communion of saints, stretching across space and time, the disciple is never alone: when Athanasius for example was exiled and isolated for upholding the *homoousias* in the Nicene Creed, he was upheld by the communion of saints. When Terry Waite was held captive and largely solitary in Beirut for four years from 1987 to 1991, he was upheld by the communion of saints.[31] The communion of saints is an eschatological partner in the prayer and ministry of the church: it is not that the saints pray *for* us, but that they glorify and enjoy God *with* us.

Less precisely, but just as significantly, communion is something believers find with themselves, one another, the stranger and the creation. We have seen above how this constitutes community, for example in how every form of combination with one another as the church seeks to be permeable to the stranger and engaged with the enemy. A neglected dimension of communion is what it means for disciples to find communion with themselves. One translation of Psalm 4:4 reads, 'Commune with your own heart upon your bed, and be still.'[32] We saw earlier in discussing the significance of 'person' how no one can find complete peace apart from God and others. But there are degrees of communion, and the reconciling of the insistent voices of the soul, the acceptance of one's limitations, the learning to enjoy the things God gives in plenty and not pining for the things in short supply, and the striving to be what only one can be rather than

[29] Dietrich Bonhoeffer, *Sanctorum Communio: A Theological Study of the Sociology of the Church, Dietrich Bonhoeffer Works*, vol. 1, trans. Reinhard Krauss and Nancy Lukens (Minneapolis: Fortress, 1998).

[30] Bonhoeffer, *Sanctorum communio*, 283.

[31] It was the practice of his fellow members of the Church Army to wear an H on their uniforms during his captivity to indicate that one of their number was a hostage and was being upheld in prayer by their whole community.

[32] King James Version. The NRSV rather lamely reads, 'Ponder it on your beds, and be silent.'

seeking to be a poor version of someone else: these are among the gifts that can yield being in communion with oneself.

Finally, perhaps the most pertinent form of communion is what it means to be in communion with the wider creation. If we see the two principal forms of revelation as being the Holy Spirit speaking through the word of God, understood as Christ and the scriptures, and through creation, in which the works of God proclaim the ways of God, then there is a potential sign of hope. Just as communion liturgically is found through gracious and reconciling interaction with Christ, the one who was betrayed, denied and abandoned, so as humankind wakes up to the ways it has ruined, poisoned and exploited creation it may similarly look to the Spirit to broker gracious and reconciling interaction in this second place of encounter. St Francis spoke in his celebrated canticle of Brother Moon and Sister Sun, Brothers Wind and Air, Sister Water and Brother Fire, Mother Earth and even Sister Death. Among many Psalms, Psalm 8:7–8 speaks in comradely fashion of 'All sheep and oxen, and also the beasts of the field, the birds of the air, and the fish of the sea'. And contemplation of the human body discloses the many layers by which we are each bonded to the elements and minerals we share with animate and inanimate nature alike. Creation is not static; often (but not always) because of nefarious human activity, species become extinct, and ecosystems alter. An expanded notion of the communion of saints would encompass the ever-present-to-God dimension of those forms of created life that the world will not see again; not as a discouragement to ecological activism, but as a further stimulus to disciples to live God's future now.

INHIBITING COVENANT, COMMUNITY AND COMMUNION

The Festival of Nine Lessons and Carols, first held in 1880 and now enjoyed around the world, has a rather different notion of what the Bible is about from the one offered in this chapter.[33] Its traditional

[33] The service was devised by the succentor George Walpole (later Bishop of Edinburgh) and E. W. Benson (then Bishop of Truro and later Archbishop of

bidding prayer enjoins worshippers to 'read and mark in Holy Scripture the tale of the loving purposes of God from the first days of our disobedience unto the glorious Redemption brought us by this Holy Child'. This neatly summarises the scriptural story as it is widely understood: a story of God's grace peeping between the pervading pillars of sin until the climax of Christ's cross, whereupon sin is vanquished (or guilt assuaged) and humankind is delivered. This redemption story is about sin, whereas the incarnation story is about glory; the redemption story is about deficit, the incarnation story about abundance; the redemption story is about a transformative confrontation, the incarnation story about constant vigilance; the redemption story is about solving human problems, the incarnation story about entering God's embrace.

The incarnation story is not fundamentally about the overcoming of evil, sin, suffering and death. It is about God's abundant life, embodied in Jesus, inhabited in covenant, community and communion. That does not mean it has no account of evil, sin, suffering and death – but that they are no longer the focus of attention. Two key texts are Colossians 1:15–20 and Ephesians 1:3–14. The Colossians passage both tells a story and identifies Christ as the centre of that story. The story is that everything was created through and for Christ, the firstborn from the dead and the agent of reconciliation between God and all things. Christ is identified as the visibility of God, the embracer of all things, the head of the church, the embodiment of the fullness of God, the reconciler of earth and heaven, and, in short, peace. The cross features in this story, but not as the reason for the story or even the key moment in the story: the story is about the one in whom all things hold together, and about how Jesus holds those things together. The Ephesians passage also tells a story – a story about glory. Before the foundation of the world God chose us in

Canterbury) and celebrated on 24 December 1880 in the wooden pro-Cathedral while Truro cathedral was still being built. In 1918 Eric Milner-White introduced the service to King's College, Cambridge, from where the BBC began to broadcast it in 1928. The first reading is the fall narrative from Genesis 3:1–6.

Christ to be holy, adopted us in Christ, forgave us in Christ, made known in Christ the divine purpose to gather up all things in Christ, gave us an inheritance in Christ and sealed us in the Holy Spirit. Again there is reference to forgiveness through the cross – but this is one among perhaps seven dimensions of the story, rather than the story's centre and focus. The initiative in both passages lies with God, God's purpose before the foundation of the world, the covenant, community and communion for which God is preparing and for which God is shaping us, and the enjoyment and glory that surround the whole unfolding mystery.

These two key texts encompass the story of covenant, community and communion I have outlined in this chapter. They place that story on a cosmic level: but they do not otherwise differ from the story I have been relating. Covenant, community and communion do not offer a story that underestimates or ignores evil, sin, suffering and death. Their story simply decentres evil, sin, suffering and death from the story – because it is a story about God's abundance and not about our scarcity. Let us consider them in the light of the story of covenant, community and communion. Immediately we may divide them into two groups: death and suffering (provided that suffering is not malevolent) are manifestations of life's constraints and limitations; evil and sin are expressions of life's perversities.

Death is the most explicit symptom of existence's finitude. Finitude is the definitive difference between existence and essence. Essence lasts forever: existence does not. The mystery of which we read in Ephesians 1 is that God intends from before the foundation of the world (we may say from before the inception of existence, or creation) eventually to draw us into essence. Thus we shall in the fullness of time be in the realm where there is no death. But that is not the realm we are currently in. We shall also one day be in the realm where there is no birth: this is the realm of creation, that is the realm of re-creation. Thus as we transition to the realm of essence there are losses as well as gains. In essence we do not die; but neither do we create, or bring to birth. In essence Christ makes all things new – but does not create new things. There is novelty, discovery, adventure, epiphany – but not birth. There is endless new encounter in what has already, previously, been created. Death names the profound loss in that equation: but in Christ, death turns out not to be a roadblock but a gate. Covenant, community and communion are not abolished by death: they continue, and in the fullness of time we reinhabit them in God's eternal realm. The whole of life is a series of more or less painful lettings-go that prepare us for the final letting-go into the embrace of the God who never lets us go.[34]

Suffering can be broken down in several ways. There is suffering that lasts until death, and suffering that lasts a limited period. The former is enfolded in the discussion about death, above. The latter is an encounter with the rawness of existence and the fragility of the human condition. This rawness and fragility includes *misfortune*, which is largely accidental; *muddle*, which is clumsy or thoughtless; *malice*, which is deliberate and willed, either directly to cause harm or indirectly as a by-product of an intent to do damage elsewhere; and *martyrdom*, in which suffering and death are humbly accepted or knowingly risked out of faithfulness in the face of malign threat. Malice and martyrdom interface with evil and sin, and are best addressed there. Thus suffering is largely a matter of misfortune and

[34] A prayer of Jim Cotter from his service of Compline captures this sense perfectly:

> O living God, in Jesus Christ you were laid in the tomb at this evening hour, and so sanctified the grave to be a bed of hope to your people. Give us courage and faith to die daily to our sin and pride, that even as this flesh and blood decays, our lives may still grow in you, that at our last day our dying may be done so well that we live in you for ever. Amen.
>
> Prayer at Night: A Book for the Darkness, *3rd ed. (Exeter: Cairns 1986), 53*

A meditation in the same book is even more acute:

> When we receive the forgiveness of another... it means the worst in us has been accepted – and that means a kind of death. ... We want to make conditions, so that there can be a core still under our control. To let go completely – this is death – but it is necessary if we are to find life. To let go into God – this is death. So receiving forgiveness is to prepare ourselves for the final letting go, for the decisive moment of truth, by a little dying, a little letting go.
>
> *(79)*

muddle. Much human endeavour and intercession concerns a condition like cancer, which may present as misfortune but may turn out to have been exacerbated by lifestyle choices, and thus be closer to muddle, and earthquakes or hurricanes, which seem like misfortune but on closer scrutiny of building methods or locations may be closer to muddle or even malice. Much of the ecological debate is about whether the current crisis is due to muddle or malice. When Jesus in Luke 13 discusses the Galileans whose blood Pilate had mingled with their sacrifices and the eighteen who were killed when the tower of Siloam fell on them, he is distinguishing between the misfortune (perhaps including muddle) of the latter and the malice of the former. The key point, again, about suffering is that suffering does not preclude covenant, community and communion. Indeed there are instances where through transfiguration the suffering of an individual can bind a community together in an experience of communion and become that community's defining moment; and there are occasions where suffering can lead to a deepening of covenant. The exile was perhaps an example for Israel of both of these phenomena. Suffering demands community, community requires covenant, and both can issue in communion. It is not always so: but once one recognises that the shape of the scriptural story is to cultivate covenant, community and communion rather than simply abolish suffering and death, a richer notion of what it means for Christ to gather all things together emerges.

Evil is not sin with a loud voice: they are qualitatively different. Sin is where you have transgressed. You know it is wrong, but you tell yourself a false story – everyone does it, no one will notice, it is only a small thing, no one is really hurt by it, look at all the good things I have done that outweigh it, no one need ever know, I am not a bad person. But evil has an alternative logic: you tell yourself what you are doing is actually good. Your story has dispensed with guilt and shame and replaced them with pride. I am not shooting innocent people in the back; I am denazifying a whole country. I am not doing it behind the bike sheds; I am doing it in the village square. Evil is like a virus.

It tells a false story that justifies sacrificing other people and pillaging creation for a hideous false god. Sin is living in a world without God, without good and bad, without judgement. But evil is creating a whole new and demonic god, and reshaping your entire life to assert that terrible things like cruelty and murder are actually noble. Evil on a national scale creates a mythical story that appeals to a grotesque past that needs honouring and projects a phantom future where those who slaughter so-called enemies will be rewarded.

In the light of the story above, sin is that which undermines covenant, dismantles community and inhibits communion. If we were made to enjoy God forever, sin comes in two forms. We *enjoy what should be used*, putting something else in place of God, our gratification, power, acclaim, even life: this is *idolatry*. We become fixated on one thing or person and lose sight of many other good things. Idolatry is when we lose sight of the one who made us to respond in companionship, and instead we invest in other gods, often of our own making. Or, *we use what should be enjoyed*, invoking the name of God for unworthy purposes, turning covenant, community and communion into instruments for our own aggrandisement, pleasure or advantage: this is *blasphemy*. Fraud, sexual assault and boasting are all forms of blasphemy. Blasphemy is when we forget that something or someone is precious, honoured and loved, and turn it or them into a means to our own ends. The account in Exodus 32:1–14, about the people making and worshipping a golden calf, is an account of the two kinds of sin in narrative form. The people blaspheme by turning God's liberation into part of their own project of survival. Meanwhile they commit idolatry by making their jewellery into an object of worship. It is a repeat of the Adam and Eve story, where the first couple blaspheme by eating the fruit that should be left on the tree and idolatrise by making the serpent, rather than God, their authority.

When Jesus tells the parable of the wheat and the weeds (Mt 13:24–30), in which the darnel is so tangled up in the wheat that it cannot be removed, he is often assumed to be commending humility – that evil must be sought, found and rooted out, but that there are bound to be casualties, because all one can do amid the reality of good and evil is try to discern amid many flawed and unsatisfactory possibilities the one that expresses and achieves the greatest good and the least evil. But the parable commends not humility but patience. It says if you set about rooting up evil, you root up the good too. It says taking it upon yourself to rid the world of evil shows a lack of faith that that is exactly what God will do at the end of history. The patience of God is Jesus himself. In Jesus we see God's patience. Jesus names and encounters the reality of evil from the beginning of his ministry. In the temptation narrative (Mt 4:1–11) Jesus does not destroy the devil. Neither does he hide himself away in a fantasy field of pure wheat. What he does is to maintain a faithful presence in the face of evil, speaking the truth, empowering a community, modelling the fruits of the Spirit, bringing about reconciliation, taking in his own body the cost of witness. Thus he endures beyond evil, waiting until the time of God's justice comes. In other words, staying faithful to covenant, community and communion. No killing the enemy, no rooting out evil, no premature summary action, no naïve attempt to make a field without evil. Instead, revolutionary patience, resting entirely on trust in God's final judgement. And this is exactly what he does on the cross. To defeat evil takes more than weapons. It requires a very different kind of story. Jesus told stories and lived a story that said he came to bring abundant life and the truth will set you free (Jn 10:10, 8:32). He overcame evil by outlasting it and discrediting the story that made it seem good. He did not destroy evil. Instead, he lived and told a better story.

Here is that better story – a somewhat different story from that told at a Festival of Nine Lessons and Carols, and one truer to the scriptures as a whole. Before there was anything – a universe, a Big Bang, let alone life – there was God. God is the name of what there was when there was nothing – in other words, when there was no existence, only essence. There was already plurality within God: that is what Trinity means. But God wanted there to be plurality *outside*

God, not just within. This was because God is fundamentally relationship, and God wanted there to be relationship with other, not just with same. Relating to someone different from you has a quality unlike relating to someone the same. The word we use to describe God's relationship with other is Jesus. Jesus is the embodiment of God's original desire to be in relationship across difference. It is that desire that triggered creation, the existence of the universe. It is a desire that issues in covenant, seeks community and will one day be fulfilled in communion. But relationship across difference is fraught with risk. I may misunderstand you, and construe our relationship not as gift but as burden, so turning grace into resentment. I may try to make our relationship exclusive, and envy anyone else you want to include. I may seek to use our relationship to gain some benefit beyond the relationship itself. I may seek to set our relationship alongside other relationships that undermine and dismantle it.

We may call all these dangers the Divine Risk. The divine risk is the possibility that humanity will forget that relationship with God in covenant, community and communion is the reason for its existence, and turn to other gods; and that it will fail to realise that all its other relationships – with self, one another, the stranger and the creation – are opportunities to practise the joy of discovery, appreciation and growth as an echo of its relationship with God. That risk makes God's goodness and mercy vulnerable to the contagion of sin. Sin is the name of the poison that inserts itself into the distance between us and God, and inhibits, dismantles or destroys all other relationship.

Making and restoring relationships is what life is all about. This is what covenant, community and communion mean. Relationships happen when two parties resolve to take a risk and say, 'The distance between us is an invitation not just to find surprising commonalities, but to explore our differences with wonder and delight.' Good relationships are ones where the parties enjoy their differences and the distance between them, even to the point of seeing setbacks and disagreements as part of the fun of a developing association. But the risk in every relationship is that the distance and difference between the parties will not by enjoyment lead to delight and discovery but, by attempts at use, will be regarded as threats to be controlled, avoided or destroyed.

The name for what occupies the distance between us is Jesus. Jesus' are the arms that stretch to fill the gap between us and God and between us and one another – the gap that would otherwise be filled by the poison of suspicion, mistrust or hostility. Jesus informs, illuminates and inspires covenant, community and communion. He embodies God's utter enjoyment of us, and our utter enjoyment of God. In him there is no use at all. He fills the distance between God and us with grace and truth, until we are utterly with God, and we enjoy one another forever.

3 Being with God

In this chapter I seek to draw out the scriptural and especially incarnational aspects of the notion of being with. Being with is inherently incarnational, but in my treatments of the notion elsewhere I have not always drawn out its full theological breadth as I do here. *A Nazareth Manifesto* makes a case for being with as the incarnational form of God's purpose and the eschatological shape of human destiny.[1] To locate being with means to distinguish it from three other ways of relating – working for, working with and being for. Working for and being for centre themselves entirely as the providers of solutions and perceive deficit in those seen as problems. Working with brings together coalitions and partnerships, and relocates problems from people to situations – but still tends to remain preoccupied with configuring those situations as problems needing solutions. Only being with engages with people for their own sake and seeks to enjoy rather than change them. The central theological claim is that God enjoys us, by contrast with conventional theological accounts, in which God is mostly concerned – even required – to change us, or at least ameliorate our situation.

A Nazareth Manifesto elucidates eight dimensions of being with, rooted in the inner-Trinitarian relationships and in eschatological anticipation.[2] These have considerable significance for theology, ethics, missiology and pastoral studies. In a number of related

[1] Samuel Wells, *A Nazareth Manifesto: Being with God* (Oxford: Wiley-Blackwell, 2015).

[2] The distinctions between the four kinds of relationship are first explored in Samuel Wells and Marcia A. Owen, *Living without Enemies: Being Present in the Midst of Violence* (Downers Grove, IL: IVP, 2011).

books, I have extended this exploration to a range of fields.[3] In this chapter I assume that foregoing exploration, and do not reprise it: instead I tie the notion of being with more explicitly to scripture in general and incarnation in particular. I take each dimension of being with in turn and investigate its scriptural resonance and incarnational capacity. Having identified covenant, community and communion as three focal elements of God's purpose, and recognised how each of these is a way of talking about incarnation, here I affirm how each one is a form of being with. Because being with is not always appreciated as a multi-layered concept, I take time to set out its eight dimensions, so that it becomes clear how textured this notion truly is, and how it informs a perspective on the theological and ethical implications of the incarnation.[4]

PRESENCE

To say that being with concerns presence is a commonplace, although what that presence necessarily entails in an era of video conferencing and online platforms is increasingly in question. But the characteristics of presence itself are less often scrutinised. It is helpful to consider the constituent of time as well as space.

The scriptures narrate many moments in which protagonists are present – yet one feels the weight of past and/or future upon them.

[3] Two books work in detail with the eight dimensions of being with in ministry and mission: see Samuel Wells, *Incarnational Ministry* and *Incarnational Mission: Being with the World* (Grand Rapids, MI: Eerdmans, and Norwich: Canterbury, 2018). A further two books discuss in more general terms being with and the cross of Christ: Samuel Wells, *Hanging by a Thread: The Questions of the Cross* (Norwich: Canterbury, 2016) and *A Cross in the Heart of God: Reflections on the Death of Jesus* (Norwich: Canterbury, 2020). I address the implications of a theological ethic of being with for Christian social and political engagement in Samuel Wells, Russell Rook and David Barclay, *For Good: The Church and the Future of Welfare* (Norwich: Canterbury, 2017).

[4] While I believe that my exploration of being with is unique in theology, Stephen Darwall has addressed the concept in moral philosophy. He perceives it as a kind of empathy based on an openness to mutual relating, rooted in sincerity, receptivity and honesty. See his 'Being With', *Southern Journal of Philosophy*, 49 (2011), 4–24, and his *The Second-Person Standpoint: Morality, Respect and Accountability* (Cambridge, MA: Harvard University Press, 2006).

One such is Nehemiah 8. The people have been hard at work rebuilding their culture, their city, their whole society. They come together, and Ezra reads to them the Torah. Ezra speaks for five hours at a time, from dawn to midday. Everyone stands up. Then Ezra blesses God, and everyone presses their heads to the ground. And the Levites interpret, or maybe translate from Hebrew to Aramaic. Whereupon the people are so moved they begin to weep – because suddenly the whole truth of themselves, and of God, and of their sin, and of God's grace, and of those fifty wasted years, and yet of a future that is full of promise – all of it becomes vivid and true and real and present at this very moment. God went ahead of Moses and made ready the Promised Land before the people got there. God went ahead of the people and was in Babylon before the exiles reached it. God went ahead of the returning exiles and was in Jerusalem while Jerusalem was still a wasteland. And only when Ezra reads them the story do the people grasp it, and recognise their sin, but realise that their sin was just a pretext for God to reveal indescribable constancy, incomprehensible faithfulness, inconceivably patient loving-kindness. Israel may have broken the covenant, but God never did.

More obviously, in Luke 1 Gabriel announces to Mary that she is to be with child. In so doing, he portrays the story of Israel coming to fruition in her womb. In calling her 'favoured one' he invokes language not heard since David. In calling the child 'holy' he cites the covenant made with Moses. In speaking of the house of Jacob he enfolds the era of the patriarchs. In calling herself the servant of the Lord, Mary is going all the way back to the obedience abrogated by Adam and Eve. And in uttering the words 'Let it be', Mary returns to the Genesis 1 creation story itself. The annunciation account is saying that the whole story of God, right back to the very beginning, is in this child. Every moment of yesterday is present today. Incarnation means not just the presence of God, but the presence of the story of God – yesterday and forever.

Likewise the resurrection story in John 20 is the presence of past and future in one moment. It is the new creation. It is the new exodus.

It is the new covenant. It is the new nativity. It is the transformation of Good Friday. And it is an anticipation of the last day. The scriptural narratives transcend time by making past and future present today – and continue to do so as they are read and proclaimed among the faithful.

But while these engagements with time are significant, presence is most obviously about space. God is present everywhere, at all times. 'Where shall I go from your Spirit? Or where shall I flee from your presence?' says Psalm 139:7. That presence is awesome: 'Oh that you would rend the heavens and come down, that the mountains might quake at your presence – as when fire kindles brushwood and the fire causes water to boil— to make your name known to your adversaries, and that the nations might tremble at your presence!' (Isa 64:1–2). Simply being in God's presence exposes waywardness and becomes unbearable to the transgressor: 'And they heard the sound of the Lord God walking in the garden in the cool of the day, and the man and his wife hid themselves from the presence of the Lord God among the trees of the garden' (Gen 3:8). Yet to the one who longs to be with God, God's presence is the epitome of glory and grace: 'Hannah said to her husband, "As soon as the child is weaned, I will bring him, so that he may appear in the presence of the Lord and dwell there forever"' (1 Sam 1:22); 'Cast me not away from your presence, and take not your Holy Spirit from me' (Ps 51:11). Indeed, being in God's presence is integral to eschatological fulfilment: 'You make known to me the path of life; in your presence there is fullness of joy; at your right hand are pleasures forevermore' (Ps 16:11). God's presence is not always something we enter; sometimes God takes the initiative and finds us: 'Surely goodness and mercy shall follow me all the days of my life, and I shall dwell in the house of the Lord my whole life long' (Ps 23:6).

In times of movement the pillars of cloud and of flame signal God's guiding presence (Ex 13:21–22). In settled times, the definitive form of God's presence for Israel is the ark of the covenant and specifically the mercy seat that covers the ark, eventually enclosed in the temple. But there is a characteristic term that indicates God's abiding with Israel, and that is the bread of the presence: twelve loaves, standing for the twelve tribes of Israel, arranged in two rows of six, and changed every sabbath, the priests eating what had been displayed (Lev 24). This anticipates the Eucharist, and particularly the tradition of the reserved sacrament and of benediction, as constant renderings of God's presence. Here are communion and covenant conjoined with presence. Hebrews confirms the confidence that in the incarnation all these scriptural notions of presence find their embodiment in Christ: 'For Christ did not enter a sanctuary made by human hands, a mere copy of the true one, but he entered into heaven itself, now to appear in the presence of God on our behalf' (Heb 9:24).

The complexity of presence is explored when a companion is present, but not yet identified. Two such moments stand out. Joseph leads his brothers a merry dance before finally declaring, 'I am Joseph.' His brothers are 'dismayed at his presence' (Gen 45:3). The presence of Joseph is almost the presence of God, because Joseph's presence reveals the extraordinary revelation that God was with him – and them – despite and even by means of the breakdown in their relationship. Meanwhile Easter is the most vivid moment of confused presence. Mary Magdalene takes Jesus for the gardener; the disciples on the road to Emmaus have no sense of Jesus' presence until he breaks the bread – but in retrospect realise their hearts were on fire as he walked with them (Jn 20:11–20; Lk 24:13–35). The episode is a microcosm of the whole gospel story: the incarnate one is misunderstood, yet his story transcends incomprehension. Presence alone is not enough for being with: except in retrospect.

The joy of pilgrims making their way to Jerusalem indicates that being with God, in God's presence, is the summit of human aspiration, and the heart of God's purposes for Israel, and thus humankind. 'Happy are those whose strength is in you, in whose heart are the highways to Zion. ... A day in your courts is better than a thousand elsewhere' (Ps 84:5, 10). The incarnation is the confirmation that this was always so, and can be fulfilled in one who is fully human and fully divine, and will be the heavenly joy of all God's people.

ATTENTION

Attention turns mere presence into genuine interaction – with the emphasis on receptivity. To offer someone attention is to say, 'For the time being (and that can be very short or very long), there is nothing in the world more important to me than you.' We may distinguish two kinds of attention. One is open-ended, obedient attention, entirely content to let the other party set the agenda, but receiving not just words but all other forms of communication available: it could be a guest being enjoyed or a client being listened to or a panorama being taken in. Another is focused attention, willingly scrutinising a particular sentence or voice or perspective, associated with the injunction 'Pay attention', perhaps with the warning, 'I'm only going to say this once': it could be the view down a microscope, the words of an expert witness or a desire to see how a magician performs a trick.

Perhaps the definitive moment of attention in the Old Testament is Moses at the burning bush: 'He looked, and the bush was blazing, yet it was not consumed' (Ex 3:2) – surely a depiction of Israel in perfect relationship with God. God calling for Moses' attention is an insight into the depth of God's attention to Moses and his people: 'I have observed the misery of my people who are in Egypt; I have heard their cry on account of their taskmasters' (Ex 3:7). A humbler model for the receptive kind of attention is the young Samuel under the authority of Eli. When Samuel is troubled by a voice calling his name, Samuel eventually, on Eli's instruction, replies, 'Speak, Lord, for your servant is listening.' It turns out that the Lord has something to say to Samuel that makes 'both ears of anyone who hears of it tingle' (1 Sam 3:10–11): the covenant has been broken.

The Old Testament prophets demand the second, focused kind of attention. Seventeen times the phrase 'pay attention' or 'give attention' arises in relation to the prophets seeking to direct the people back to the terms of the covenant and walk with God anew: Jeremiah is the most frequent in making this plea. Jeremiah conveys God's distress to the people of Judah, saying,

> Amend your ways and your doings, and let me dwell with you in this place. Do not trust in these deceptive words: 'This is the temple of the Lord, the temple of the Lord, the temple of the Lord.' For if you truly amend your ways and your doings, if you truly act justly one with another, if you do not oppress the alien, the orphan, and the widow, or shed innocent blood in this place, and if you do not go after other gods to your own hurt, then I will dwell with you in this place, in the land that I gave of old to your ancestors for ever and ever.
>
> *(Jer 7:3–7)*

In the language of this chapter, we can hear Jeremiah saying, 'Being with doesn't just mean presence: it means attention – and attention means honouring the covenant.' Elsewhere, Esther turns presence into attention when she says to Mordecai, 'Go, gather all the Jews to be found in Susa, and hold a fast on my behalf, and neither eat nor drink for three days, night or day. I and my maids will also fast as you do' (Esth 4:16). Attention intensifies presence: rather than relying on her presence at court, Esther realises she needs to be entirely focused on her people and (although the divine name is not mentioned) her God.

The gospels offer definitive accounts of receptive attention, focused attention – and a third dimension: inattention. When Jesus visits Martha and Mary, Martha is present, but Mary is attentive. Mary offers a paradigm of what true attention to God entails. Martha implies that Jesus is ungrateful – and inattentive to her. She then orders Jesus to criticise her sister and to instruct her to leave Jesus alone and join her in working for him rather than being with him. Her anger is such she cannot use her sister's name. Jesus points out that Martha is distracted by many things: Mary is alert to one thing only. Martha thinks Jesus is not enough; for Mary, Jesus is more than enough. Jesus exalts Mary because Mary portrays God. In the incarnation, God is not concerned about many things; God is alert to one thing only. Martha is 'serving' Jesus; but entirely on her own terms. She is not giving him the only thing he wants: her attention. Martha offers food; Mary shares communion.

The focused attention of the disciples is tinged with irony almost throughout. Most poignantly, they hang on Jesus' every word at the Last Supper: 'Peter said to him, "Even though I must die with you, I will not deny you." And so said all the disciples' (Mt 26:35). Yet hours later Peter denies him three times. Earlier in the same chapter there is an ironic contrast: the focused devotion of the unnamed woman who pours on Jesus' head an alabaster jar of very costly ointment, preparing his body for burial, sits uncomfortably alongside Judas, who prepares to betray Jesus for thirty pieces of silver (Mt 26:6–14). And this presages the definitive moment of inattention in the gospels: Gethsemane. Jesus confesses he is deeply grieved, even to death; but three times he returns to Peter, James and John to find them sleeping (Mt 26:36–45).

The gospel narrative is one in which the Father's attention to the Son, and through the Son and the Holy Spirit to their creation, is always greater and more embracing than humankind's attention to God. As in the story of Martha and Mary, so in the Sermon on the Mount, the alternative to anxiety is attention. Attention assumes trust, because in order to focus entirely on one thing, you need to be confident someone else is looking after all the other things. Martha lacks that trust; Mary has it. Trust is the better part of faith. Anxiety chips away at trust by consistently gnawing away at its roots and crowding in information that distracts attention. God has reason not to trust, but has faith in us anyway. God's attention is on us. Accordingly, Jesus tells his disciples not to worry about their life, what they will eat or drink, or about their body, what they will wear. He encourages them to look at the birds of the air, which neither sow nor reap nor gather into barns, and yet their heavenly Father feeds them. He asks, 'Are you not of more value than they?' He directs his disciples' attention to the lilies of the field, how they grow; yet even

Solomon in all his glory, he says, was not clothed like one of these (Mt 6:25–29). Thus attention dismantles anxiety. Later, reassuring those sent on mission that they should not fear, Jesus adds, 'Are not two sparrows sold for a penny? Yet not one of them will fall to the ground unperceived by your Father. And even the hairs of your head are all counted' (Mt 10:29–30). Attention dispels anxiety, and trust creates faith, just as it does among the persons of the Trinity. In showing the Trinity to humankind and humankind to the Trinity, the incarnate Jesus is creating a community that beholds one another as the persons of the Trinity indwell each other.

MYSTERY

In many ways mystery is the key to the transformation of perception I am advocating in this book. Christian theology often regards creation in general and humankind in particular as a problem for God to fix, rather than as a mystery that God enters.[5] A problem is something God might address as a detour, a setback that occupies time and energy and no doubt some skill and proficiency, but does not exercise God's very being. Just as a person hires an accountant to sort out a complex tax return or finds a friend with a ladder to get a cat down from a tree, humanity calls on God to deliver it from the plight of guilt and mortality – and once the job is done, God and humankind can go their separate ways. But the incarnation is not like that. It is not built around fixing an anomaly and then returning to normal. The incarnation is not a detour. It is at the very heart of God: it is inherent in essence. We may discern four mysteries and one truth. Mystery one is why God wanted to conceive creation as a theatre in which to share glory with humankind in the incarnate Christ: hence, 'He was destined before the foundation of the world, but was revealed at the end of the ages for your sake' (1 Pet 1:20). Mystery two is why God continued to seek relationship before and after the coming of the

[5] I owe the distinction between a problem and a mystery to Gabriel Marcel. For an account of Marcel, see my *A Nazareth Manifesto*, 129–32.

fleshly Jesus, given the repeated rejection of covenant, community and communion, reaching its apex in the crucifixion of Christ: hence, 'In this is love, not that we loved God but that he loved us' (1 Jn 4:10).[6] Mystery three is why God still seeks relationship, through the Holy Spirit. And mystery four is how we shall find relationship with the Father in Christ through the Holy Spirit and share that relationship with one another and the renewed creation. The truth is, God entered all these mysteries in the incarnation from before the foundation of the world.

The scriptures speak of two kinds of mystery: the one that is wrapped in endless complexity and takes all one's powers and energies to unravel, and the one that engulfs one's whole being, indeed the whole being of the universe, and yet still can never be fathomed. Daniel 2 is particularly concerned with the first kind. The mystery buried in Nebuchadnezzar's dream is beyond the skill or imagination of all the wise among the Chaldeans. To Daniel is revealed the mystery at the heart of the revelation: one that concerns the empires that will follow upon the demise of Nebuchadnezzar. The mystery is really about the unfolding of history according to God's purpose. It takes great understanding and insight to unravel, but it is simply a further portal into the mystery of God.

That latter mystery is explored in Ephesians and Colossians. 'Mystery' sums up the opening verses of Ephesians – and that mystery is the mystery of God's will and purpose, which he set forth in Christ (Eph 1:9); a mystery referred to no fewer than five times two chapters later, and described as 'the plan of the mystery hidden for ages in God who created all things' (Eph 3:9). Likewise Colossians refers four times to mystery, and each reference highlights the centrality of the incarnation, a mystery hidden for ages and generations but now revealed to the saints (Col 1:26).

[6] Augustine recognises this when he says, 'The Father loved us also before, not only before the Son died for us, but before he created the world.' Augustine, *On the Trinity*, trans. Edmund Hill OP (Hyde Park, NY: New City Press, 1991), 355 (book 13, section 15).

Emphasising the way Ephesians and Colossians perceive the incarnation as a mystery is vital because the tendency in Christian theology is to treat the incarnation as a means to an end – that end being some kind of judicial, redemptive or ritual atonement.[7] While rooted in Paul's letters, these metaphors contrast with Jesus' simpler offer of present and everlasting relationship. Jesus' words are not in the spirit of fixing a problem: he says of the poor in spirit, the meek, the pure in heart and the persecuted, 'Theirs is the kingdom of heaven … they will inherit the earth … they will see God … theirs is the kingdom of heaven' (Mt 5:3–10). There seems no problem to solve here by believing in a notion of atonement; but there is a great mystery of the transformation of earthly hardship into heavenly glory. The Father is one who knows how to give good gifts to those who ask, is found by all who seek and opens doors to any who knock (Mt 7:7–11).[8] Meanwhile in Luke, Jesus says (7:50) to the woman who bathes his feet with her tears, 'Your faith has saved you', and (23:43) to the repentant criminal beside him on the cross, 'Today you will be

[7] Stephen Finlan, in his *Problems with Atonement: The Origins of, and Controversy about, the Atonement Doctrine* (Collegeville, MN: Liturgical Press, 2005), 50–57, shows how Paul speaks of several kinds of transactions: sacrificial –ritual cleaning and killing of a victim; scapegoat – ritual sending-away of sin; judicial – a writ of acquittal in the divine court; and economic – purchasing the freedom of captives or slaves. Finlan adds that the notion of Christ dying for others recalls the Hellenistic notion of a noble death with vicarious saving power: thus martyrdom becomes a fifth mode of atonement.

[8] Stephen Finlan, in his *Problems with Atonement*, points how 'Christ died for us' can mean he died as a martyr, he died as a substitute in our place, he ransomed us, he made a sufficient sacrifice or he took on his shoulders our curse. Finlan speculates, on the basis of Paul's disclosure that he has become all things to all people that by all means he might save some (1 Cor 9:22), that Paul gladly used such soteriological motifs as persuaded people in his Mediterranean milieu. Finlan laments 'the danger with atonement metaphors, however rhetorically effective they may be: they carry their baggage with them, and leave these bags like time bombs in the railway stations of our thinking, prepared to explode into manifestations of fear, suspicion, and scapegoating' (62). He adds, 'The open-hearted message of faith and sincerity that is clearly Jesus' central teaching … tends to be brushed aside by the intense emotions of repentance and yearning and the mental construct of affirming certain soteriological formulas' (61). He also notes, again pointedly, 'Paul could never say, "Blessed are the pure in heart, for they will see God" (Matt 5:8), for there *are* no pure in heart in Paul's view' (60).

with me in Paradise.' These are invitations to enter a mystery; they can hardly be said to fix a problem, for the woman is still a notorious sinner, and the criminal is still about to die on the cross.

The problem–mystery distinction is perhaps the most revealing contrast between two different understandings of the incarnation. The gospels portray Jesus as one who knew he had to go to Jerusalem and face execution there (he predicts it three times in all the synoptics); but not as one who believed this was the thrust of his incarnation, his message or his ministry. Instead, he came to live God's future now, or, in his words, to say, 'The kingdom of God is among you' (Lk 17:21).

DELIGHT

Delight comes in two forms, which have some overlap but are not the same. One is the exultant joy one takes in something or someone worthy of praise; the other is the rich assets one finds in something or someone in whom it would be more common or more likely only to see deficits. In broad terms the former is a human characteristic, in the Bible, particularly in relation to God; the latter is a divine characteristic, particularly in relation to humankind.

While the latter is the focus of my concern here, it is worth pausing to recognise the forms in which the former arises. The Psalms are the embodiment of the first kind of delight. They have thirty-five references to delight; Psalm 119 alone has ten references, every one of which is about law, commandments, statutes or, in two cases, testimonies: thus, 'I long for your salvation, O Lord, and your law is my delight' (Ps 119:174). This is a portrayal of love for and rejoicing in God, on an individual and national level: an ideal embodiment of covenant. Likewise Israel is called to inhabit the covenant with joy, and thus live as a healthy and thriving community, at peace and in communion with God: 'I delight to do your will, O my God; your law is within my heart' (Ps 40:8). The reciprocal side of this relationship is the way Israel seeks to evoke delight in God, and recognises those actions or rituals that do not evoke that delight: Hence, 'Our steps are made firm by the Lord, when he delights in our way' (Ps 37:23), and, by contrast, 'Sacrifice and offering you do not desire, but you have given me an open ear' (Ps 40:6).

But delight is not fundamentally about an appropriate and joyful response to blessing or faithfulness. Delight becomes significant when it is a transformative response of abundance in the face of scarcity, perceiving asset where most would see only deficit. Thus expression of delight requires training of the moral imagination. The Bible was not written by those who felt God had given Israel its just punishment for abrogating the covenant and would give the gentiles similar judgement once the covenant embraced them. The Bible was written by people who rejoiced that God had shown grace rather than due measure, and had in Christ raised humankind beyond its deserts rather than condemned it to desolation. The most evocative moment of this kind is perhaps Isaiah 62:4–5, where, out of waywardness and exile, Israel still finds favour in God's sight:

> You shall no more be termed Forsaken, and your land shall no more be termed Desolate; but you shall be called My Delight Is in Her, and your land Married; for the Lord delights in you, and your land shall be married. For as a young man marries a young woman, so shall your builder marry you, and as the bridegroom rejoices over the bride, so shall your God rejoice over you.

Israel's deficits (infidelity) are turned to assets (marriage), and Israel's isolation (forsaken) is transformed into companionship (delight).

Jesus models delight in encounter after encounter. Perhaps definitively, he says Peter, Andrew, James and John will turn from those who catch fish (and at key moments, not very many) to those who catch people, and Peter from a fisherman into a rock on which the church is built (Lk 5:10; Mt 16:18). He enables Simon Peter, Thomas, Nathanael of Cana, the sons of Zebedee, and two others to see not the scarcity of fishing on one side of the boat but the abundance of fishing on the other side (Jn 21:1–8).[9] But his delight is

[9] Surely a reference to taking the gospel not to the Jews only but also to the gentiles.

everywhere: he regards not the paucity of loaves and fish, but what they can become in God's realm, not a failed party but an occasion for an overflowing of wine (Jn 6:9, 2:10). He sees in Zacchaeus not a tax collector depleting Israel but a benefactor enriching Israel (Lk 19:1–10). On the one occasion he betrays himself and does see deficit in the Syrophoenician woman, on the grounds that she is not an Israelite, she corrects him by asserting the asset of her lowly status and Jesus accordingly responds (Mk 7:24–30). When the angry crowd sees a woman only as an adulterer deserving of stoning, Jesus sees her as a future disciple and encourages her to go her way without fear for her safety (Jn 8:10–11). When Jesus encounters a man born blind, he perceives not a person defined by his deficit but one in whom the works of God may be revealed (Jn 9:3). And this action of Jesus inspires those who follow: Paul implores Philemon not to define Onesimus by the deficit of his former slave status, but as a brother in the faith and a co-worker (Philem 16).

But beyond these gestures in which Jesus portrays salvation as building on assets, Jesus' incarnation itself is an embodiment of delight. Many times God speaks of delight – but in Jesus, God delights in humankind in a far more profound way. Thomas Aquinas says, 'Grace does not destroy nature, but perfects it': this is truly a statement about Jesus' incarnation, which is the summit of God's purpose – a purpose expressed in the humbler ways described above.[10] In the incarnation God does not destroy humankind, and does not reject the covenant with Israel: God perfects human nature and brings the gentiles into the covenant with Israel. The incarnation is the ultimate form of God's delight. In contrast to the traditional portrayal of humankind as damaged, even totally depraved by the fall, the

[10] Thomas Aquinas, *Summa theologiae*, 1.1.8, in Latin/English Edition of the Works of St Thomas Aquinas, vol. 13, trans. Laurence Shapcote, ed. John Mortensen and Enrique Alarcón (Lander, WY: Aquinas Institute for the Study of Sacred Doctrine, 2012), 12. For an extended study on the Protestant and Catholic understandings of this statement, see Kathryn Tanner, *Christ the Key* (Cambridge: Cambridge University Press, 2010), 58–139.

incarnation takes the asset of human nature and elevates it to be alongside God's own nature in one person. In the same vein, Pentecost is not regime change for Jesus' fitful followers: it builds on th,eir assets and empowers them to do unbelievable things (Acts 2:4) The church's mission is made up of ordinary people doing things they never thought they could do, and able people putting their skills to uses of which they never dreamed. Once one sees the effervescent abundance of the Father's creation and the Spirit's bestowal of gifts it becomes easier to perceive that God has given everything that is needed. Fulfilment does not mean replacement of the flawed by the perfect: it means the Holy Spirit inducing the assets of all to blossom so fully that they take up all the space and obscure any deficits. This is incarnational transformation.

PARTICIPATION

Participation is in many ways the heart of being with, because it affirms the centrality of with for its own sake, with no thought to succeed, achieve, change, rescue or save. Participation removes the sense of goal, and consequent urgency, from relationship and just relishes the relationship itself. Whereas attention is focused, even fierce, and delight is joyful, even playful, participation is simple and steady. It says, 'There is no being without being with you.' There is no ancillary gain, pleasure, profit or transferable enhancement from so doing; the relationship is all that is sought. This is the way, we must assume, Jesus spent the hidden years of his life, from his arrival in Nazareth (perhaps after a sojourn in Egypt, following Matthew's account) until his appearance at the Jordan to be baptised by John. Around 90 per cent of his life was devoted to participation with his family and neighbourhood. Even his discussion with the teachers in the temple, usually recalled for his apparent disobedience and the alarm he causes in Mary and Joseph, is simply a demonstration that his participation is not limited to Nazareth, but that it in a significant sense belongs in the temple, in the place of Israel's participation with God (Lk 2:41–50).

The day of celebrating participation is the sabbath. As the famous hymn puts it, 'O Sabbath rest by Galilee, O calm of hills above, where Jesus knelt to share with thee the silence of eternity, interpreted by love!'[11] The sabbath is usually noted for the work that cannot be performed on it: but it is perhaps better to see the restraint from labour as an encouragement to be with one another with no thought to any end product. This is something that some of the Israelites failed to do when they went searching for manna on the seventh day, despite the reassurance that the food collected on the sixth day would suffice (Ex 16:27–30). This is territory where Israel has long understood something the church has been slow to grasp: 'There is a realm of time where the goal is not to have but to be, not to own but to give, not to control but to share, not to subdue but to be in accord. Life goes wrong when the control of space, the acquisition of things of space, becomes our sole concern.'[12] On the sabbath humankind and God participate with one another, with no plan being devised or energy being conserved for tasks ahead.

The stories of Jesus in the gospels mostly concern the remarkable deeds of his ministry and the momentous days of his passion. But on a closer look, there are plenty of occasions when he spent time with people apparently simply for the joy of their company, even if

[11] 'Dear Lord and Father of Mankind', written in 1872 by the American Quaker poet John Greenleaf Whittier as part of his longer poem 'The Brewing of Soma'. The original context for the hymn is a plea to attend to the 'still small voice' heard by Elijah and not to infest Christianity with 'music, vigils, incense drear'.

[12] Abraham Joshua Heschel, *The Sabbath: Its Meaning for Modern Man*, with wood engravings by Ilya Schor (New York: Farrar, Straus and Young, 1951), 3. Heschel adds, 'The seventh day is like a palace in time with a kingdom for all. It is not a date but an atmosphere' (21). He goes on, 'Unless one learns how to relish the taste of Sabbath … one will be unable to enjoy the taste of eternity in the world to come. … The Sabbath is not for the sake of the weekdays; the weekdays are for the sake of the Sabbath. It is not an interlude but the climax of living' (14). Further,

> The Sabbath, thus, is more than an armistice, more than an interlude; it is a profound conscious harmony of man and the world, a sympathy for all things and a *participation* in the spirit that unites what is below and what is above. All that is divine in the world is brought into union with God. This is Sabbath, and the true happiness of the universe.
>
> (31–32, italics added)

what we hear about is a notable direction the conversation took. Most of these occasions involve meals: such meals were no rushed affair. We have noted how Jesus visited Martha and Mary, at a time when a male visiting an unmarried female was a transgressive act. Likewise we have seen how Jesus was at supper at the house of Simon the Pharisee, even though at this early stage in the story he has already been in controversy with the Pharisees more than once (Lk 7:36; see also 5:21, 5:30, 6:2, 6:7); he can hardly have been compelled to be there. In fact, Luke's gospel is a series of meals where Jesus participates with others in ways that may not end with simple companionship, but begin so. Jesus first eats with Levi the tax collector (5:29). Then a sinful woman washes Jesus' feet with her tears at the house of Simon the Pharisee (7:38). Then at the feeding of the 5,000 Jesus offers Israel manna in the wilderness (9:16). Next at a Pharisee's house Jesus speaks about notions of purity, and then on his way to another Pharisee's house Jesus heals a man with dropsy (11:37, 14:2). (The significance of the Pharisees is that their rules were especially preoccupied with how to eat.) Then Jesus goes back to a tax collector's house, that of Zacchaeus, whereupon Zacchaeus embarks on a radical programme of reparation and restoration (19.5). The seventh and eighth meals – the Last Supper and Emmaus – clearly have more resting on them than simply fellowship (22:14, 24:30). But the earlier ones do not, other than testing the boundaries of what fellowship entails and whom it includes. The aspiration of fellowship is identical to the notion of participation: simply being with one another with no ulterior aim.

But participation in relation to the incarnation is about a great deal more than Jesus being with people for no other reason than to relish their company. The words of 2 Peter 1:3–4 hint at a cosmic agenda: 'His divine power has given us everything needed for life and godliness, through the knowledge of him who called us by his own glory and goodness. Thus he has given us, through these things, his precious and very great promises, so that through them you may ... become participants in the divine nature.' Participation, especially for the Orthodox, as we shall see in the next chapter, becomes a vital way of expressing what it means for humanity to be elevated into the company of God. While for Orthodox theologians this tends to focus on the relationship of God and humankind, we may legitimately expand the notion to incorporate human relations with one another and with the restored creation in God's eschatological company. In Ephesians 2:6 we read that God raised us up with Jesus 'and seated us with him in the heavenly places in Christ Jesus': the mention of seats might be taken as an indication of status, but could just as well be a sign of being invited into conversation, and perhaps food-sharing, with Christ – genuine fellowship rather than simply elevation of dignity.

It is close to the heart of the New Testament that if we participate in Christ's passion, we may anticipate sharing in his resurrection. This is both a positive and a negative thing. 'Rejoice insofar as you share Christ's sufferings, that you may also rejoice and be glad when his glory is revealed' (1 Pet 4:13): here we find the conviction that humankind may actually participate in the cross and thereby participate in Christ's future beyond the cross. Paul speaks similarly: 'We are children of God, and if children, then heirs, heirs of God and joint heirs with Christ—if, in fact, we suffer with him so that we may also be glorified with him' (Rom 8:16–17). We participate both as children and as fellow sufferers. Jesus insists, 'If any want to become my followers, let them deny themselves and take up their cross daily and follow me' (Lk 9:23). This is an intense form of participation. It is not pious endurance of suffering or zealous violent action but the voluntary non-violent journey with Christ into the heart of conflict with evil and alienation from God. The negative side of the coin is that if we will not participate in Christ's path to the cross, we will not be with him beyond the cross: 'Peter said to him, "You shall never wash my feet." Jesus answered him, "If I do not wash you, you have no share with me"' (Jn 13:8). Thus acts of obedience, of faithfully following in Christ's steps to the cross, rather than, for example, taking up the cause of Barabbas, the Sanhedrin or Pilate, are ways of actually participating through the Holy Spirit in Christ's incarnate life.

PARTNERSHIP

The difference between participation and partnership is the difference between being with and working with. Participation means it does not matter what we do, or whether we do anything at all, so long as we do it together; partnership says if you exercise your role and/or skills, and I employ my attitude and aptitude, we can go further and do better than we could ever have done alone. Partnership is not 'back to back', in the sense that we act for one another without significantly interacting with each other; it is more 'side by side', in that we work alongside each other in complementary ways.[13]

The most prominent form of partnership in the Bible relates to providence. When Joseph reframes his brothers' penitent dismay, he explains how he, Pharaoh and the brothers have each partnered with God in bringing God's people to safety. 'Do not be distressed, or angry with yourselves, because you sold me here; for God sent me before you to preserve life. ... God sent me before you to preserve for you a remnant on earth, and to keep alive for you many survivors. So it was not you who sent me here, but God' (Gen 45:3–8). God's partnership with humankind continues to choose unlikely co-workers: perhaps most notably, Cyrus is anointed to open doors for Israel and cut through the bars of iron (Isa 45:1). Israel's return from exile as narrated in Ezra and Nehemiah is a study in God's partnership with various human agents, just as Moses becomes a key partner of a more conventional kind in Exodus. Perhaps fundamentally, Abraham is called to partner with God in bringing blessing to the nations (Gen 12:2–3).

Paul describes the experience of being God's partner when he relates his mission to preach Jesus' resurrection: 'by the grace of God

[13] For a more extensive account of marriage as face to face, side by side and back to back, see my *How Then Shall We Live? Christian Engagement with Contemporary Issues* (Norwich: Canterbury, 2016), 85–90; US ed. (New York: Church Publishing, 2017), 109–14.

I am what I am, and his grace towards me has not been in vain. On the contrary, I worked harder than any of them – though it was not I, but the grace of God that is with me' (1 Cor 15:10). In this resonant phrase 'I . . . though . . . not I', Paul sums up what it means to partner with God. An earlier, and perhaps less agreeable, epiphany of partnership comes to Joseph of Nazareth, when it is made known to him that the child conceived in Mary is from the Holy Spirit, and that Joseph is to name him Jesus (Mt 1:18–21); in this he is nonetheless a more willing partner than John the Baptist's father Zechariah (Lk 1:8–20).

The most explicit notion of partnership in the New Testament is the practice of intercessory prayer. Jesus promises, 'If two of you agree on earth about anything you ask, it will be done for you by my Father in heaven. For where two or three are gathered in my name, I am there among them' (Mt 18:19–20). This is an account of how prayers are carried by the Spirit to Jesus at the right hand of the Father. It is amplified by Paul in his vivid description of how intercession is a partnership with the Holy Spirit: 'Likewise the Spirit helps us in our weakness; for we do not know how to pray as we ought, but that very Spirit intercedes with sighs too deep for words. And God, who searches the heart, knows what is the mind of the Spirit, because the Spirit intercedes for the saints according to the will of God' (Rom 8:26–27). All prayer is such a partnership, but intercession particularly so.

The most characteristic account of partnership comes in Jesus sending his disciples on mission. When Jesus instructs the twelve, he tells them to announce to the lost sheep of the house of Israel, 'The kingdom of heaven has come near.' Their most profound experience of partnership comes in the face of hostility: 'When they hand you over, do not worry about how you are to speak or what you are to say; for what you are to say will be given to you at that time; for it is not you who speak, but the Spirit of your Father speaking through you' (Mt 10:7, 19–20). Their mission is truly an enterprise shared with Christ and the Holy Spirit: 'Whoever welcomes you welcomes me, and whoever welcomes me welcomes the one who sent me'

(Mt 10:40). This becomes even more explicit on the mount of Ascension, when Jesus commissions the eleven disciples to make disciples, baptise and teach – but assures them they are never alone: 'I am with you always, to the end of the age' (Mt 28:20).

Partnership is a recognition that being with is not inimical to working with: 'with' is more determinative than 'being'. While in eschatological terms there is no work to do, and thus being with is the only mode of dwelling and relating, short of the last day working with is a perfectly fitting dimension of being with; hence partnership is one of the eight dimensions of being with – so long as the goal of working with is to lead to being with. But to work with is not to assume that the two parties are always equals: to partner with the Holy Spirit is not to regard one's own contribution as of corresponding validity. The whole wonder of Israel and the church is that the Holy Spirit could have done it all alone: it is a matter of grace and gift that humankind has been ushered into covenant ways of shaping community and being in communion. Grace is not God doing everything for us: grace is God involving us even though we are unsteady partners. Working for is so often the easier path: but it sets in place habits and assumptions that often make it very difficult to transfer into working with, let alone being with. God's means and God's ends are identical: God comes to be with us forever by coming to be with us in the incarnation. Purpose and method are the same.

ENJOYMENT

Enjoyment is the seventh dimension of being with and the one that contains the previous six. It is rooted in Augustine's distinction between what we use, which is of limited value, and what we enjoy, which is of unlimited value. For Augustine, only God comes into the latter category, and thus we use all things that we may enjoy God.[14] I prefer to reshape Augustine's proposal to suggest that being with entails coming to enjoy things, and especially people, that might

[14] Augustine, *On Christian Doctrine*, 1.4.4, www.ccel.org/a/augustine/doctrine.

often, even normally, be used – such that for example congregation members might describe their loyalty to their local church by saying, 'Everywhere else – at work, at home – I am used, but here I am truly enjoyed.'[15] Like so many things, our vocation to enjoy is well expressed by Thomas Traherne:

> All things were made to be yours. And you were made to prize them according to their value: which is your office and duty, the end for which you were created, and the means by which you enjoy. *The end for which you were created is that by prizing all that God hath done, you may enjoy yourself and him in blessedness.*[16]

Thus Traherne expresses that God enjoys us, and we enjoy God, and other things accordingly.

My concern about conventional theological portrayals of the incarnation as occasioned by the fall and the need to address human guilt and mortality is that they portray the Trinity in general, and Jesus in particular, as someone to be used rather than enjoyed. Any account of the incarnation where some notion of the atonement shapes the reason for and narrative of Jesus' purpose in coming is almost bound to fall into this trap. If, as I argued in the previous chapter, blasphemy is using what should be enjoyed, while idolatry is enjoying what should be used, an argument that the incarnation is governed primarily or wholly for the objective of reversing the fall and thus alleviating our human plight qualifies as blasphemy – because it uses what should be enjoyed. I understand the eschatological hope as being that there will be a realm where everyone is perpetually enjoyed and no one is ever used; and the same is true of the renewed creation. There can be no using on the way to enjoying: the only way to enjoyment is through gradual, increasing, and eventually complete enjoyment.

[15] For Augustine's account of using and enjoying see my *A Nazareth Manifesto*, 137–41. For what it is like to be enjoyed where elsewhere one is accustomed to being used, see my *Incarnational Ministry*, 96–97.

[16] Thomas Traherne, *Centuries*, 1:12, in *Selected Poems and Prose*, ed. Alan Bradford (London: Penguin, 1991), 190.

Consider Nicodemus: he comes to Jesus by night, not wanting to unsettle his social and religious standing yet drawn to the truth (Jn 3:1–10). By saying, 'No one can see the kingdom of God without being born from above', Jesus is telling Nicodemus there is no use trying to take the gospel 'in one hand', combining it with other commitments – he needs to take it 'in both hands' as if he were beginning life all over again. Likewise the rich man wants to inherit eternal life, but is shocked and grieved when he is advised by Jesus to 'go, sell what you own, and give the money to the poor, and you will have treasure in heaven; then come, follow me' (Mk 10:21). Jesus is saying that the gospel cannot be used as a mechanism to inherit eternal life; it can be enjoyed only by adopting Jesus' lifestyle. The most notorious case of using something that should be enjoyed is the request of James and John. They say to Jesus, 'Grant us to sit, one at your right hand and one at your left, in your glory' – thus turning glory into a status game, and seeking attention on themselves rather than on Jesus (Mk 10:37). They are instructed instead to enjoy discipleship, by becoming servants.

The notion of enjoyment makes unambiguous that Christ's incarnation is not dependent on the fall. The incarnation comes about so that creation, and in particular humankind, may utterly enjoy God in Christ, and thus reflect and fittingly reciprocate the way, in Christ, God utterly loves creation, and in particular humankind. Any other account of the incarnation uses what should only be enjoyed. It treats Christ as something or someone who has a limited purpose, and can be dispensed with once that task is achieved. And it focuses its attention on what humankind needs, rather than what God longs to give. In that sense it is shaped around human scarcity rather than God's abundance.

The parables are transformed from techniques to earn God's favour to depictions of the enjoyment of God when we begin to interpret them from God's point of view. Thus in Matthew 13:45–46 we read, 'The kingdom of heaven is like a merchant in search of fine pearls; on finding one pearl of great value, he went and sold all that he had and bought it.' The parable is transformed if we realise that we are not the merchant; we are the pearl. God risks everything to be with us in Jesus. This turns a moralistic tale into an occasion for worship – and a vision of the way God enjoys us. Similarly the morality of Luke 16:1–9 is unfathomable if we try to make sense of ourselves as the dishonest manager currying favour with his master's clients before being fired; but if we see Jesus as the manager forgiving and befriending before judgement day it becomes a subversive tale of the kind of radical lives we might lead if we were to imitate Christ's abundant mercy. Again, the parable of the labourers in the vineyard in Matthew 20:1–15 is a story of rank injustice if we try to treat it as a moral tale; but if we see it as an account of what it means for God to enjoy us, and see the wages as forgiveness and eternal life, for which double or triple amounts are absurd attempts to commodify and thus use what can only be enjoyed, the narrative makes complete sense.

Enjoyment is being with in a nutshell – because it reveals that all other forms of relationship are inclined to use for some ulterior end, whereas enjoyment is simply for its own sake. This is how God considers humankind. This is the utterly abundant reason for the incarnation. This is the gospel in miniature. In the words of an ancient prayer, 'God of time and eternity, if I love thee for hope of heaven, then deny me heaven; if I love thee for fear of hell, then give me hell; but if I love thee for thyself alone, then give me thyself alone.'[17] To enjoy God is to love as God loves in the incarnation – not to gain heaven, nor to evade hell, but for 'thyself alone'.

GLORY

Glory emerges in three senses as the eighth dimension of being with. It refers definitively to God being with God, that is with the persons of the Trinity being with each other – the all-sufficient wondrousness of

[17] Jane Hirshfield's translation of the mystic Rabi'a's original prayer goes as follows: 'O my Lord, if I worship you from fear of hell, burn me in hell. If I worship you from hope of Paradise, bar me from its gates. But if I worship you for yourself alone, grant me then the beauty of your Face.' See Rabi'a, 'Oh My Lord', trans. Jane Hirshfield, Poetry Foundation, www.poetryfoundation.org/poems/55267/o-my-lord-56d236a947ec8 (accessed 12 March 2024).

the divine interactions and coinherence, including the original incarnational decision of God never to be, except to be with us in Christ. It describes, second, the experience of humankind and the creation's being in the presence of God, and thus eternally, their being with God in each of the eight dimensions: hence Jesus' statement 'Father, I desire that those also, whom you have given me, may be with me where I am, to see my glory, which you have given me because you loved me before the foundation of the world' (Jn 17:24). It reviews, third, the process, particularly as seen in retrospect, of how, through Christ and the Spirit, humankind and the creation come to be with God forever.

Perhaps the only place where we witness something approaching the first sense, the inner-Trinitarian relationship, is in Jesus' transfiguration. In Exodus 34:29–30 we are given a profound account of the second sense, humankind being in God's presence, when, returning from Mount Sinai, 'Moses did not know that the skin of his face shone because he had been talking with God.' It is from this portrayal that the significance of the appearance of Moses and Elijah on the mountain with Jesus, in which Jesus' 'clothes became dazzling white, such as no one on earth could bleach them', becomes clear (Mk 9:3). The transfiguration is a moment when the disciples, in time, see the nature of Christ's eternal relationships, and by his discourse with two great figures of Israel, who embody revelation because they represent the law and the prophets, see the life God has prepared for all humankind. It is an earthly window into heaven. From the disciples' point of view, it is glory in the second sense: being in the presence of God. But excluding the disciples for one moment, it is glory in the first sense: the active dialogue within the Godhead, in which the Father's voice is the only one actually heard, speaking of the need to listen to the beloved Son (Mk 9:7). What it affirms is that eschatological hope should focus on a future that is interpersonal, conversational, glorious, involving – and centred on Christ.

Turning to the second kind of glory, there are many scriptural references to what it means to be in the presence of God, specifically in the person of Jesus. These begin with Luke's account of the throng of angels that fill the sky at Jesus' birth, singing, 'Glory to God in the highest heaven, and on earth peace among those whom he favours!' (2:14). Thus shepherds come to be, besides Mary and Joseph, the first to enter the presence of God through the presence of God in Christ on earth. In the hour of his passion, Jesus calls on the Father to 'glorify your Son so that the Son may glorify you' (Jn 17:1); he later explains to the disciples on the road that his suffering preceded his entering into glory (Lk 24:26), a state in which we see him 'crowned with glory and honour' (Heb 2:9).

The third sense, of the process by which humankind and the creation come to be with God in Christ forever, is made mode explicit in Ephesians, where the first chapter is the New Testament's principal account of how we are brought into the presence of God by a purpose initiated 'before the foundation of the world' (1:4). The notion of glory is repeated at different moments along this narrative: thus the Father 'destined us for adoption as his children through Jesus Christ, according to the good pleasure of his will, to the praise of his glorious grace that he freely bestowed on us in the Beloved' (1:5–6). The same Father destined those who were the first to set their hope on Christ to 'live for the praise of his glory' (1:12). Accordingly the Holy Spirit marked those first believers with a seal as a pledge of their inheritance, again 'to the praise of his glory' (1:14). Finally this comprehensive account of how we come to be with God in Christ forever is completed with reference to 'the riches of [God's] glorious inheritance among the saints' (1:18).

I trust this account of the eight dimensions of being with has offered a compelling portrayal of both the scriptural depth and the incarnational character of all eight dimensions, each of which seek to render the life of the Trinity, the eschatological hope, the pattern of Christ's life and the most fitting ways to live God's future now. Being with is simply our best understanding of how God is with God, how we shall be with God, one another and the renewed creation, how God is with us in Jesus, and how we may live faithful lives of discipleship, ministry and mission in the spirit of Christ's incarnation and in anticipation of God's ultimate glory.

PART II An Emerging Story

4 Orthodox Foundations

The purpose of Part I of this book was to investigate what the priority of the incarnation entails and to establish its scriptural basis. The purpose of Part II is now to explore how that priority has been addressed in the three eras in which it has become an important focus of theological reflection. This chapter and the two that follow examine how theologians have historically taken up the question of God's purpose as understood in and through the incarnation, seeking to identify the key arguments that could support (and salient ones that might oppose) the incarnational rendering of the story of God outlined in Part I.

I begin with the Eastern Orthodox tradition, because this is where the question of God's purpose first arises in earnest. By the Eastern tradition I refer to those authors writing in Greek (and later also Russian), beginning with Irenaeus in the second century, majoring on the Cappadocian theologians of the fourth century, coming to a head with Maximus the Confessor in the seventh century, touching on Nicolas Cabasilas in the fourteenth century and continuing beyond the demise of Constantinople all the way to Sergei Bulgakov in the twentieth century and David Bentley Hart in the twenty-first.

This chapter seeks to answer three questions. The first is, how do Eastern theologians configure the way the incarnation is rendered as God's original intention, and how significant is that insight? The answer is that this is central to their portrayal of God's purpose. The second question is, what precisely is God's purpose in the incarnation? The answer lies in the notion of deification, our being made divine, a concept pivotal to Eastern theology – and yet one that seems in significant respects problematic. Thus the third question becomes, are there ways in which Eastern theologians portray God's purpose that are less problematic, yet equally integral to their notion of God's original and constant purpose? The answer is, yes there are, and I conclude with a consideration of what I judge to be three key motifs that I find more transferable yet nonetheless wholly authentic to the Orthodox theological imagination.

INCARNATION

I begin with the centrality of the incarnation from an Orthodox perspective. While the overwhelming Eastern emphasis is on exploring Christ's role beyond simply putting right the damage of the fall, theologians in this tradition are largely content to take the scriptural record as it is and not speculate about counterfactual scenarios.[1] No theologian is claiming that Christ's incarnation was unconcerned with the fall – just that it is prior to and not exhausted or determined by redemption. The divine plan is much more than the restoration of humankind to Eden: it is to bring about a new creation, or to fulfil the ultimate purpose of creation. Thus Christ's purpose has a negative side – liberation from original sin; but even more, it has a positive side: the completion and fulfilment of humankind's original potential.

The closest any Eastern theologian gets to denying any redemptive purpose in the incarnation is Isaac of Nineveh.[2] With withering sarcasm, Isaac pours scorn on the notion that we have received untold blessings because of sin, and on the implication that sin gave us the very thing we would have been unworthy of had we continued in justice.

[1] By 'counterfactual scenarios' I mean the question associated with the medieval Franciscans and explored in Chapter 5 below – 'If there had not been a fall, would Christ still have come?'

[2] Isaac of Nineveh (sometimes called Isaac the Syrian) lived from about 613 to around 700. He spent large stretches of time as a hermit, and his ascetical and mystical writings have been much studied. In addition to his views on redemption, he also questioned whether the notion of eternal punishment was compatible with the love of God.

> By no means did the death of the Lord take place that he might redeem us from sins, nor on account of anything else, but only that the world might experience the love that God had toward creation. If all the wonderful operation had been only on account of the remission of sins, it would have sufficed for him to redeem us in some other manner. Who would have opposed him if He had done what he did [redeem us] by a simple death? He did not die a simple death, but experienced it in the hard suffering of the cross, that you might understand what kind of a mystery this is [namely, of love].[3]

Isaac cannot envisage an account of redemption that does justice to what he regards as the true reason for the incarnation – a manifestation of God's love in order to receive a return of love. Here Isaac presents an account of the cross that emphasises the way it demonstrates the mystery of God's love – but does not attach to the cross any sophisticated soteriological construal. Nonetheless even Isaac recognises that redemption has some place in the economy of incarnation.

A more thorough and balanced account comes from Isaac's contemporary Maximus the Confessor.[4] Maximus puts the incarnation at the centre of God's purposes – before we can even speak of God's purposes: at the very heart of what it means for God to be God. Referring to the incarnation, he says,

> This is the great and hidden mystery, at once the blessed end for which all things are ordained. It is the divine purpose conceived before the beginning of created being. In defining it we would say that

[3] Dominic J. Unger OFM, Cap., 'The Love of God the Primary Reason for the Incarnation According to Isaac of Nineveh', *Franciscan Studies*, 9/2 (June 1949), 146–55 at 147. Unger provides a translation of Isaac's work *De vita spirituali et de mysteriis divinis et iudiciis et tentatione*, from which this quotation is taken.

[4] Maximus the Confessor lived from around 580 to 662. He was a senior assistant to the Byzantine Emperor before becoming a monk and exercising his vast learning both in theological treatises and in campaigning against Monothelitism, the view that maintained that Christ, though he had two natures, had only one will; his campaigning led to his having his tongue cut off and his right hand removed. His view nonetheless prevailed at the Third Council of Constantinople shortly after his death.

> this mystery is the preconceived goal for which everything exists, but which itself exists on account of nothing. With a clear view to this end, God created the essences of created being ... The Logos, by essence God, became a messenger of this plan when he became a man and, if I may rightly say so, established himself as the innermost depth of the Father's goodness while also displaying in himself the very goal for which his creatures manifestly received the beginning of their existence. Because of Christ – or rather, the whole mystery of Christ – all the ages of time and the beings within those ages have received their beginning and end in Christ. For the union between a limit of the ages and limitlessness, between measure and immeasurability, between finitude and infinity, between Creator and creation, between rest and motion, was conceived before the ages.[5]

This quotation epitomises the Eastern understanding of the way the incarnation is the definitive revelation and disclosure of God, summing up God's purpose and creation's destiny, the reason for the story, the shape of the story and the end of the story. The incarnation is both mysterious and fully revealed. Everything depends on it, but it depends on nothing. It is the innermost depth of God and yet the most visible act of God. It happens in the middle of the story, but it is the origin and destiny of the story. It was conceived before the foundation of the world, but is not fully comprehended until the end of the world.[6] This means the incarnation is not dependent on the fall, as David Bentley Hart explains:

[5] Maximus the Confessor, *Questions to Thalassius*, 60, in *On the Cosmic Mystery of Jesus Christ: Selected Writings from St Maximus the Confessor*, ed. Paul M. Blowers and Robert Louis Wilken (Crestwood, NY: St Vladimir's Seminary Press, 2003), 124–25. I am grateful to Geoffrey Ready for highlighting the significance of this quotation. Maximus adds, 'This mystery was conceived by the Father, the Son and the Holy Spirit before all time': the Father, by proper consent, the Son, through personal experience, and the Spirit through cooperation. See Lars Thunberg, *Man and the Cosmos: The Vision of St Maximus the Confessor* (Crestwood, NY: St Vladimir's Seminary Press, 1987), 41.

[6] The whole history of divine providence is for Maximus divided into two great periods: the first, which culminates in the incarnation of the Logos and is the story of divine condescension; the second, which is the story of human ascension into the

> God can both allow created freedom its scope and yet so constitute the world that nothing can prevent him from bringing about the beatitude of his Kingdom. God did not will the fall, and yet always wills all things toward himself. The entire history of sin and death is in an ultimate sense pure contingency, one that is not as such desired by God, but that is nevertheless constrained by providence to serve his transcendent purpose.[7]

We could call Maximus' words above the foundational statement of the Orthodox perspective on the incarnation. For Maximus, the incarnation is more than reversal, more than restoration, more than return. It reveals the true possibility of humankind; it elevates humanity to a true likeness of God; it replaces potential with perfection. It realises the telos of the creation of human beings, and brings the human race into the presence of God. Thus the nativity of Christ is, in Basil of Caesarea's phrase, 'the birthday of the whole human race'.[8] Liberation in Christ provides a much larger context for humankind than it would otherwise have had. It detaches humanity from evil and attaches it to Christ; thereby relativising evil and sin. Sin tells a smaller story than incarnation. Sin does not reach back to humanity's origin or forward to humanity's destiny. A human being can be enslaved by sin, but need not be. Being formed in God and destined to be with God forever, humankind is part of a story broader, longer and deeper than evil and sin.[9] These are among the ways in which Christ's incarnation

glory of deification – an extension of the incarnation to the whole creation. See Georges Florovsky, 'Cur Deus Homo? The Motive of the Incarnation', in *Evharisterion: Hamilcar Alivisatos* (Athens, 1957), 70–79.

7 David Bentley Hart, *The Doors of the Sea: Where Was God in the Tsunami?* (Grand Rapids, MI: Eerdmans, 2005), 83.

8 See Kallistos Ware, *The Orthodox Way* (Oxford: Mowbray, 1979), 93. Basil of Caesarea was Bishop of Caesarea in Cappadocia, Asia Minor. He upheld the Nicene Creed and opposed Arianism and Apollinarianism.

9 See especially Panayiotis Nellas, *Deification in Christ: Orthodox Perspectives on the Nature of the Human Person*, trans. Norman Russell (Crestwood, NY: St Vladimir's Seminary Press, 1987), 41.

incorporates a great deal more than simply overcoming the consequences of the fall.[10]

Sergei Bulgakov articulates this conviction about the primacy of Christ succinctly when he describes the incarnation as the final cause of creation.[11] This is helpful because, without dwelling on which came first, Bulgakov orders the doctrines of incarnation and creation, highlighting that the incarnation is the reason for creation. The incarnation expresses and advances the purpose of God; indeed, it *is* the purpose of God. Citing Aristotle's notion of causation, he speaks of the final cause – the 'why' of God's action, in this case in creation:

> The incarnation is the interior basis of creation, its *final cause*. God did not create the world to hold it at a distance from him, at that insurmountable metaphysical distance that separates the Creator from the creation, but in order to surmount that distance and unite himself completely with the world; not only from the outside as Creator, nor even as providence, but from within: 'the Word became flesh'. That is why the incarnation is already predetermined in humankind.[12]

Bulgakov's introduction of the language of final cause offers a perfect way to articulate the primacy of Christ in line with Col 1:15–20. The

[10] Elsewhere, in his *Difficulty* 7, Maximus speaks of a threefold embodiment of the Logos: (1) in the *logoi* of created beings at the creation of the world and in the four elements, (2) in the *logoi* of scripture, when the Spirit inspired its authors, and (3) in the incarnation of the Logos in our flesh, when the Spirit covered the virgin with his shadow. Lars Thunberg, in his *Man and the Cosmos*, 75, comments, 'This threefold embodiment represents an economy of salvation more fundamental than one which is motivated only by the fall.' The title *Difficulties* (or *Ambigua*) refers to Maximus' lengthy dialogue with the work of Gregory of Nazianzus.

[11] Sergei Bulgakov was born in 1871 around 200 miles south of Moscow. He rejected Orthodoxy and became a noted Marxist. Through reading Vladimir Soloviev he returned to the church. He was exiled from Russia in 1922, and in 1925 established the St Sergius Theological Institute in Paris, which he led until his death in 1944.

[12] Sergei Bulgakov, *Du verbe incarné* (Paris: Aubier, 1933), quoted in Andrew Louth, 'The Place of Theosis in Orthodox Theology', in Michael J. Christensen and Jeffrey A. Wittung, eds., *Partakers of the Divine Nature: The History and Development of Deification in the Christian Traditions* (Cranbury, NJ: Associated University Press, 2007), 32–44 at 36, italics original.

observation that humankind is predetermined in incarnation corresponds with Paul's words 'He is the firstborn of all creation.' Now the full teleological power of the final cause can take shape: everything is oriented towards being with God in Christ. The mystical theologian Nicolas Kabasilas grasps this teleological capacity fully:[13]

> It was for the new man that human nature was originally created; it was for him that intellect and desire were prepared. We received rationality that we may know Christ, desire that we might run towards him. We possessed memory that we might bear him in us, since he was the archetype for those who have been created. For the old Adam is not the model for the new, but the new a model for the old.[14]

Kabasilas portrays all human faculties as bestowed not for some independent goal of flourishing, but for a very precise reason: the better to apprehend Christ temporally and interact with him eternally. This is a true teleological theology of being with, as applied to creation. It includes external actions ('run towards him') and internal dispositions ('bear him in us'). It includes cerebral rationality and sensual feeling. Kabasilas' account implies that the phrase from Genesis 1:27 ('in the image of God he created them') is both a gift and a goal, a possession and a destiny: both being and potential.[15] Adam was 'a type of the one to come' (Rom 5:14), and we are too – the rough draft, from which we are called to grow into 'the measure of the stature of the fullness of Christ' (Eph 4:13).

Thus what we have so far seen is that, though the question is not explicitly raised among the theologians of the early centuries, a consensus emerges among the Eastern theologians, particularly from Maximus onwards, that the purposes of the incarnation predate and

[13] Nicolas Kabasilas was born in Thessalonica and lived from around 1320 to 1392. He is known for his works that describe union with Christ and the liturgy.

[14] Nicolas Kabasilas, *The Life in Christ*, trans. C. J. De Catanzaro (Crestwood, NY: St Vladimir's Seminary Press, 1974), quoted in Nellas, *Deification in Christ*, 34–35.

[15] I owe these three balanced pairs of attributes to Nellas, *Deification in Christ*, 37.

outweigh righting the wrong of the fall. These theologians offer a rich breadth of larger purposes, crystallising in the notion that the reason for existence is that Christ be with us in creation, eventually to elevate us to be with him in eternity. This is precisely the vision outlined in Part I above – a vision that we can see is deeply rooted in Orthodox thought.

But things are not quite that straightforward. There is a phrase above in the quotation from Sergei Bulgakov that I did not highlight and that the quotation from Nicolas Kabasilas does not explain: that is when Bulgakov speaks of God being united completely with the world.[16] Here Bulgakov touches on the flashpoint of Eastern theology's account of the incarnation and its purpose: the motif of deification. The dispute arises because of the frequent implication that our ultimate becoming (like) God in glory threatens the distinction between creator and creature. Are the Eastern theologians aspiring to something incompatible with the created nature of humankind? That is what we must now investigate.

DEIFICATION

Two early theologians, Irenaeus of Lyons and Athanasius of Alexandria, set in train a consistent theme in the early church: the characterisation of God's purpose as a glorious exchange.[17] Thus Irenaeus says, 'In his immense love, he became what we are, that he

[16] Nellas is more careful. He says, 'The essential gulf between created and uncreated nature is absolute and infinite. But the equally infinite goodness of God, *without abolishing that essential gulf*, has been pleased to bridge it in a real way from the beginning.' Nellas, *Deification in Christ*, 31, my italics.

[17] Irenaeus lived from around 130 to 202. He grew up in Smyrna, on the west coast of Asia Minor, and was thus a Greek speaker, but he became a bishop of Lyons, in France, and thus in the Western sphere. He was a notable defender of the faith against heresies, especially Montanism and Gnosticism. Athanasius, who lived from around 297 to 373, was Bishop of Alexandria for forty-five years, a period that included five exiles, as a result of his tireless defence of the Nicene faith against Arianism.

might make us what he is.'[18] Christ shared our life and our death that we might be delivered from death and share in the life of God.[19] Likewise Athanasius says, '[The Word of God] became human that we might become God; and he revealed himself through a body that we might receive an idea of the invisible Father; and he endured insults from humans that we might inherit incorruption.'[20] These statements set an agenda for what became known as deification (sometimes divinisation – in Greek, *theōsis*), understood as the goal and counterpart of incarnation in Orthodox theology to this day.[21]

God became human, that humans might become God. This wondrous exchange is the succinct answer to Anselm's celebrated question of why God became a human.[22] Divine *kenosis* leads to human *theōsis*.[23] A key text is 2 Peter 1:3–4, which speaks about

[18] Irenaeus, *Adversus haereses*, trans. Alexander Roberts and William Rambaut, 5, preface, www.newadvent.org/fathers/0103500.htm. The early Latin theologians called this *admirabile commercium* (wonderful exchange).

[19] William G. Witt and Joel Scandrett characterise Irenaeus as always looking for unity in contrast to gnostic dualism: thus he perceives unity between (1) the creator God and the God of Jesus, (2) creation and salvation, (3) Israel, the apostles and the church, (3) Old and New Testaments, (4) God and humanity in Christ, (5) humanity and Christ through the Spirit and (6) human beings and their bodies in creation and resurrection. See their *Mapping Atonement: The Doctrine of Reconciliation in Christian History and Theology* (Grand Rapids, MI: Baker, 2022), 17.

[20] Athanasius, *On the Incarnation of the Word*, trans. Archibald Robertson, 54, www.newadvent.org/fathers/2802.htm. Athanasius places a heavy emphasis on the incarnation, and stresses how it redivinises us. For him, the resurrection is vital for how Christ overcomes the central challenge, which is death. But he is certain that there is no question of an incarnation without the fall. In that sense he is the epitome of the way theologians have been captivated by and consequently shaped their theology around the deficit of sin and evil. It is interesting that in their book *Mapping Atonement: The Doctrine of Reconciliation in Christian History and Theology* (Grand Rapids, MI: Baker 2022), William G. Witt and Joel Scandrett consider Athanasius in their chapter on the incarnation – but acknowledge unambiguously, 'According to Athanasius, the entire purpose of the incarnation was that Jesus might die to save the fallen human race' (30, referencing Athanasius, *De incarnatione*, 4.21).

[21] The term *theopoiesis*, or divinisation, is first used by Clement of Alexandria. See George A. Maloney SJ, *The Cosmic Christ: From Paul to Teilhard* (New York: Sheed and Ward, 1968), 117.

[22] See the treatment in Chapter 5 below.

[23] Bruce L. McCormack, in his *The Humility of the Eternal Son: 'Reformed' Kenoticism and the Repair of Chalcedon* (Cambridge and New York: Cambridge

God's threefold work: of giving us in the past 'everything needed for life and godliness through the knowledge of him who called us by his own glory and goodness', of giving us in the present 'precious and very great promises' and crucially, in the future, of 'becoming participants in the divine nature'. Another is Psalm 82:6, which proclaims, 'You are gods, children of the Most High, all of you.'[24] Another frequently cited text is 2 Corinthians 8:9: 'For you know the generous act of our Lord Jesus Christ, that though he was rich, yet for your sakes he became poor, so that by his poverty you might become rich.' For Athanasius, deification refers to the way human beings are brought into the communion of the Trinity by the incarnation of Jesus through the agency of the Holy Spirit. A definition of deification is given by Pseudo-Dionysius when he speaks of 'the attaining of likeness to God and union with [God] so far as is possible'.[25] Elsewhere Pseudo-Dionysius describes the Christian hope as unifying creation through a return brought about by purification, illumination and perfection.[26] Basil of Caesarea describes deification like this:

> When a sunbeam falls on a transparent substance, the substance itself becomes brilliant, and radiates life from itself. So too spirit-bearing souls, illumined by him, finally become spiritual themselves, and their grace is sent forth to others. From this comes

University Press, 2021), offers a contemporary treatment of the significance of *kenosis* in God being poured out into human nature while that human nature retains its integrity. He sees the Son as eternally receptive, and perceives a key role for the Holy Spirit in ensuring that the humility and obedience of Jesus are true of both the human and the divine natures of the Son.

24 In John 10:34 Jesus asks, 'Is it not written in your law, "I said, you are gods"?' Other cited Johannine passages are John 3:8, 14:21–23, 15:4–8, 17:21–23; 1 John 3:2, 4:12.

25 Pseudo-Dionysius the Areopagite was a Neoplatonic theologian who was born in the late fifth century and died in the early sixth century, and whose writings identify with the figure Dionysius the Areopagite, mentioned in Acts 17:34 as one who came to faith in Athens.

26 Pseudo-Dionysius the Areopagite, *Ecclesiastical Hierarchy*, trans. John Parker, 1.3, www.tertullian.org/fathers/areopagite_14_ecclesiastical_hierarchy.htm, and *Divine Names*, trans. John Parker, www.tertullian.org/fathers/areopagite_03_divine_names.htm. See Paul M. Collins, *Partaking in the Divine Nature: Deification and Communion* (London: T & T Clark, 2010), 104–05.

> knowledge of the future, understanding of mysteries, apprehension of hidden things, distribution of wonderful gifts, heavenly citizenship, a place in the choir of angels, endless joy in the presence of God, and becoming like God, and, the highest of all desires, becoming God.[27]

Here Basil expresses the full characteristics of eternal sanctification, exploring the way those deified attain significant divine attributes and become a means of grace and a blessing to others. There is no reference to the need to overcome the legacy of the fall: this is a process that would have taken place even had there been no fall. Meanwhile he touches on the profound ambiguity of whether this entails simply attaining immortality or actually becoming God: a momentous line to cross.

The significance of deification is that, unlike Western notions of redemption, it is not a return to a human condition prior to the fall: its focus is on future destiny – a face-to-face encounter with God. This is fundamentally about fulfilling original potential, and not so much about restoring something lost. God created the world so as to be united with it. The incarnation marks the way Jesus assumes the appointed role of the one who fulfils and completes the place of the universe in God's purpose. Deification is also about a social, political, collective destiny. One characteristic of Irenaeus in his tussle with the Gnostics of his day was how much he invested in the human body, and consequently human society. Body and society were not, for him, things to be escaped or superseded, but things to be perfected in a new, social Jerusalem.[28] This is about God's original purpose, not about what God did to deal with that purpose being thwarted. Human

[27] Basil of Caesarea, *On the Holy Spirit*, trans. Blomfield Jackson, quoted in Torstein Tollefsen, 'The Metaphysics of Maximus: Becoming One with God', in Daniel Haynes, ed., *A Saint for East and West: Maximus the Confessor's Contribution to Eastern and Western Christian Theology* (Eugene, OR: Cascade, 2019), 223–30 at 223.

[28] See Denis Minns OP, *Irenaeus* (Washington, DC: Georgetown University Press, 1994), 138.

greatness lies in its being donned by Christ and in its destiny. Human uniqueness lies not in its biological distinctiveness, in its being a rational or political animal, but in its being a deified animal – one whose existence has received the command to be a god. Humanity is not just a microcosm but a mystical church – 'a vast new world within the small old one'.[29] Humankind was created to be a microcosm of the cosmos.

In a compelling image, the contemporary Orthodox theologian Andrew Louth describes a great arch stretching from creation to deification, portraying God's original and current intention – to bring into being a universe, and for human beings in due course to share in the divine life. On account of humankind's failure to work in accordance with God's purpose, progress along this arch has been hindered. Within this greater arch there is a smaller arch, stretching from fall to redemption. The purpose of this smaller arch is to restore the functioning of the greater arch. As Western theology came to be less enthusiastic about the notion of deification, it consequently focused almost entirely on the smaller arch. Louth observes that the consequences are 'a loss of the sense of the cosmic dimension of theology, [and] a tendency to see the created order as little more than a background for the great drama of redemption, with the result that the incarnation is seen simply as a means of redemption, the putting right of the fall of Adam'.[30] The task of this book is, in part, to redirect attention towards the greater arch. The reason why Western theology

[29] This is expertly expressed by Nellas, *Deification in Christ*, 30.

[30] Louth, 'The Place of Theosis in Orthodox Theology', 35. Vladimir Lossky puts the point more subtly, suggesting that Western accounts of redemption have been unduly dominated by juridical and forensic categories. See Vladimir Lossky, *In the Image and Likeness of God* (Crestwood, NY: St Vladimir's Seminary, 1985), especially chapter 5. Daniel B. Clendenin resists the tendency to overdraw the characterisation of Western accounts as uniformly legal and Eastern as unanimously about the mystical union. He helpfully points out a series of contrary examples. See his 'Partakers of Divinity: The Orthodox Doctrine of Theosis', *Journal of the Evangelical Theological Society*, 37/3 (September 1994), 365–79. Perhaps a better distinction is to see the West as preoccupied with assuaging the guilt of sin, whereas the East is more concerned with overcoming the problem of mortality.

became nervous about the term 'deification' was that it seems to downplay the creator–creature distinction, turning humankind into something other than human.

The central question that arises in relation to Orthodoxy is this: is deification the way to restore the incarnation to the centre of God's purposes? Is deification a synonym for being with God?[31] Is deification what it means to be partakers of the divine nature and human partners to share the divine life? Sergei Bulgakov portrays deification succinctly: 'God comes in the cool of the day to talk with [humankind], as with a friend, and that "conversation" was no *donum superadditum* [added gift] in relation to [humankind's] corrupt nature, but, on the contrary, that conversation was something quite normal.'[32] Andrew Louth comments that such intimacy as speaking with God as with a friend is precisely what deification means. He adds that deification does not transcend what it means to be human, but fulfils it. He notes that in 1 Corinthians 13:11 Paul speaks of seeing God face to face, and in John 15:15 Jesus calls his disciples friends. We seem to have on the one hand a heritage of language that speaks of 'becoming God', and on the other hand a consensus of contemporary interpretation that suggests that means 'being perpetually in the presence of God'. Orthodox theologians insist on the language of deification, but maintain that it does not mean what it seems to mean;

31 In his *Difficulty* 10, Maximus comes close to this when he says, 'God makes himself human for the sake of man though his philanthropy, in the same measure as man, fortified by charity, divinises himself for God; man is enraptured by God in mind to the unknowable, so far as man has manifested, through virtues, the God by nature invisible' (Lars Thunberg, *Man and the Cosmos*, 10). Here Maximus relies on his distinctive notion of reciprocity, by which Christological and anthropological convictions are always in complete harmony. This notion of reciprocity has significant overlap with my notion of partnership, articulated in Chapter 3 above.

32 Sergei Bulgakov, *Kupina neopalimaya* (Paris: YMCA Press, 1927), 25, quoted in Louth, 'The Place of Theosis in Orthodox Theology', 39. A *donum superadditum* is a gift provided in addition. The subtle references are to Genesis 3:8, when God walks through Eden in the cool of the day, just after the forbidden fruit has been eaten, and Exodus 33:11, 'Thus the Lord used to speak to Moses face to face, as one speaks to a friend.' This quotation does beg the question of why Bulgakov thinks there was an incarnation of the Son, since these depictions seem almost to be an incarnation of the Father.

instead it means something very much like my notion of being with, though largely shorn of that notion's social and ecological aspects.

Louth acknowledges that 'our final encounter with God is an encounter, an engagement, with an Other; it is not to be dissolved in the Ultimate. But that encounter is on our part also a transfiguration- . . . in which we shall be "like him."'[33] The story of the transfiguration brings the disciples, Moses and Elijah face to face with God, a moment of which Paul speaks in 2 Corinthians 4:6 as an experience of 'the light of the knowledge of the glory of God in the face of Jesus Christ'. Meanwhile we are told in 1 John 3:2, 'We shall be like him, for we shall see him as he is.' In Chapter 3 above I recognised transfiguration as a vital dimension of how we may understand glory. But I also distinguished between three kinds of glory – the glory of God being with God within the Trinity, the glory of being in the presence of God and the glory of the process of coming to be with God. What we seem to have here is a confusion between the first and second kinds of glory – the glory of God's own co-inherence, which humankind, even glorified, cannot enter, and the glory of being perpetually in the presence of God, which is our true destiny.

The danger of deification is that it loses the distinctness of humanity from God, both by eliding the difference between essence and existence, and by so strongly suggesting a sense of union that humanity seems to become part of God.[34] The issue is not so much the disputed question of whether deification means 'becoming God'

[33] Louth, 'The Place of Theosis in Orthodox Theology', 40.

[34] There is an analogy to be drawn here between the swallowing-up of humankind in the final divine encounter and the absorption of Christ's human nature by his divine nature in the heresy of Monophysitism. Nellas, *Deification in Christ*, 39–40, helpfully draws attention to the anthropological consequences of various other Christological heresies.

> Arianism, by teaching that Christ is a creature, inevitably limited life in Christ to the created order. Nestorianism, by teaching that the human and the divine natures are contiguous but not really united, ended up by maintaining that [humankind] can approach the infinite but cannot penetrate it. On the other hand, Monophysitism by regarding [humankind's] salvation as his absorption into God ended up by preaching the annihilation rather than the salvation of [humankind].

(and thus ceasing to be human): it is that the fulfilment of God's original and sustained purpose is to be *with* us – and deification too often suppresses or supplants that. Louth's emphasis on encounter and engagement withstands the danger that the world loses its integrity and identity and is collapsed into God. This is where I propose that being with is a richer notion than deification. It is so because like deification it celebrates the transfigured state of humankind and creation and rejoices in communion with the divine – but precisely keeps the 'com', and does not conceive only of the 'union'. Moreover, references in Orthodox theology to our being with one another and the creation in the presence of God are scarce. What being with offers is not just an account of being with God in a state of presence, attention, mystery, delight and so on – but being with one another and the creation in the same spirit. What is missing from deification is this genuinely corporate sense of destiny. And only this corporate sense of destiny does justice to the richness of the creation God has so elaborately made.

I very much warm to the language of transfiguration, of friendship, and of seeing face to face. I entirely share the lament that Western theology has lost the cosmic dimension and stayed within the lesser arch. But I remain chary of the term 'deification'. I humbly assert that being with is a notion that incorporates all the helpful connotations of deification while remaining free from the more problematic ones. My concern is not just with eliding the creator–creature distinction, or with the many occasions when humankind seems to be promised absorption into God, which offers bliss at the price of loss of identity, or even accusations of pantheism, which is clearly a misunderstanding. Whatever their sometime florid descriptions, none of the Eastern theologians believe the essence of human nature is lost. Transformation is relative, not absolute. The believer is united with God, but there is no fusion or confusion, no loss of the integrity of

Nellas identifies precisely the point that concerns me in relation to deification – that it can fall under Nellas' account of Monophysitism.

human nature. Humankind does not participate in the essence of God. It remains distinctly human by nature but participates in God by grace. Its humanity is never abolished. We are elevated to something better, not reduced to something less.[35]

Yet the descriptions of what deification entails tend to be preoccupied with a moment of encounter, rather than describing an ongoing, eternal relationship. Bulgakov's citation of a conversation as with a friend that reinhabits Moses and echoes Eden offers a much more promising indication of what kinds of interactions glory involves, and how the Holy Spirit governs and animates such activity. But in general, deification, while commendably drawing attention to the larger arch, focuses insufficiently on the practices that constitute its everlasting life with God.[36] In relation to human virtue and growth in holiness, this is clearly not the case, for it is a slow, dedicated process on the human side.[37] But a thick description of how the heavenly divine–human and God–humanity–creation relationships

[35] Daniel P. Clendenin lists a host of images taken from the *Philokalia* that describe *theōsis*: transformation, union, participation, partaking, intermingling, elevation, interpenetration, transmutation, commingling, assimilation, reintegration, adoption, recreation. He adds that divinisation implies our being intertwined with Christ, an influx of the divine, or the attainment of similitude with God. See his 'Partakers of Divinity', 374. The *Philokalia* is a collection of mystical texts from the fourth to the fifteenth centuries compiled by two monks of Mount Athos in 1782. It became hugely influential. See St Nikodemos of the Holy Mountain and St Makarios of Corinth, *The Philokalia: The Complete Text*, trans. G. E. H. Palmer, Philip Sherrard and Kallistos Ware (London: Faber and Faber, 1979–84).

[36] Origen provides a description that amplifies the notion of contemplation while offering no account of genuine interaction with one another, the renewed creation or God:

> The mind, when it has come to perfection, still feeds on appropriate and suitable food in a measure which can neither admit of want nor of superfluity. But in all respects this food must be understood to be the contemplation and understanding of God, and its measures to be those that are appropriate and suitable to this nature which has been made and created.
>
> *On First Principles*, 2, 11, 7, trans. C. Butterworth (New York: Harper Torchbooks, 1966), 153–54, quoted in Maloney, *The Cosmic Christ*, 261

[37] In this the Orthodox notion of deification has much in common with the Wesleyan notion of sanctification. See Randy L. Maddox, 'John Wesley and Eastern Orthodoxy: Influences, Convergences and Differences', *Asbury Theological Journal*, 45/2 (1990), 29–53 at 39–40.

are actually conducted seems not to be forthcoming. What is at stake here is whether God is fundamentally a noun or a verb: whether God is perpetual activity of conversation, interaction, and appreciation, as I suggest, or whether perfection is a static moment of arrival with no subsequent narrative.

In the rest of this chapter, I explore how Orthodox theologians respond to this challenge with the notions of communion, participation and transfiguration.

COMMUNION, PARTICIPATION AND TRANSFIGURATION

Maximus strives to avoid the pitfalls that frequently attend deification.[38] He explores how God can be all in all (1 Cor 15:28) while maintaining a fitting distance between the human and the divine, and still incorporating the whole creation, of which humanity is a microcosm. He finds his answer in the hypostatic union, by which Christ is two natures, human and divine, in one person, Jesus. The divine and the human natures interpenetrate each other in each deified human being, without contravening the four Chalcedonian strictures – confusion, change, division and separation.[39] As we saw in Chapter 2, this unfortunately roots communion in the union of Christ's two natures rather than Christ's interaction with human beings.[40] Not only does this fail to render a full distinction between Christ and human beings, but it places too much weight on the distinction between the divine and human nature – treating them almost as if they were two distinct beings, rather than two natures in one being.

In Maximus' writings, deification can refer to the purpose of creation (and incarnation), human moral endeavour and divine grace,

[38] For Maximus, 'Unity without annihilation is the supreme divine goal.' Thunberg, *Man and the Cosmos*, 76.

[39] The declaration of Christ's one person in two natures, declared in 451 and known as the Chalcedonian definition, states that Christ is 'acknowledged in two natures unconfusedly, unchangeably, indivisibly, inseparably'.

[40] We shall observe in Chapter 6 that Kathryn Tanner makes the same move.

or sharing in the divine attributes, especially immortality. He sees God and humanity as paradigms of each other: they co-inhere without either changing its nature.[41] Deification is chiefly accessible through the sacraments: baptism incorporates the believer into Christ, and in the Eucharist a genuine exchange takes place and the believer becomes a partaker of the divine nature, being filled with Christ.[42] Instead of the bread of communion becoming part of us, we become part of God; the bread is not consumed by us: it consumes us.[43] This latter in particular helps the notion withstand the accusation of being too focused on the individual.

Maximus addresses the question of overemphasis on the individual head-on. He speaks of the way grace draws humankind, in freedom, into a dynamic, perichoretic relation with God, and how there is a perichoretic exchange between the human and divine will in Christ, forming a genuine communion. Humanity is called to this synergy of communion manifest in Christ.[44] In a passage with striking resonances with the themes of community and communion I outlined in Chapter 2, Maximus describes a profoundly corporate, collective notion of church and heavenly congress:

> Men, women and children, profoundly divided as to race, nation, manner of life, work, knowledge, honour, fortune ... the Church recreates them all in the Spirit. To all equally she communicates a divine aspect. All receive from her a unique nature which cannot be broken asunder, a nature which no longer permits one to take into

[41] See the summary in Collins, *Partaking in the Divine Nature*, 106–08. Maximus' emphasis on the hypostatic union becomes more significant in light of his embattled defence of it in the face of the Monothelites, who said Christ had only one will.

[42] The sacramental dimension was especially emphasised by John of Damascus and Symeon the New Theologian.

[43] This is a particular emphasis of Gregory of Nyssa. See Maloney, *The Cosmic Christ*, 156, 273.

[44] Collins, *Partaking in the Divine Nature*, 180. Note again the significance of the Monothelite controversy in the reference to the exchange between Christ's divine and human will.

> consideration the many and profound differences which are their lot. In that way all are raised up and united in a manner which is truly catholic. In her none is in the least degree separated from the community, all are grounded, so to speak, in one another by the simple and indivisible power of faith ... Christ, too, is all in all, he who contains all in himself according to the unique, infinite and all-wide power of his goodness – as a centre upon which all lines converge – that the creatures of the one God may not live as strangers or enemies one with another, having no place in common, where they may display their love and their peace.[45]

Thus the answer to misgivings about what Maximus and companions say about deification lies in what they say about communion. Here is a rich conception of communion that breaks down barriers, builds up faith, meets each in their own context, enriches the other and centres on Christ. It is a rousing portrayal of peace. Humanity will contemplate the mystery of God's love for each human being; yet never fully comprehend.[46]

We saw in Chapter 2 above that communion elevates the heritage of covenant and the practices of community to the threshold of divine destiny. Communion offers a vocabulary to affirm the aim of the language of deification while avoiding the pitfalls that can beset it. Communion speaks of both union, the being of God embracing humanity, and presence, the character of God being with humankind. It emphasises both aspects: with and in. But we have seen here that

[45] Maximus the Confessor, *Mystagogia*, trans. in Maloney, *The Cosmic Christ*, 279.

[46] See Maloney, *The Cosmic Christ*, 113. Irenaeus, in *Adversus haereses*, 5.1.1, speaks of atonement as communion:

> The Lord thus has redeemed us through his own blood, giving his soul for our souls, and his flesh for our flesh, and has also poured out the Spirit of the Father for the union and communion of God and [humanity], imparting indeed God to [humankind] by means of the Spirit and, on the other hand, attaching [humankind] to God by his own incarnation, and bestowing upon us at his coming immortality durably and truly, by means of communion with God.

communion is not a helpful way to describe the relation of divine and human natures in the person of the incarnate Jesus. Christ exhibits the way human beings come into the full relationship with God for which they were created. Divine–human communion is the purpose of all things, and the reason for the incarnation.[47] That communion is modelled on the way Christ relates to us – the pattern of being with witnessed in his incarnate life – rather than, as Maximus would have it, humankind and divinity perfectly co-inhering in Christ's person.[48]

Communion has a definitive form: the relationship of God and humankind. But it can be extended to two further dimensions: communion between human beings and one another; and communion between God, humanity and the wider creation. In both these additional dimensions there are areas of promise and areas of under-exploration in the Eastern tradition. Beginning with the relations of human beings with one another, contemporary Orthodox theologians are beginning to recognise the degree to which Eastern theology has long assumed the focal leadership of an emperor. The rich Byzantine traditions developed in this imperial context; but Orthodoxy is emerging from a half-millennium of oppression, and is in danger of reverting from being colonised into becoming the coloniser. The question of what kinds of relationships, both political and ecclesial, mirror and enhance the participation of the world in God remains acute, and is often focused in precise social and political arrangements. One commentator notes,

[47] Aristotle Papanikolaou, 'Orthodoxy, Postmodernity, and Ecumenism: The Difference That Divine–Human Communion Makes', *Journal of Ecumenical Studies*, 42/4 (Fall 2007), 527–46, describes this conviction as the ultimate non-negotiable for contemporary Eastern Orthodox theologians, and their principal contribution to ecumenical dialogue. One commentator describes the growing likeness of the human soul to God in its most intimate phase: 'It is more than knowledge, though it is less than ecstasy: "communion", perhaps is its nearest equivalent in English.' R. B. Tollinton, *Clement of Alexandria*, vol. 2 (London: Williams and Norgate, 1914), 99–100, quoted in Maloney, *The Cosmic Christ*, 119.

[48] This is a point deftly articulated in Edwin Chr. van Driel, 'Sharing in Nature or Encountering a Person: A Tale of Two Different Supralapsarian Strategies', *Scottish Journal of Theology*, 75 (2022), 193–206.

> The particular challenge for the Orthodox Church is to find a way in which the very heart of its tradition, the realism of divine–human communion in the person of Jesus Christ, is able to permeate and shape its institutional structures so as to enable responses to 'political' questions that are faithful to all that is entailed in this principle of divine–human communion. Such faithfulness means working to create a world in which particularity, otherness, difference, relationality, and freedom are the norm and reflect the glory of God, which is the presence of God's love that is always striving to show itself'[49]

Communion offers much promise to respond to the postmodern challenge of navigating difference.

As to the relationship between God, humankind and the wider creation, this is a theme that is on the whole neglected among the early Greek theologians; yet it is one where communion has great potential, particularly when one ponders the priestly role of humanity in bringing all creation in worship to the throne of God. The exception to the neglect is Clement of Alexandria. Among the early Greek theologians, he has a uniquely positive estimation of the world – both as people and as institutions, and as non-human life and wider creation. For example, he perceives the Logos communicating to all people in every generation: to ancient philosophers, Old Testament prophets and consistent theophanies since the time of Christ. Pseudo-Dionysius built on this more expansive notion of the wider creation with his distinctive account of celestial hierarchy:

> A hierarchy is a sacred order, a state of understanding and an activity approximating as closely as possible to the divine. . . . The goal of a hierarchy is to enable things to be as like as possible to God and to be at one with him. . . . Hierarchy causes its members to be images of God in all respects, to be clear and spotless mirrors reflecting the glow of primordial light and indeed of God himself.

[49] Papanikolaou, 'Orthodoxy, Postmodernity, and Ecumenism', 545–46.

> It ensures that when its members have received this full and divine splendour, they can then pass on this light generously and in accordance with God's will to beings further down the scale.[50]

Hierarchy is a radiant display that reaches out from God to the whole created world and draws it back into union with the Trinity. It connotes not separation and exclusion (as in contemporary use), but union and inclusion. For Pseudo-Dionysius, the cosmos is constituted by rank upon rank of angels, reflecting and praising God's glory, drawing in human beings to be transformed by worship. Maximus describes how the pattern of the Eucharistic liturgy achieves this vision by portraying and embodying the exchange between the emptying of God in the incarnation and the deification of humankind in return. Ascetic discipline and contemplation, by which the human will is united to the will of God through the incarnation, provides the counterpart to this corporate experience. Here is a communion in which the whole creation can rejoice.

It seems that the language of communion and participation can convey the profound *with* of eternal relationship and articulate all that is intended by the term 'deification' without jeopardising the creator–creature distinction. George Pattison argues convincingly in this vein. He denies that deification means that human beings get a new essence or substance, or that they stop being human beings. Instead, he maintains, 'In our most decisive personal being we come to know ourselves as we are in and through the relation to the personal God.' He goes on to suggest, deftly employing the language of 2 Peter 1:4, that 'To come to know who we truly are is to come to know ourselves as we are in and as participants in the divine conversation, finding ourselves being partakers of the divine way of being, namely this being-as-conversation itself.'[51] Here we arrive at the

[50] Pseudo-Dionysius the Areopagite, *Celestial Hierarchy*, 3.1f: 164D–165A, quoted in Andrew Louth, *Maximus the Confessor* (London: Routledge, 1996), 31.

[51] George Pattison, *A Short Course in Christian Doctrine* (London: SCM, 2005), 40, quoted in Collins, *Partaking in the Divine Nature*, 182.

crystallisation of what deification, participation and communion all point to: the discovery that the Trinity is a constant conversation, and that God's purpose for humankind is for it to be a full – but distinct – participant in that conversation. Participation is thus the outward form of what communion involves inwardly. John Scotus Eriugena offers an allusive but nuanced articulation of what this means: 'Everything that is, is either participant, or participated, or participation, or (both) participated and participant at once.'[52] This participation begins with the incarnation.

The most vivid portrayal of being-as-conversation in the New Testament is the account of the transfiguration. The transfiguration portrays the incarnate Jesus, illumined as at no other time in the gospel story; a conversation with the Father, indicated in the words 'This is my Son, the Beloved; listen to him!' (Mark 9:7 – the instruction to listen, not given at Jesus' baptism, is a further encouragement to discourse); dialogue with Moses, representing the law, and Elijah, the prophets; and less congruent dialogue with Peter, James and John. Here is a portrayal, not perfect, yet illustrative and suggestive, of eternal being-as-conversation; of everyone being participant, or participated, or participation; of both the created purpose and the ultimate destiny of humankind, yet one that is experienced in the present tense. Transfiguration is the moment in time in which we see our relationship with God in eternity. It is the episode in which the full implications of the incarnation are disclosed. It is the bringing-together of historical revelation (Moses and Elijah) with present experience. It is a vision through the veil of existence into the wonder of essence.

Maximus offers no fewer than eighteen interpretations of how the transfiguration scene harmonises and balances ways of knowing.

[52] John Scotus Eriugena, *Periphyseon*, 3, quoted in Collins, *Partaking in the Divine Nature*, 114. John Scotus Eriugena was a Neoplatonist philosopher and poet who was born in Ireland and lived from 815 to 877. He was almost unique in the West in being able to translate Greek texts, and is considered the outstanding Western philosopher of his era.

These include legal and prophetic, wisdom and kindness, knowledge and education, ascetic struggle and contemplation, the sensible and the intelligible. He then summarises the significance of the transfiguration in these words:

> He accepted to be unchangeably created in form like us and through his immeasurable love for humankind to become the type and symbol of himself, and from himself symbolically to represent himself, and through the manifestation of himself to lead to himself in his complete and secret hiddenness the whole creation, and while he remains quite unknown in his hidden, secret place beyond all things, unable to be known or understood by any being in any way whatever, out of his love for humankind he grants to human beings intimations of himself in the manifest divine works performed in the flesh.[53]

In this passage the transfiguration becomes, for Maximus, the definitive display of the incarnation. It exhibits Christ's humility ('he accepted'), God's purpose in him ('immeasurable love'), his embodiment of the eternal logos ('type and symbol'), his as-yet-not-fully-disclosed identity ('secret ... unknown ... hidden') and his awesome revelation ('intimations'). These are a sample of the many layers of significance of the transfiguration, and of the many dimensions that Jesus' obedience entails. Elsewhere Maximus translates the transfigured presence of Jesus from an event in history into an understanding of what happens when words of the gospels become manifest and radiant to the disciple.[54] Maximus maintains that the shining of Jesus' garments can refer to the way the disciple can discern the Word either in scripture or in creation: both can be forms of

[53] Maximus the Confessor, *Difficulty* 10, 31c, trans. in Louth, *Maximus the Confessor*, 132. Maximus teaches that the shining vestments of the transfigured Christ represent the way, when God is revealed to the human soul, all the *logoi* of things intelligible and sensible in scripture and nature appear as if they were with him. See Thunberg, *Man and the Cosmos*, 76.

[54] Maximus the Confessor, *Centuries on Theology and the Incarnate Disposition of the Son of God*, 2, 14, trans. in Louth, *Maximus the Confessor*, 46.

illumination.[55] Thus Moses received written revelation, the commandments, while God spoke to Elijah through earthquake, wind, fire and echoing silence. Transfiguration becomes a key motif for explaining how humankind can come face to face with God without ceasing to be human, and how human beings can know God despite their limitations.

GLEANINGS

Now that I have surveyed distinctive features brought by Eastern theologians in relation to the reasons for the incarnation, and the reflections of some contemporary contributors and commentators, it is time to glean key themes and insights to guide my constructive proposals to follow in Part III.

In relation to **incarnation**, there is almost unanimity that the incarnation is about the completion and fulfilment of humankind's original potential, which is to be brought face to face with God. The incarnation tells a much bigger story than that circumscribed by fall and redemption. In this larger story sin and evil do not play a determinative part, and while they remain significant, neither humankind nor God in Christ is defined in relation to them. Sin does not reach back to humanity's origin or forward to humanity's destiny. The incarnation is the final cause of creation: all aspects of human nature were created that we might be in relationship with Christ – to apprehend him temporally and interact with him eternally.

As to the nature of **eternal life with God**, I encountered some difficulties with the key Orthodox notion of the divine exchange – whereby God in Christ became what we are that we might become what God is. I concurred with the conviction that God's purpose was not limited to returning humanity to its condition prior to the fall, and was instead focused is on its future destiny. But I regretted that deification too readily envisages our union with God, and is too reticent about precisely what activity and interaction genuinely

[55] See Louth, *Maximus the Confessor*, 95.

describe our being with God, one another and the renewed creation. I was glad to find some awareness of wider society and the creation, and wished to discover further ways of their being incorporated into the aspiration of being face to face with God. I argued that 'being with' incorporated the thrust of the deification doctrine, yet offered more explicit distinction between the glory of being with God and the glory of God's essence itself, and also provided a richer account of being with one another and the renewed creation than is generally found in Orthodox theology.

More specifically in regard to what being with God entails, I found three fertile and generative motifs. Divine–human **communion** is the purpose of all things, and the reason for the incarnation: but this communion precisely means intimate and general perpetual exchange – in silence, touch, gesture, food and words. Communion is not just between humanity and God, but an encounter where the creatures of the one God do not live as strangers or enemies to one with another, but display love and peace. Communion also has a sacramental dimension: baptism and Eucharist are the most tangible human entry points to the wondrous exchange. This notion of communion is entirely congruent with the one I set out in Chapter 2 above.

A second motif is that of **participation**, a richer concept than deification because it specifically describes (rather than tacitly implies) ongoing interaction. Participation means joining the divine conversation, partaking of the divine nature, engaging in being-as-conversation itself. The Trinity is a constant conversation, and God's purpose for humankind is for it to be a full participant in that conversation. Everything that is, is either participant, or participated, or participation. This account enriches the notion of participation outlined in Chapter 3 above as the fifth dimension of being with.

The final motif is **transfiguration**. Transfiguration is the moment in time in which we see our relationship with God in eternity. It is the episode in which the full implications of the incarnation are disclosed. It is the convergence of historical revelation with present experience. It is a vision through the veil of existence into the wonder of essence. Transfiguration offers a key theme in explicating how humankind can come face to face with God without ceasing to be human, and how human beings can know God even though their faculties are limited. A whole other area is that transfiguration challenges any strong distinction between theology and ethics, because it is a genuine entering into conversation, which has been described as precisely what ethics is all about.[56] Ultimately transfiguration, which I identified in Chapter 3 above as the most distinctive characteristic of glory, emerges as a vital theme for our exploration of the theological reach of being with.

[56] Herbert McCabe, *What Is Ethics All About?* (Washington, DC, and Cleveland, OH: Corpus Books, 1969), 92.

5 Medieval Debates

This chapter explores medieval debates about the incarnation. Like many scholastic debates, the controversies are intense and complex, and, while greatly assisted by expert exponents of the various major contributors to the issues, it is not my intention to explore the detail of those discussions here. Neither is the particular debate that caused a rift between Scotists and Thomists, that of whether, had Adam not fallen, Christ would still have come, my principal focus. Rather, I highlight points that advance my larger argument about the centrality of incarnation for the whole of Christian doctrine.

REASONS FOR THE INCARNATION

The outpouring of reflection on Christ's incarnation that characterised the Franciscan scholastics of the thirteenth and fourteenth centuries was triggered by Anselm of Canterbury's work *Cur Deus homo*, composed over the period 1094–98, while he was Archbishop of Canterbury. Anselm responds to two kinds of critics of the incarnation: Jews who deny the dignity of the incarnation, and secular teachers who focus entirely on Christ's commission to defeat the devil. Anselm focuses the issues back on God. He gives a reason for creation: that humankind should find eternal bliss. Humankind, however, lost that blessed state through sin. That sin cannot be ignored, because there can be no true mercy without justice, and because due order requires a calling to account. Thus the only way to remit the sin is through satisfaction.[1] But the human realm is one of freedom, and it

[1] Satisfaction, for Anselm, is the restoration of due honour to a lord after an affront to his dignity. Sin is that affront; and Christ offers the payment or punishment required to restore due order and fitting relationship. His innocent life becomes a recompense for the dishonour accumulated by humankind's sins.

has a dignity that must be respected. This yields a stand-off: God alone can re-order and restore creation; but humanity alone should.[2] Hence the incarnation of Jesus – both God and human.[3]

Anselm's account of the reason for the incarnation – that Christ was required to provide recompense for the affront to God's honour accumulated by human sin – was largely endorsed by Thomas Aquinas.[4] But it brought about a backlash that lasted 300 years, led

[2] David Bentley Hart, *The Beauty of the Infinite: The Aesthetics of Christian Truth* (Grand Rapids, MI: Eerdmans, 2003), 360–73 at 370 offers a fascinating alternative reading of *Cur Deus homo*:

> Far from an arbitrary arrangement of jurisprudential transactions calculated to effect a kind of forensic reconciliation between humanity and God, the atonement at *Cur Deus Homo* depicts it is an assumption of solidarity with us by an infinitely merciful God in order to fulfil in us that beatitude intended in our creation, by accomplishing on our behalf what, in our impotence to do good and in his unwillingness to employ unjust means, could never otherwise have been brought to pass.

In their account of Anselm, *Mapping Atonement*, 61–81, William G. Witt and Joel Scandrett trace three receptions of his theory: antagonistic (which alleges he is rationalistic, Nestorian and, in the language of Joanne Carlson Brown, a portrayer of cosmic child abuse ('Divine Child Abuse', *Daughters of Sarah*, 18/3 (1992), 24–28)), critically appreciative (which follows Richard Southern in lamenting Anselm's grounding in medieval feudalism and argues that his view of sin, death and punishment is extrinsic and forensic rather than intrinsic and ontological) and harmonistic. Hart, along with George Sumner and John McIntyre, represents the harmonistic position.

[3] It is notable, but not often acknowledged, that Anselm's theory displaces altogether the widespread notion of the devil's rights, a view for example significant for Augustine. See his *On the Trinity*, 357–60 (book 13, sections 16–18). See also Michael Robson, 'Saint Bonaventure', in G. R. Evans, ed., *The Medieval Theologians* (Oxford: Blackwell, 2001), 187–200 at 191.

[4] Thomas Aquinas equivocates on the question, seeing validity on both sides. The reason he finally opposes the notion that Christ would have come even had there been no fall is that, while nothing would have prevented the incarnation in a sinless world, scripture gives us no ability to decide the question either way. See his *Summa theologiae*, 3.1.3, in Latin/English Edition of the Works of St Thomas Aquinas, vol. 19, trans. Laurence Shapcote, ed. John Mortensen and Enrique Alarcón (Lander, WY: Aquinas Institute for the Study of Sacred Doctrine, 2012), 8–10. His key notion is fittingness. This is manifest in five forms: (1) human beings know how much God loves them, and are stirred to love in return; (2) humankind is set an example of obedience, humility, constancy and justice; (3) Christ not only delivered humankind from sin but merited justifying grace and the glory of bliss; (4) this makes human beings less likely to sin; and (5) as a man was deceived and overcome by the devil, so a man overcame the devil; and as humankind deserved death, by a human by dying vanquished death (3.46.3). Answering the question 'Why the incarnation?' he finds

by friars of the Franciscan order. This backlash was not just cerebral jousting. Franciscan practice and disposition emphasised not so much God's omnipotence, omniscience and transcendence, as generosity, mercy and benevolence. God is endlessly creative, loving like an artist who constantly seeks to evoke dynamic and generous human responses. The Franciscans who played a major role in the medieval debate about the incarnation were seeking not a detached vision of God, but an encompassing and compassionate embrace with practical and social dimensions.[5] This concerned whether faith was about belief in an ethereal configuration of divine justice, or about a truly incarnate form of life and pattern of relationships. The Franciscans wanted not simply to win an intellectual contest, but to affirm the artistic, generous, utterly responsive character of God. For my purposes in this study, this is not a niche sideshow, but a key insight: it concerns the very nature and entire purpose of God – and there are stark alternatives.

The holistic nature of the Franciscan vision is not restricted to the incarnation alone. The emphasis of the Franciscan tradition on creation and the importance it attaches to incarnation are complementary. Francis of Assisi cherished creation as God's gift centred on the definitive gift, which was Jesus Christ. Franciscan Christology has thus always been characterised by its cosmological context. This is highlighted in Alexander of Hales, mentor to Bonaventure. Like the Cappadocian theologians of the fourth century, Alexander saw Christology as rooted in a Trinitarian understanding of God. In this perspective, the doctrine of God is inseparable from a notion of

ten reasons, among them that it raises hope, excites charity, removes presumption and liberates from servitude (3.1.2).

[5] Mary Beth Ingham, *Scotus for Dunces: An Introduction to the Subtle Doctor* (St Bonaventure, NY: Franciscan Institute, 2003), 109. Maximilian Mary Dean FI maintains that Duns Scotus' views were originally those of Francis of Assisi, and Scotus' work is the translation of Francis' contemplative theology into academic terms. See his *A Primer on the Absolute Primacy of Christ* (New Bedford, MA: Academy of the Immaculate, 2006), 41.

incarnation, but the incarnation cannot be conceived without an account of creation.[6]

We have already seen that the debate about Christ's incarnation, and the intention behind the incarnation, is wide-ranging and far-reaching. It concerns God's purpose and the exercise of God's will; the identity of Christ; the reason for creation; the nature of salvation; and the destiny of humankind. The enquiry that focuses this chapter is generally taken to begin with Rupert of Deutz.[7] Rupert was a Benedictine monk who was concerned that arguments like those of his older contemporary Anselm open the door to two kinds of problem. The first is that if the incarnation is considered to be always God's intention, then sin and evil must accordingly be part of that same intention. This means that sin and evil are willed by God at creation. The second is that, if one cannot countenance that God wills sin and evil, then the incarnation arises as an unwelcome change of plan, which jeopardises notions of God's sovereignty, omnipotence and immutability.[8] Rupert addressed the second problem by maintaining that God had foreordained the incarnation from all eternity: God had always intended the Word to have an earthly role in the divine plan for the chosen people. As to the first problem, Rupert acknowledged that sin and evil were of humankind's and the devil's making; Christ's sacrificial response to them in the atonement was not foreordained. Rupert remains comfortable with the notion of the atonement – he just denies that soteriology governs Christology, in

[6] Here I follow the insight of Ilia Delio, 'Revisiting the Franciscan Doctrine of Christ', *Theological Studies*, 64/1 (2003), 3–23. Alexander of Hales, like Robert Grosseteste, William of Ware and John Duns Scotus a native of the British Isles, lived 1185–1245.

[7] Rupert of Deutz lived from around 1075 to around 1130. He was Abbot of St Heribert in Deutz, now a suburb of Cologne. His work on these questions is found in his *De gloria et honore Filii hominis super Mattheum*, in Corpus Christianorum Continuatio Mediaevalis, 29 (Turnhout, Belgium: Brepols, 1971).

[8] These points are highlighted by Daniel P. Horan OFM, 'How Original Was Scotus on the Incarnation? Reconsidering the History of the Absolute Predestination of Christ in Light of Robert Grosseteste', *Heythrop Journal*, 52 (2011), 374–91 at 377. See also John H. Van Engen, *Rupert of Deutz* (Berkeley: University of California Press, 1983), 354–56. Horan points out that Rupert had previously addressed these two positions in his *Commentary on Genesis* and his *Commentary on John* (c.1114–16).

other words that the need to deal with sin constitutes the reason for the incarnation. Nonetheless he begins a whole tradition, at least in the West, by taking the focus away from the fall and asserting a counterfactual: that, if humanity had not sinned, God would yet have become incarnate.[9]

THE BEAUTIFUL SONG OF CREATION

While those who agree with Rupert offer fertile material for our exploration, there is just as much fruit to be found in others who emphasise the primacy of Christ according to Colossians 1:15 ('he is the firstborn of all creation') yet equivocate on Rupert's counterfactual assertion. Among these are Bonaventure of Bagnoregio and Robert Grosseteste.[10] Bonaventure's emphasis in relation to the incarnation is on completion and the fulfilment of God's purpose. This is a

[9] I do not here discuss all the theologians who followed Rupert of Deutz in this trajectory. In addition to Alexander of Hales, among those discussed by Juniper B. Carol in his extensive study *Why Jesus Christ? Thomistic, Scotistic and Conciliatory Perspectives* (Manassas, VA: Trinity Communications, 1986), 120–479, are Honorius of Autun (1080–1151), Albert the Great (unlike the others, a Dominican, c.1200–80) and William of Ware (1260–1305). (Curiously he hardly dwells on Robert Grosseteste.) Ilia Delio notes, for example, that Matthew of Aquasparta (1240–1302) 'held that the Incarnation was supposed for the perfection of the natural order', and that Raymond Lull (a lay theologian, 1232–1316)

> asserted that the primary aim of the Incarnation was to show forth the love of God. In his *Libre de Sancta Maria* Lull wrote: 'The nature of Jesus Christ is the most eminent and most noble of all creatures, because it is the end, the beginning and the crown of all other things since all things that God made, he created to be clothed with this human nature, born of our Blessed Lady.'
>
> 'Revisiting the Franciscan Doctrine of Christ', 7

Trent Pomplun adds to this list the Franciscan Archbishop of Canterbury John Peckham (c.1230–92). See his 'The Immaculate World: Predestination and Passibility in Contemporary Scotism', *Modern Theology*, 30/4 (October 2014), 525–51 at 530.

[10] Born Giovanni di Fidanza, and an Italian Franciscan, bishop, cardinal and seventh Minister General of the Franciscan Order, Bonaventure of Bagnoregio lived 1221–74. He perceives that God foresaw the possibility of the fall and thus structured humankind in relation to redemption. Thus he keeps the sense that the principal reason for the incarnation does not come from something external to God, but nonetheless recognises that the incarnation is shaped by redemption. See Zachary Hayes, *The Hidden Center: Spirituality and Speculative Christology in St. Bonaventure* (New York: Franciscan Institute, 1992), 190.

significantly different emphasis from that which assumes the incarnation was ordered to address the problem of sin and evil.[11] For Bonaventure, the human predicament is not so much one that stems from the fall as that arising from humankind's status as a creature. How can that creature relate to God, in creation, and in the final life of glory? Thus in a sermon at Christmas, the feast of the incarnation, he preaches:

> It is in the Word that we discover the perfection of that greatness of heart which brings all reality to its consummation and completion, since the figure of the circle attests to the perfection of bodies both in the macrocosm and in the microcosm. ... But this figure is not complete in the universe. Now, if this figure is to be as perfect as possible, the line of the universe must be curved into a circle. Indeed, God is simply the first. And the last among the works of the world is man. Therefore, when God became man, the works of God were brought to perfection. This is why Christ, the God-man, is called the alpha and the omega, the beginning and the end.[12]

God is the first; humanity is the last; Christ brings first and last, alpha and omega, together in the incarnation. Here we see Trinity, incarnation and creation held tightly in an account of God's ultimate purpose – formulated before the foundation of the world, and fully disclosed at Christmas. This is the foundation of a truly incarnational theology.

Rather than see creation and incarnation in some kind of tussle for pre-eminence, Bonaventure exalts both. The Trinity exudes

[11] Justus H. Hunter, in his *If Adam Had Not Sinned: The Reason for the Incarnation from Anselm to Scotus* (Washington, DC: Catholic University of America Press, 2003), 7, explains that when Bonaventure considers 'the primary reason for the incarnation', his underlying concern is how we can discern God's reasons for any action. So he rephrases the counterfactual question in terms of primacy among reasons – hence the expression 'the primacy of Christ'.

[12] Bonaventure, 'Sermo II in nat. Dom.', IX, 107, trans. as 'Sermon II on the Nativity of the Lord', in *What Manner of Man? Sermons on Christ by St. Bonaventure*, 2nd ed., trans. Zachary Hayes (Chicago: Franciscan Herald, 1989), 73–74, quoted in Delio, 'Revisiting the Franciscan Doctrine of Christ', 10.

dynamic, self-diffusive, communicative and expressive goodness. Creation shares in the mystery of the procession of the Son from the Father. Thus creation mirrors, to a limited degree, the infinite and dynamic love between the Father and the Word, emerging from this relationship and exploding into a thousand forms in the universe. Bonaventure crystallises this insight in a memorable image: 'Creation is like a beautiful song that flows in the most excellent of harmonies, but it is a song that God freely desires to sing into the vast spaces of the universe. Creation is simply the loving outflow of a loving God whose infinite dynamic goodness is shared in a limited dynamic way.'[13] Here we see the vitality of creation in artistic, poetic, stirring creativity.

As to the Trinity, on the one hand, God is infinitely fecund and self-communicative within God's self; yet God desires to create, because God is love. It is in the nature of perfect love not to be content to be contained in itself; it bursts out, to be shared with another. This is the notion of effervescence to which I referred in Chapter 1. While it is impossible to claim knowledge about precisely what initiated creation, my argument throughout this book, here endorsed by Bonaventure, is that creation is the setting for the Trinity to be with an other through the incarnation of the Son. That other is humankind.[14]

We may distinguish two connected notions here. *Exemplarism* refers to the way the fecundity of divine ideas, centred on the Word of God, is the template for all existence. The Father, who is unbegotten and effervescent, pouring forth like a fountain, is the source of Son, the Holy Spirit and all that showers down from them. *Expressionism*

[13] Bonaventure, I *Sentences*, d. 44, q. 1, a. 3, concl. (I, 786a). See the critical edition of his works, *Doctoris Seraphici S. Bonaventurae opera omnia*, ed. PP. Collegium S. Bonaventurae, 10 vols. (Quaracchi: Collegium S. Bonaventurae, 1882–1902). See also Delio, 'Revisiting the Franciscan Doctrine of Christ', 12.

[14] I am suggesting that effervescence is a more helpful notion than the 'nature of perfect love', since the latter is a term that may be used in a great many contexts. It is partly to nuance the complication of a term like 'perfect love' that I have developed the dimensions of being with as explored in Chapter 3.

refers to the urge to bring forth and generate – originally in the Father's generating Son and Spirit, but subsequently and accordingly in every aspect of creation. This expression is at the epicentre of all reality. All creatures derive from the expression of the Word by the Father, and themselves find life in the Word through the Spirit. Thus all in creation emerges out of the Word; it externalises and objectifies and makes visible the inner Word known previously only to the Father and the Spirit. Expression is a key element of creation – and a key characteristic of humankind.

Hence it is fitting to describe the whole creation as incarnational, because the whole creation takes its lead from the creativity of the Word. Likewise all creation has the potential for union with God. (Thus does eschatology peep in at the very outset of creation.) Jesus manifests the potency of creation to be brought to completion. As Bonaventure puts it, in the Christ child, 'The perfection of the entire order is realised, for in that one being the unity of all reality is brought to consummation.'[15] Bonaventure is particularly fond of what he calls the coincidence of opposites. He sees this perfectly expressed in Christ, who unites divine and earthly, eternity and time, beginning and end. This is how Bonaventure understands completion and perfection, and how he sees both embodied in the incarnation. For Bonaventure, all creation is made for Christ. A world without Christ (that is, one in which Christ had not come because there had been no fall), would have left creation incomplete.

Many bracket out Bonaventure from this discussion simply because he does not concur with the exact conclusion to Rupert's counterfactual assertion.[16] This is to miss the ways in which he expands the Franciscan imagination and resources the project of this book. We have seen how he offers an account of creation and incarnation that has an integrity separate from any urgency Christ has in

[15] Bonaventure, 'Sermon II on the Nativity', 74. See also Delio, 'Revisiting the Franciscan Doctrine of Christ', 12–15.

[16] Juniper Carol assigns him merely two pages in his 500-page study. See his *Why Jesus Christ?*, 27–29.

addressing the legacy of the fall. In exemplarism and expressionism he provides a rich description of the dynamics of creation. He emphasises completion and perfection as the key roles of Christ's incarnation. In this he furnishes extensive notions that may enrich an account of the priority of incarnation.[17]

INCARNATION AND FULFILMENT

Like Bonaventure, Robert Grosseteste is, after much deliberation, finally unpersuaded by Rupert's way of framing the question; yet he offers fertile thoughts on the matter.[18] These can be distinguished into intrinsic arguments, which refer to the absolute goodness of Christ's humanity, and instrumental ones, which relate to the perfection or elevation of humanity – and do not necessarily only apply to overcoming sin and death.[19]

[17] Justus Hunter, in his *If Adam Had Not Sinned*, 220–22, maintains that these intense medieval debates are largely reconcilable on a proposal he draws largely from Bonaventure but believes is within Aquinas' scope. It is as follows. (1) No necessary reasons for the incarnation can be given. (2) The hypothetical question is generically insoluble. (3) Hypothetical speculation can (and should) be engaged so long as resemblance (with our actual world) is upheld. (4) The question of the motive for the incarnation can be asked more precisely in the form of the primacy question (i.e. which is the most significant motive). (5) Reasons from divine attributes are congruous or fitting (i.e. it seems more appropriate if a freely willed divine action accords with a divine attribute). (6) These proposals render the question salutary for Christian reflection on the incarnation (i.e. faith seeking understanding).

[18] Robert Grosseteste was Chancellor of Oxford University and Bishop of Lincoln, a scientist as well as a scholastic theologian. He lived from 1175 to 1253. See Dominic J. Unger OFM Cap, 'Robert Grosseteste Bishop of Lincoln (1235–1253) on the Reasons for the Incarnation', *Franciscan Studies*, 16/1–2 (March–June 1956), 1–36, for Grosseteste's views on incarnation and primacy. Unger (27–34) reduces Grosseteste's nineteen arguments to ten. Daniel Horan, 'How Original Was Scotus on the Incarnation?', reduces them to five. Here I simply select the ones I find most pertinent. Interestingly Horan (386) suggests that Grosseteste was 'probably unfamiliar with Rupert's work.' James McEvoy, in his *Robert Grosseteste* (New York: Oxford University Press, 2000), 129, notes, 'A theologian of Grosseteste's bent, one who preferred the positive study of the sources of theology to the more systematic application of dialectical method, could not be completely content with giving an unreservedly positive answer to a question that was not raised in the Scriptures or discussed by authoritative commentators.'

[19] Brendan Case, 'More Splendid Than the Sun': Christ's Flesh among the Reasons for the Incarnation", *Modern Theology*, 36/4 (2019), 1–20.

Christ's primacy, in the language of Colossians 1:15–20 and Ephesians 5:32, is an intrinsic argument. Grosseteste points out that Christ is the head and final cause of all creation and of the church, for which all creation was made. Since Christ is the end of all creation, he is therefore the first in God's plan of creation, because the final purpose is always first. Meanwhile God, the highest love, loves creation in the highest manner, and so seeks to be united with it in the highest manner: which is the personal union of incarnation. Moreover, if Christ had not come, the church would have no head.[20] Likewise Grosseteste refers to Ephesians 1:3–10, which states that Christ was intended by God as the source of all blessings for humankind, and as the unifying principle of all creation, on earth as in heaven.

In the same intrinsic vein, but more subtly, Grosseteste argues that incarnation, which he describes as an essence, cannot arise from a defect. Both guilt and punishment, he says, are defects of essences and not essences themselves, and so they cannot be the cause of the capacity for union, which is something positive; in fact, it is the greatest positive good.[21] Creation is so ordered that it is receptive to God's goodness. God offers the universe the maximum goodness it can receive. That maximum good is the incarnation. No lesser good, and certainly no privation, such as evil, can be the rationale for creation.[22] Grosseteste regards as absurd the idea that that our sinful world, because it provides sufficient grounds for the incarnation, is in

[20] Edwin Chr. van Driel, 'God and God's Beloved: A Constructive Re-Reading of Scotus's Supralapsarian Christological Argument', *Heythrop Journal*, 63 (2022), 995–1006 at 997, finds these kinds of arguments problematic, because (a) they are necessitarian, i.e. they bind God to an extraneous obligation, and (b) they suggest the incarnation happens to further a larger good, such as a perfect creation, rather than seeing the incarnation as itself that larger good. While I am inclined to agree with van Driel, at this stage I am simply attending to the variety of arguments brought into the debate around the incarnation and God's purposes.

[21] Unger, 'Robert Grosseteste, Bishop of Lincoln', 28–29.

[22] For more in this territory, see Horan, 'How Original was Scotus on the Incarnation?' 380.

fact a much better world than a sinless world could have been.[23] This is a sly reference to the famous words *felix culpa* in the Exsultet, part of the Latin liturgy for the Easter Vigil; a perspective that this discussion renders deeply problematic.[24]

By contrast, in an instrumental line of argument, Grosseteste asserts that God willed the Eucharist, thereby to be most intimately united with all creation in the most perfect manner.[25] Later, he cites Augustine to say that humanity, in order to be perfectly happy, must be entirely beatified; which Grosseteste takes to mean both the transformation of human intellectual and the enhancement and purification of human feeling. God became a human being in order that these latter, sentient faculties might have a divine object that perfectly satisfies them. The incarnation enables humankind to be completely beatified, lest it have a capacity that might be perpetually unfulfilled.[26] Thus the Eucharist is not fundamentally about the honouring of the passion of Christ: it has a much wider scope than that. It is about the elevation of the temporal to the eternal. In particular, Grosseteste emphasises Christ's beauty:

> The flesh of the Lord Jesus Christ will be manifested after the resurrection as more splendid and more beautiful than the sun and every corporeal creature, because in comparison with the splendour of the flesh of Christ, the sun will seem not to shine. . . . For no mere bodily creature will be able to have as much beauty and splendour as will the glorified flesh of the Lord Jesus Christ.[27]

[23] Case, 'More Splendid Than the Sun', 7.

[24] 'O happy fault that earned for us so great, so glorious a Redeemer.' This sense – that more benefit had accrued to humankind subsequent to the fall than would have done had the first couple remained innocent – appears in Ambrose, Augustine and Aquinas.

[25] Unger, 'Robert Grosseteste, Bishop of Lincoln', 27.

[26] This is not a statement of ableism. Grosseteste is referring to humankind as a whole, rather than human beings singly.

[27] Robert Grosseteste, *De cessatione legalium*, 3.1.24, ed. Richard Dales and Edward King, Auctores Britannici Medii Aevi, 7 (London: Oxford University Press, 1986), 129. For translation, see Case, 'More Splendid Than the Sun', 9.

This is a reference to the light of God, which outshines sun and moon in the new creation (Rev 22:5) and the transfigured face of Jesus (2 Cor 4:6). It is worth noting that, without this communion, the life of heaven would be impoverished, being 'deprived of a profound good for which there is no substitute'.[28] Brendan Case points out that 'the good of fleshly communion with God in Christ offers a sufficient reason for the Incarnation even apart from its role in redeeming us from sin'. He adds that 'The life of heaven is a great Eucharistic liturgy, in which the body of Christ, no longer veiled by the appearances of bread and wine, is offered as the object in which the human senses find their perfect fulfilment.'[29] Thus Grosseteste is arguing that the incarnation is necessary for eternal human happiness, including the apprehension of beauty – something qualitatively different from, above and beyond (though in most accounts closely related to) redemption from sin and death, and much closer to the Orthodox notion of deification explored in Chapter 4.

In his intrinsic and instrumental arguments, and particularly in his attention to beauty, Grosseteste offers plentiful resources for a truly incarnational theology, regardless of his final judgement on Rupert's question.

GLORY AND ELECTION

John Duns Scotus eschews the speculative question of what might have happened had Adam not sinned.[30] Instead he begins with the

[28] Case, 'More Splendid Than the Sun', 9.

[29] Case, 'More Splendid Than the Sun', 19. Case makes a deft point at 19–20: Grosseteste has established that Christ achieves real goods for us apart from salvation from sin. So the person who argues that the incarnation was a response to the fall must either suppress those goods, or entertain exactly the kind of speculation about alternative worlds that renders suspect the view that Christ would have come regardless of the fall.

[30] John Duns Scotus was born in Duns, Scotland, c.1265/66 and died in Cologne in 1308. He studied in Oxford, became Franciscan regent master at Paris, and finally taught in Cologne.

given of the incarnation.[31] He has a very pointed question of his own: 'Does Christ's predestination to grace and glory, and consequently to his position as end of all creatures beneath him, depend on the permission of sin? In short, is the universe sin-centric or Christocentric?'[32] Thus the first theme that emerges in our study of Scotus is election.[33] In Scotus' words,

> It does not seem to be solely because of redemption that God predestined [Christ's] soul to such glory, since the redemption or the glory to be redeemed is not comparable to the glory of the soul in Christ. Neither is it likely that the highest good in the whole of creation is something that merely chanced to take place, and that

[31] Van Driel, 'God and God's Beloved', 997, explains why this matters:

> The Reformer John Calvin, an avid infralapsarian, would later speak of vague speculations that captivate the frivolous and the seekers after novelty'. In fact, he says, whoever desires to say more, 'shows that he is not even content with the very Christ who was given to us'. To this, Scotus would have a simple answer. His account is not an exercise in speculation about a counterfactual situation, but an investigation into the very Christ who was given to us. His point is that the claims of the biblical narrative about God's character and God's relationship to the world as it is suggest a richness to the act of incarnation that goes beyond a divine measure to counter sin.

[32] Allan Wolter OFM, 'John Duns Scotus on the Primacy and Personality of Christ', in Damian McElrath, ed., *Franciscan Christology: Selected Texts, Translations and Introductory Essays* (New York: Franciscan Institute of St Bonaventure, 1980), 139–82 at 141. Justus Hunter maintains that the suggestion that Aquinas and Bonaventure are sin-centric is unfair, although I am not convinced by his argument (see his *If Adam Had Not Sinned*, 231). Daniel Horan articulates another widely perceived impression of how Scotus differs from his predecessors:

> While it is true that he invokes some New Testament passages, unlike his predecessors it is exceptional rather than the rule. It is in this way that Scotus is often viewed as 'highly philosophical', in that he selected to approach the subject from a rigorously rational angle. … It is through natural reason, not revelation, that Scotus believes we are able to delve into the question of the Incarnation and it is with reason that he makes his case.
>
> 'How Original Was Scotus on the Incarnation?', 385

[33] Justus Hunter, in his *If Adam Had Not Sinned*, 224, identifies the origin of this theme in the logic of the will: 'The universally ordinate willer seems first to will that which is closest to the end.' John Duns Scotus, *Ordinatio* 3. d. 7. q. 3, in *B. Ioannis Duns Scoti opera omnia*, vol. 9 (Civitas Vaticana: Typis Vaticanis, 2006), 287.

> only because of some lesser good. Nor is it probable that God predestined Adam to such a good before he predestined Christ. … God selected for his heavenly choir all the angels and [people] he wished to have with their varied degrees of perfection, and all this before considering either the sin or the punishment of the sinner.[34]

Thus there are two aspects to Scotus' sense of election: the election of Christ and the election of humankind, Christ's companions. The central notion for Scotus is that Christ's election precedes ours. For Scotus, there is what we might call an infinite qualitative difference between the glory of redeemed souls and Christ's human nature. For him, it is unimaginable that the restoration of such souls to grace and glory could be the principal reason for the instigation of Christ's soul, and its assumption by the Word. It is even more difficult for Scotus to see rectifying the fall as the reason behind Jesus being from the beginning supernaturalised by grace and glorified with the beatific vision.[35] It is impossible to exaggerate the centrality of Christ to Scotus' whole understanding of the Trinity, creation and the eschatological fulfilment of God's purposes.[36]

Beyond election, the second theme that emerges from our scrutiny of Scotus is glory. Scotus is putting the eschatological dimension of the incarnation on a whole other level than the soteriological dimension. He does not dismiss the soteriological dimension; he simply refuses to let it set the agenda, as it has so consistently done in Western theology.[37] Again there is this consistent note that the

[34] John Duns Scotus, 'Concerning the Predestination of Christ', in Wolter, 'John Duns Scotus on the Primacy and Personality of Christ', 149–51.

[35] For this point, see Wolter, 'John Duns Scotus on the Primacy and Personality of Christ', 140.

[36] Allan Wolter helpfully summarises Scotus' key point here: Scotus 'makes the human nature of Christ the *motif* the Divine Architect was to carry out in the rest of creation. In Christ's soul God saw mirrored the choirs of angels; after his body the visible world was sculptured. The whole universe is full of Christ.' See his 'John Duns Scotus on the Primacy and Personality of Christ', 141, italics original.

[37] Trent Pomplun expresses the infinite qualitative difference between them: 'The glory that accrues to Christ's soul on account of the hypostatic union exceeds the

incarnation is about glory first and foremost – and only secondarily about rescue. Jesus would have come whether sin had appeared or not. In concentrating on the predicament of sin, humankind could easily forget not one but two more significant dimensions: our very existence (creation), and our final dwelling in the presence of God. Neither of these is inherently related to sin.[38] Perfection and completion replace redemption and salvation in the central configuration of the incarnation.[39]

Beyond glory and election, there is in Scotus a third connected theme: that of a reasonable and ordinate (i.e. appropriately measured and sober) love. This takes the discussion away from the abrasive logic of the debate about election to a gentler tone of receptivity and grace. We may imagine loving inordinately as a good, passionate thing: after all, how could one provoke censure by loving too much? Scotus disagrees. When you love inordinately, you lose sight of the intrinsic value of the person or thing you love. You confuse the *way* you love with the *one* you love, turning the means into an end and the end into a means. This is not how God loves. The end of all perfect love is God, who attracts and offers perfect and infinite love. No human will is capable of reaching perfection or fulfilling its ability to love without loving God to the fullest extent. Meanwhile, God's love is ordinate. The love the persons of the Trinity have for the truly lovable essence they share is neither jealous nor selfish. Here Scotus follows Richard of St Victor, saying, 'The perfect lover wishes the beloved to be loved.' It is for this love that God created humankind. God draws each

glory of a redeemed soul as the infinite exceeds the finite.' See his 'The Immaculate World', 532–33.

[38] Once again Mary Beth Ingham puts it well: 'The purpose of the Incarnation is not to remove something bad; it is to facilitate a higher perfection.' Ingham, *Scotus for Dunces*, 76–77.

[39] After reviewing the three locations Scotus discusses the reason for the incarnation in detail, Justus Hunter, in his *If Adam Had Not Sinned*, 227, concludes, 'The prevision of sin and fall is subsequent to both the volition for the highest glory to Christ and the volition to personal union with Christ's human nature. And it is apparent that this order is justified by the fundamental orientation of the divine will to the divine glory and divine self-love.'

creature to love in precisely this way – because this is the purpose of creation.[40]

This is how the dynamics of love interact with creation, glory and election. God is looking to identify the creature best able to receive the full measure of goodness and glory, and return it to the greatest extent. Predestination is the moment God seeks good and wills that such good be shared and returned by another. God wills perfectly, and cannot will anything less than perfection. Thus Christ would have come in the maximal glory of creation – even if there had been no fall.[41] Jesus is the centre of God's purposes and not subject to or dependent on any other power or event, but he does not dwell alone: creation is ordered around him. So God intends ultimate glory, and incarnation and creation lead to that end.[42] Here Scotus picks up many of the themes addressed by his predecessors, including the headship of Christ and the creative, architectural purpose of God that makes Christ God's glorious work of art.[43]

[40] Allan Wolter, 'John Duns Scotus on the Primacy and Personality of Christ', 141–42, describes ordinate love in these very helpful terms. Richard of St Victor, who lived 1110–73, was a Scottish philosopher and mystic and was prior of the Augustinian Abbey of St Victor in Paris for the last ten years of his life.

[41] John Milbank, in his *Being Reconciled: Ontology and Pardon* (London and New York: Routledge, 2003), 64 is sceptical: 'Scotus' Christology undid the vital link between forgiveness and incarnation, thereby inaugurating the reign of aspiration to purely negative forgiveness which... cannot be achieved and effects no reconciliation.' See *Being Reconciled*, 61–78, for the whole discussion. In Chapter 10 below I offer an account designed to withstand Milbank's criticism.

[42] Here I follow the helpful summary of Delio, 'Revisiting the Franciscan Doctrine of Christ', 8.

[43] A lot of attention is given by commentators to the extent to which Scotus' statements had been anticipated by his forebears – thus begging the question of why this whole debate is principally associated with him. Juniper Carol, *Why Jesus Christ?*, 276, offers three explanations, as follows. (1) Scotus was the first to teach that the primary reason for the existence of Christ was the fact that God's first wish (*ad extra*) was to have someone who would return love and worship in a supreme manner. (2) Scotus was the first to give theological precision to the argument based on the nature of predestination, by pointing out that predestination is a totally free act on the part of God and hence cannot depend on any creaturely factor. (3) His formulation of the argument based on the hierarchy of values exerted an unparalleled influence on the theologians of subsequent centuries.

The incarnation represents God's intention from before the foundation of the world to raise humankind to ultimate glory by uniting it with divine nature. Scotus brings into proximity the perfect mutuality between divine and human nature in the incarnation, and the intercommunion and mutual indwelling of the three divine persons of the Trinity. This naturally leads to the language of communion, through which all created humanity, all creation beyond humankind, and God dwell in abiding, loving, utter, mutual and eternal relationship. This invites a sacramental connection, noted above in connection with Bonaventure: that the Eucharist, as a nourishing, rather than saving, rite would have been instituted even without the fall, because it profoundly connects the believer with the incarnate Christ, which is the purpose of the incarnation.[44]

The full significance of what Scotus is presupposing only emerges when we step away from the text and place his thoughts in a larger narrative – one that does not simply have to choose between glory and sin as the reason for the incarnation. Mary Beth Ingham does so in a telling direction. She reflects that God could perhaps have created all things, and, seeking relationship, have drawn us into communion by leaving clues in the world and among our fellow creatures. But this was not, apparently, enough for God. What God was seeking was a more profound relationship than recognition, appreciation, or admiration. God desired to establish a covenant. In language that echoes my treatment in chapter 2 above, she describes a covenant as

[44] This is artfully articulated by Trent Pomplun:

> Even if Adam had not sinned, I think it supremely fitting to think that we would still be united to God, indeed deified, by the most sacred blood of Christ. Such saving blood would not, however, be shed, but shared. Indeed, I am inclined to think it fitting to believe that Christ would have preserved us from sin by sharing His body and blood in the very way in which He now does – in the Eucharist.
>
> Pomplun, 'The Immaculate World', 551

Here Pomplun introduces an element of redemption ('preserved us from sin') in a preventative rather than restorative vein, thereby keeping Scotus' emphasis on the priority on incarnation.. Along the same lines, Pomplun notes (551 n. 69) that 'Grosseteste argued that Adam and Eve would have consumed the Body and Blood of Christ even if there had been no fall.'

'an intentional act of relational initiative, taken by God as part of his loving desire, not only to make a world, but to be personally *present* to that world and to the creatures in it.'[45] This covenant is God's way of inviting us into the ultimate goal, the telos of creation: our joining the glory of divine life. She might almost be saying the universe was created that we God might be with us in Christ.

Scotus understands God's purpose as the offer of divine relationship to all that exists ('to make his glory known': Rom 9:23). It is this that causes creation, because thus there are beings to behold that glory. And this is about more than mere existence – it means sharing the divine life in an act of self-revelation: hence the covenant. This covenant is the declaration of those standards for human behaviour that enable the social fabric to remain intact and sustain the relationship of the person to God. The real message of Jesus is that God's only wish is to be present with us and with all creatures. The covenant is 'about relationship and unconditional commitment'. Jesus as the Word of God translates 'the reality of God into a language we might understand. That language, that reality, is love and mercy, self-gift and generosity, the infinite outpouring of grace and glory that is God's own internal experience. … The Incarnation is the centerpiece to the covenant and represents for the Franciscan tradition the Christological point of entry toward understanding the trinitarian nature of God.'[46]

We have arrived at the point where Trinity, covenant, creation, eschatology and incarnation all coincide. Creation leads to the creation of those creatures apt to respond and relate to the Trinitarian God, that is, humankind, possessed with rationality, the capacity for understanding and free choice. For the relationship to be fulfilled, this human nature must become capable of receiving the Trinitarian glory and sharing relationship. To enable this to happen, the divine and human nature are united. The incarnation unifies the human and divine natures in Jesus Christ. 'The move from the metaphysical

[45] Ingham, *Scotus for Dunces*, 71.
[46] Ingham, *Scotus for Dunces*, 72–74.

relationship of the essential order to the revealed relationship of covenant and Incarnation is contained within one single, intentional divine act of love.'[47] God's decision to become incarnate took place long before the created order came into being. The reason for creation was to provide a theatre in which God could become incarnate. It is not that creation, covenant and incarnation provide largely independent routes through which to come to know and love the Trinity (the third positioned above the first two, by its relation to redemption). It is a clearly ordered sequential account.

The whole vision is thus laid out in ways that are not antagonistic to, or that seek to defeat, the Anselmian account, but instead tell a much more encompassing story. This is a story about divine desire, and the measures undertaken to fulfil that desire, not a story about needing to fix the problem of sin. God acts entirely freely, generously, unconditionally and perfectly – 'according to the good pleasure of his will, to the praise of his glorious grace that he freely bestowed on us in the Beloved' (Eph 1:5–6). This larger story encompasses the smaller story of the fall: the presence of God is itself transformative. The effect of the incarnation is to glorify human nature: this is what God being with us brings about.[48] God's intent to initiate and sustain relational presence, attention, delight and so on, even when humankind fails to respond, is part of what it means for God to be free.[49]

[47] Ingham, *Scotus for Dunces*, 74–75.

[48] Ingham, *Scotus for Dunces*, 78. Intriguingly Ingham (77), again from within the Franciscan imagination, points out why Scotus would find Anselm's argument so problematic: if the incarnation had been the result of sin, we would have reason to rejoice at another's downfall. ('No one therefore is predestined simply because God foresaw that someone would fall, lest anyone have reason to rejoice at the misfortune or sin of another.' John Duns Scotus, *Ordinatio* 3. d. 7, q. 3, in *Opera omnia*, vol. 9, 289.) For a Franciscan like Scotus, shaped by the Admonitions of St Francis (notably Admonition XI, discouraging followers from taking any pleasure in the sin of another), this situation was unthinkable.

[49] Edwin Chr. van Driel, 'God and God's Beloved', offers a correction to one aspect in which Scotus' argument falls short. He points out that Scotus presents not only an account of the ordering of God's will, but additionally an account of the ordering of God's love. The account of God's will 'tells us only that incarnation is first in the order of divine willing, but it does not tell us anything about the divine intentions in

GLEANINGS

Now that we have surveyed significant contributors to the medieval debate about the reasons for the incarnation, and the reflections of some helpful commentators, it is time to glean from this discussion key themes and insights that resonate with my themes in Part I and that will guide my constructive proposals to follow in Part III.

God the Holy **Trinity** is characterised less by ancient attributes (omniscience, transcendence, immutability) than by interpersonal dimensions of love, such as generosity, mercy, patience. God is not static, but like an artist, even a theatre director or orchestrator, creating out of an abundant imagination. God seeks not just encounter but embrace: this is a dynamic rendering of God's being with creation. Divine expression is vital to creation, and God is the example on which all creation is founded. The ultimate divine goal, for which all has been made, is to invite us to join in the glory of divine life. Love is at the centre of the universe, and its face is Christ – Christ beholding the Father and the Spirit, and Christ beholding creation.

On the **incarnation**, there are three related themes. First, the incarnation was not a change of plan consequent upon the fall. God did not will sin and evil as a device to draw humanity into relationship through Christ. Assuming that the incarnation came about as a response to the fall is an absurdity, because it attributes the highest good of all to a defect. It also implies that a sinful world is much better

becoming incarnate. It is a formal argument without material theological content' (995). It is God's love that discloses God's actual motivation. God becomes incarnate for the sake of love: to become incarnate is first in God's intentions towards that which is not God. Thus love is at the centre of the universe. This love has a human face: Christ. But whose love is in question, and for whom? Van Driel points out that Scotus abrogates his Chalcedonian principles by suggesting God becomes incarnate in order to be loved by Christ's human nature, thus appearing to detach Christ's two natures unfortunately from one another. This notion also misses the impetus of the incarnation to expand the circle of love beyond God and God's incarnate one, so as to encompass other creatures. Van Driel resolves this anomaly by proposing that the incarnation is 'not an expression of divine self-love but an expression of love for others' (1003). This more adeptly orders the relationship between Trinity, election, incarnation and creation, while still affirming the primacy in Scotus of the purpose of love.

than an unfallen world would have been. It breaks a Franciscan principle that one should not rejoice in another's downfall. The narrative of existence is fundamentally about God and blessedness, not about us and sin. The purpose of the incarnation is not to remove something bad; it is to facilitate a higher perfection. The story is about glory, not about rescue.

Second, there is the sense that the incarnation's eschatological elements are constitutive of any soteriological account. Divine presence is salvific in its presence alone. The incarnation itself redeems and glorifies human nature, thereby revealing the divine desire to be with us. That presence, because it is God, heals and saves. The glory that accrues to Christ's soul on account of the hypostatic union exceeds the glory of a redeemed soul as the infinite exceeds the finite.

Third, the incarnation has a validity independent of soteriology or eschatology. The incarnation reveals God's freedom to initiate and sustain relational presence regardless of the human response. The incarnation is an expression not just of divine self-love but of love for others. Long before the created order was brought into being, God had already decided to become incarnate. This world was created as a theatre in which to do so. In the incarnate Jesus the unity of all reality is brought to consummation. The incarnation offers intrinsic and instrumental goods. Not all instrumental goods relate to sin and redemption.

In relation to **creation**, there are some briefer assertions. Creation and incarnation are closely linked, rather than being separate significant doctrines. Creation is from the outset eschatological, because it is ordered toward its completion. Thus creation is made for Christ, and would be incomplete without Christ. Creation is like a beautiful song that that God freely desires to sing into the vast spaces of the universe. It is the loving outflow of a loving God whose infinite dynamic goodness is shared in a limited dynamic way.

As to **eschatology**, the following insights have surfaced. Heaven is not merely an intellectual or spiritual thing: it is sentient and corporate. The summit of creation is the communion of all persons with one another and with God. A subtle but important difference exists between utter happiness – the life of heaven – and redemption – simply being delivered from sin and death. This is embodied in the incarnation and fulfilled in heaven. The Eucharist is not simply or even primarily an encounter with the paschal mystery; there would have been a Eucharist even without the fall, because it enacts God's companionship with us, initiated in the incarnation. The Eucharist portrays the life of heaven.

Finally there is the context of **covenant**, understood as a synonym for Israel in the Old Testament, and more generally. Covenant is an intentional act of relational initiative, taken by God out of loving desire, not only to make a world, but to be personally *present* to that world and to the creatures in it. Covenant entails the declaration of those standards for human behaviour that enable the social fabric to remain intact and sustain the relationship of the community to God. The incarnation is the centrepiece of the covenant.

Here lie several of the foundations I shall build upon in the next part of the book.

6 Modern Developments

The third era in which the question of the priority of the incarnation came to the fore in Christian theology is the nineteenth and twentieth century – particularly in that it came to be such a distinctive feature of Karl Barth's *Church Dogmatics*. But as we found with Maximus the Confessor and John Duns Scotus, the counterfactual question of whether Christ would have come had there been no fall turns out not to be the most helpful way of investigating the matter. The real question is whether God's means are consistent with God's ends – whether the story of God's purpose to be with us now and always is a more encompassing narrative than the smaller story of evil, sin, suffering and death, and whether there is utter consistency between the Jesus who is with us in the incarnation and the Jesus who is with us always. In this chapter I investigate Karl Barth's proposal and, while appreciating its very significant contributions to my project, find it finally wanting on these grounds.

THE RENAISSANCE OF THE QUESTION

In a masterly study, Edwin van Driel considers three notable modern adherents of the notion that Christ's incarnation precedes and exceeds the fall.[1] He also offers a brief historical survey, which notes, among other things, that Catholic thought after the Reformation was dominated by the framework of Thomas Aquinas, but that these questions were still discussed among the Jesuits; that the Reformers were preoccupied with sin and reconciliation, and those who did take up the priority of incarnation tended to be suspect on other grounds; and that

[1] Edwin Chr. van Driel, *Incarnation Anyway: Arguments for Supralapsarian Theology* (New York: Oxford University Press, 2008).

the seventeenth and eighteenth centuries were the low tide of this exploration.[2] Hence it was Hegel and Schleiermacher whose work revived the question in Protestant theology.[3]

Before exploring in detail the work of Karl Barth, van Driel discusses Friedrich Schleiermacher. Schleiermacher's view is based on the notion of absolute dependence and divine causality. Because nothing falls outside the latter, sin must be part of the divine initiative. But because absolute dependence does not allow us to imagine alternatives to divine causality, we cannot posit a specific divine motive. God does not respond to human actions: so the incarnation cannot be the result of the fall. Sin therefore becomes instead an instrument that God uses to make us receptive to the redeemer. Our whole relationship with Christ rests on this. God seeks intimate fellowship first with Christ, and thereafter with all humankind. 'The Redeemer assumes believers into the power of his God-consciousness, and this is his redemptive activity.'[4]

Van Driel describes Schleiermacher's approach as based on redemption. He goes on to outline the views of Isaak Dorner, which he characterises as based on creation.[5] For Dorner, the relationship between God and human beings is that of a free, mutual love and embrace. Religious faith is not primarily about sin, atonement and

[2] Van Driel, *Incarnation Anyway*, 173–74. The suspect Reformers to whom van Driel refers include Andreas Osiander, Michael Servetus and Faustus Socinus. Van Driel also notes that while John Calvin insisted that the incarnation is dependent on sin, he did not perceive that Christ's role as mediator is contingent on sin – a question later explored by Abraham Kuyper, among others.

[3] For an account of Hegel see Eugene TeSelle, *Christ in Context: Divine Purpose and Human Possibility* (Philadelphia: Fortress, 1975), 86–105.

[4] Friedrich Schleiermacher, *The Christian Faith*, trans. Donald M. Baillie, ed. H. R. Mackintosh and J. S. Stewart (Edinburgh: T & T Clark, 1999), 425. See van Driel, *Incarnation Anyway*, 9–32.

[5] Van Driel, *Incarnation Anyway*, 33–62. Isaak Dorner, who lived 1809–84, was a prominent German Lutheran theologian and Professor of Theology at the University of Berlin. Dorner synthesised the thinking of a number of nineteenth-century German theologians concerned with the primacy of Christ. See I. A. Dorner, *History of the Development of the Doctrine of the Person of Christ*, vol. 3, trans. Patrick Fairbairn (Edinburgh: T & T Clark, 1878), 237–48. Though Dorner is not well known today, van Driel points out that his account of divine immutability and his description of the three persons of the Trinity as modes of being were influential on Karl Barth.

reconciliation, but about humanity's growth into community with God and the consummation of its essential nature. Religion is the reciprocal relationship of love between God and creation (in practice, humankind). This attains its perfection in the incarnation. Dorner offers an inspiring vision of the final kingdom of love, in which the beatified share reunion, mutual recognition, infinitely diversified fellowship and joy – a perpetual Sabbath, in which there is neither inactivity nor unrest in the activity; and during this Sabbath, Christ keeps the supper anew. What Dorner provides, in characteristic nineteenth-century Protestant fashion, is a far greater emphasis on sociality and community than we found in the Orthodox or the Franciscans. While the Orthodox stressed communion and the Franciscans covenant, Dorner insists on the communal dimension of salvation: thus we see our three themes of Chapter 2 evoked in the three eras of Part II.

While there is much to admire in Dorner's approach, van Driel argues that Dorner does not see the incarnation as an end in itself, but as something finally subject to a larger necessity – that of love. Human beings are

> instrumental for the greater good, created as instances of subjects capable of love, potential inhabitants of the divinely intended kingdom. ... The incarnate One is not an end in itself but a means by which the kingdom of love is ushered in – just as human beings are not ends in themselves but are created as instruments by which the kingdom is realised.[6]

The primacy of Christ is not just about his incarnation not being determined by sin – it is about it not being subject to any other agenda; including love.[7]

[6] Van Driel, *Incarnation Anyway*, 60. Van Driel suggests that the solution is for love, in Dorner's system, not to be necessary but instead to become contingent. This makes creation contingent too: but Dorner's idea of necessity cannot accommodate that.

[7] Advocates of positions like that of Dorner sprang up in a variety of places in late nineteenth-century Europe. For example, Hans Martensen (1808–94) was a professor at the University of Copenhagen and Bishop of the Diocese of Zealand. He asks a

Van Driel suggests that Schleiermacher's problem with redemption and Dorner's with creation could be addressed if one's theological account started with the end.[8] What goal had God in mind when God set creation in train? This eschatological perspective is what he sees in Karl Barth.

ELECTION AND INCARNATION

John Calvin dismisses the counterfactual consideration of what would have happened had humankind not fallen. He infers that those who so

question characteristic of the medieval Franciscans, saying, 'Are we to suppose that which is most glorious in the world could only be reached through the medium of sin?' Then he moves to an approach more associated with the Eastern theologians.

> If we recognise that apart altogether from sin, the union of the human race with God is involved in the idea of the perfection of the world; if, further, we are convinced that this union is to be one not merely of sentiment and thought, but also of human nature in its entirety, that it must accordingly embrace the body of [humankind], which is to fitted to become the temple of the divine fulness; we are led back again to the Only Begotten One, who appeared in the midst of the process of human development as the *Incarnation* of the divine nature, the *beginner* of the *world's perfection*, and as the personal manifestation and embodiment of the ways of God with [humankind]; and who, by continuing to work through the medium of the new economy of creation which he inaugurated, is still the mediator of the completion of the whole kingdom, and of every individual member thereof.
>
> *Christian Dogmatics: Compendium of the Doctrines of Christianity*, trans. William Urwick (Edinburgh: T & T Clark, 1898), 260–61, italics original

[8] One voice van Driel mentions but does not consider in detail is the Anglican Bishop of Durham B. F. Westcott. In his 'The Gospel of Creation', in *The Epistles of St John: the Greek Text with Notes and Essays*, 2nd ed. (London: Macmillan, 1886), 285–328, Westcott maintains that the 'circumstances of the incarnation were due to sin' but 'the idea of the incarnation was due to the primal and absolute purpose of love foreshadowed in Creation, apart from sin which was contingent' (288). Humankind was made in God's image to gain God's likeness; but human beings on their own did not have the capacity to attain union with God. So even without a fall, they would still have needed a mediator to sustain, deepen and perfect their fellowship with God. Creation would have had a latent tendency to dissolution and separation even without the fall, since such is a feature of growth. Humankind leads the creation in being restored to wholeness and unity. For Westcott, the incarnation is not just for redemption: it is for perfection. It is for us – and not just for our salvation (a point made first by Andreas Osiander). Like Duns Scotus, Westcott considers it unfitting to assume there was a flaw in God's original design – and better to perceive that there was potential needing fulfilment. See also Duncan Reid, 'A Reading of Westcott's Gospel of Creation: An Early Venture into Ecological Theology?', *Journal of Anglican Studies*, 12/2 (November 2014), 185–202.

speculate are unwilling to face the damage of their own sin and that they are not content with the Christ who has been given to them as the price of their redemption.[9] But Calvin does speculate. He speculates that there is an absolute decree by which some are destined for salvation while others are doomed to condemnation.[10] Karl Barth renarrates Calvin's notion of election, agreeing that God chooses before the foundation of the world, but maintaining that God's choice is not to consign some to hell but to be with us in Jesus. This is what election means for Barth:

> In the beginning before time and space as we know them, before creation, before there was any reality distinct from God which could be the object of the love of God or the setting for his acts of freedom, God anticipated and determined within himself (in the power of his love and freedom, of his knowing and willing) that the goal and meaning of all his dealings with the as yet non-existent universe should be the fact that in this Son he would be gracious toward [humankind], uniting himself with [it]. In the beginning it was the choice of the Father himself to establish this covenant with [humankind] by giving up his son for [it], that he himself might become [a human being] in the fulfilment of his grace. In the beginning it was the choice of the son to be obedient to grace, and therefore to offer up himself and to become [a human being] in order that this covenant might be made a reality. In the beginning it was the resolve of the Holy Spirit that the unity of God, of Father and Son, should not be disturbed or rent by this covenant with [humankind], but that it should be made the more glorious, the deity of God, the divinity of his love and freedom, being confirmed and demonstrated by this offering of the Father and this self-offering of the Son.[11]

[9] John Calvin, *Institutes of the Christian Religion*, ed. John T. McNeill, trans. Ford Lewis Battles (Philadelphia: Westminster, 1960), vol. 1, 469 (I/12, para. 5).

[10] Calvin, *Institutes of the Christian Religion*, vol. 2, 920–87 (III/21–24).

[11] Karl Barth, *Church Dogmatics*, vol. II/2, trans. G. W. Bromiley et al., ed. G. W. Bromiley and T. F. Torrance (Edinburgh: T & T Clark, 1957), 101–02.

For Barth, God's decision to be with humankind is self-determined. It is free, chosen, elected; but it is gracious, loving, generous: 'It is a question of grace, and that means the love of God. It is a question of election, and that means the freedom of God.'[12] This contrasts with the Calvinist notion of the absolute decree, which seems to demonstrate neither grace nor freedom – or a freedom unhinged from grace. For Barth, grace is overflowing, free, unconstrained, unconditioned: both merciful and patient. 'Merciful' means taking the other to itself, identifying itself with its need, and meeting its plight by making it its own concern. 'Patient' means not consuming the other, but giving it space and place for its own sake. Together, mercy and patience display a God who is kind as well as good.[13]

God's decision, for Barth, is eternal, formed 'before time and space as we know them, before creation', but also perpetual, stretching beyond existence. On this decision rests all subsequent understanding of God: 'Theology must begin with Jesus Christ ... Theology must also end with him.'[14] This moment is at the epicentre of Christianity: 'The election of grace is the sum of the gospel ... But more, the election of grace is the whole of the gospel.'[15] It is not revocable or transitory, but definitive. When this decision translates into history, Barth describes it as a covenant. The terms of this covenant are set by God: God institutes, maintains, shapes and directs it, and chooses the covenant partner.

Barth explains the reason for this choice, indeed this covenant: for God not to be alone in glory, but to let heaven and earth witness it. God's will for fellowship is demonstrated to the world in a way that surpasses anything that could be expected or claimed. God meets the world not in indifference or enmity but in love. God's desire for fellowship is the basis for the world's existence. That fellowship is exercised through the people of Israel and through the church, and at

[12] Barth, *Church Dogmatics*, vol. II/2, 9.
[13] Barth, *Church Dogmatics*, vol. II/2, 10.
[14] Barth, *Church Dogmatics*, vol. II/2, 4.
[15] Barth, *Church Dogmatics*, vol. II/2, 13–14.

the centre of this history is Jesus. Here Barth makes a move vital to my argument in this book: he relocates Christianity from a story about us to a story about God. Thus when he describes the message of Christmas, he says the nativity goes beyond an extraordinary event in history that we must apply to our lives, and beyond an internal event of God being born in us, or our soul. Instead, there is the external reality that 'we *were* taken up (quite irrespective and even in defiance of our own action and merits), into the fellowship with God for which we were ordained . . . and that we *are* therefore taken up into fellowship with him, this one'.[16]

A further way in which Barth distances himself from Calvin is by asserting that Jesus is not just the object of election – the chosen agent through which God's purpose will be carried out; Jesus is also the subject of election: he was with God in the beginning (Jn 1:1–2), and he was part of the choice that God made 'before the foundation of the world' (Eph 1:4). Thus for Barth the decision to be with humankind is integral to God; there is no notion of God that is not wholly invested in this decision, and there will never be any circumstances in which it could be changed or revoked. As the quotation above indicates, the decision is made from the Father, exercised through the Son and activated by the Holy Spirit. Barth summarises how this yields the incarnation as follows:

> The concept of election has a double reference – to the elector and to the elected. And so, too, the name of Jesus Christ has within itself the double reference: the one called by this name is both very God and very [human]. Thus the simplest form of the dogma may be divided at once into the two assertions that Jesus Christ is the electing God, and that he is also elected [humankind].[17]

Jesus is in the beginning with God: not just in God's omniscient awareness that he would one day come to be born, but before any

[16] Karl Barth, *Church Dogmatics*, vol. IV/2, trans. G. W. Bromiley, ed. G. W. Bromiley and T. F. Torrance (Edinburgh: T & T Clark, 1958), 270, italics original.

[17] Barth, *Church Dogmatics*, vol. II/2, 103.

created thing came to be. From eternity, the second person of the Trinity chooses to be united with the human Jesus, and chooses the human Jesus as the one with whom to be united. In Jesus, the Son of God becomes in time what he already was from eternity. Jesus is not just the revelation of the mystery of God: he is the mystery concealed within this revelation. This is not just one choice of God among many: 'in the eternal background of history, in the beginning with God, the only decree which was passed, the only Word which was spoken and which prevails' was this decision to be with humankind in covenant relationship in the person of the incarnate Christ.[18]

For Barth, election, and therefore God's purpose, is threefold: centrally to the incarnation as an end in itself; thereby to the covenant between God and humankind; and eventually to the eternal joy of the transformed creation. Creation and covenant relate to each other as the external and internal outworkings of the incarnation. Creation is defined by its future – it is the promise, expectation and prophecy of God's gracious plan and will: it is 'the road to the covenant'.[19] Edwin van Driel summarises the place of creation in God's intentions:

> Its purpose is to make possible the history of the covenant. In the strict eschatological reading of Barth though, purpose, meaning and value collapse [into one]. If the purpose of creation is the covenant, so is its meaning. And if the meaning of creation is the covenant, so is its value. . . . Creation's goodness is not derived from being created by Christ. It only derives its goodness from its future.[20]

In Barth's words, 'Salvation, fulfilment, perfect being means – and this is what created being does not have in itself – being which has a part in the being of God, from which and to which it is: not a divinised being

[18] Barth, *Church Dogmatics*, vol. II/2, 115.

[19] Karl Barth, *Church Dogmatics*, vol. III/1, trans. J. W. Edwards, O. Bussey and H. Knight, ed. G. W. Bromiley and T. F. Torrance (Edinburgh: T & T Clark, 1958), 231.

[20] Van Driel, *Incarnation Anyway*, 80–81.

but a being which is hidden in God and in that sense (distinct from God and secondary) eternal being.'[21]

Barth goes on to explain more thoroughly God's purpose in incarnation and creation.

> The primal and basic purpose of this God in relation to his creation is to impart and reveal himself – and with himself his glory. He himself being the very essence of all glory. And because all things are his creation, because he is the Lord of all things, this primal and basic purpose is the beginning of all things, the eternal reality in which everything future is already determined and comprehended. And in this purpose which is the beginning of all things God does not will at random. He wills man – not the idea of man, not humanity, not human individuals in the mass or in particular; or rather all of these, but *in concreto* and not *in abstracto*. He wills man, his man, *elected* man, man predestined as the witness to his glory and the object of his love. In this man, but only in him, he wills humanity and every individual man and what we may describe as the idea of humanity. But first and specifically and immediately he wills man, his man, man elected by him.[22]

This is the closest Barth gets to precisely articulating God's purpose in Christ and in creation.[23] Human beings in general, and Jesus in particular, are the witness to God's glory and the object of God's love. Jesus is the essence of all glory. What is utterly clear here is the centrality of Jesus at every stage in the story of God. Jesus is the beginning of the story – there is nothing to be said of any intention, motivation or design prior to the incarnation in time or logic. Jesus is the centre of the story: he conjoins Israel and church, the two embodiments of the covenant by which God exists in fellowship with

[21] Barth, *Church Dogmatics*, vol. IV/1, 8.

[22] Barth, *Church Dogmatics*, vol. II/2, 140–41. I have not attempted to de-gender this passage.

[23] Keith L. Johnson, *The Essential Karl Barth: A Reader and Commentary* (Grand Rapids, MI: Baker, 2019), 200.

humankind. Jesus is the end of the story: all was created for him, and all will find its fulfilment and salvation in him. Thus Trinity, election and creation all converge on incarnation. It appears that in Karl Barth we have found our truly incarnational theology.

RECONCILIATION

But in the very moment of articulating the centrality of incarnation, Barth transposes Christ's fundamental *partnership* into an apparently more fundamental *representation*: 'with' is supplanted by 'for'. As Barth moves to his account of reconciliation, the centrality and enjoyment of 'with' is dismantled and displaced by the urgency and directionality of 'for'. God did not in the end centre all things around being with us in Christ: instead, God placed Christ at the centre of all things in order that Christ might be our representative in achieving redemption. An incarnation for its own sake is transformed into an incarnation subordinated to redemption. It is not a truly incarnational theology after all.

We see this even as Barth describes God's primal purpose. At the start it seems that God's intention is entirely about being with us.

> What unites God and us [human beings] is that he does not will to be God without us, that he creates us rather to share with us and therefore with our being and life and act his own incomparable being and life and act, that he does not allow his history to be his and ours, but causes them to take place as a common history.[24]

Here is a vision of genuine sharing of life for its own sake. Barth speaks of a history that God wills to share with us. From here Barth goes on to describe God's ultimate purpose, salvation, which is 'fulfilment, the supreme, sufficient, definitive and indestructible fulfilment of being... being which has a part in the being of God'.[25] But God-

[24] Barth, *Church Dogmatics*, vol. IV/1, 7.

[25] Barth, *Church Dogmatics*, vol. IV/1, 8. This participation in God's being does not blur the distinction between humanity and God. Humans are still creatures.

with-us is still described in terms of the incarnation itself, rather than the interactions made possible by the incarnation, in time or eternity: it speaks of a conjoining of God and humanity in the particular event of Jesus' life and ministry. God-with-us is the most primitive relationship between God and humankind, that which was freely determined by God before there was any created being. In the very fact that humankind is, it is chosen by God for salvation; that eschaton is bestowed by God.[26] At this stage God's ends and God's means are entirely congruent: Barth thus accords with my seventh principle as set out in Chapter 1 above.

But this is the point at which God being with us for fellowship is supplanted by a more determinative notion, that of redemption. God *with* us is transformed into, and yet equated with, God *for* us. Barth sees no tension between the two – yet the difference is monumental. Here is the moment when with slides into for – a moment Barth evidently regards as an enhancement:

> 'God with us' means more than God over or side by side with us, before or behind us. It means more than his divine being in even the most intimate active connection with our human being otherwise peculiar to him. … It means that God has become [a human being] in order as such, but in divine sovereignty, to *take up our case*. … Because he is God he has and exercises the power as this [human being] to *suffer for us* the consequence of our transgression, the wrath and penalty which necessarily fall on us, and in that way to satisfy himself in our regard.[27]

In a single paragraph the account of God as with us in Christ is transformed into a God who is for us in Christ.[28] Christ stands in

[26] Barth, *Church Dogmatics*, vol. IV/1, 10.

[27] Barth, *Church Dogmatics*, vol. IV/1, 12, italics added.

[28] And this is where Barth finally pitches his tent – squarely on the territory of 'for'. 'He took our place as Judge. He took our place as the Judged. He was judged in our place. … Everything depends on the fact that the Lord who became a servant, the Son of God who went into the far country, and came to us, was and did all this for us' (*Church Dogmatics*, vol. IV/1, 273).

humanity's place as substitute and representative. Barth turns incarnation into redemption; meanwhile genuine participation is turned decisively into awareness of creaturely deficit: 'We cannot fully understand the Christian "God with us" without the greatest astonishment at the glory of divine grace and the greatest horror at our own plight.'[29] None of the talk of God's original desire and decision to be with us has materially changed the fundamental harnessing of the incarnation to a traditional model of the atonement. The incarnation is never finally detached from soteriology.[30] 'God wills *homo labilis* [fallible humankind], not in order that it may fall, but in order that when it has fallen, it may testify to the fulness of God's glory.'[31] God does not will the fall – but God's original purpose is profoundly shaped

[29] Barth, *Church Dogmatics*, vol. IV/1, 13.

[30] By the time we get to Barth's declaration that the atonement is the very special history of God with humankind and the very special history of humankind with God (*Church Dogmatics*, vol. IV/1, 157–58), Barth is clearly using the term 'with' in a very different sense from the way I am using it.

[31] Barth, *Church Dogmatics*, vol. II/2, 141–42. This is clearly unsatisfactory, as it comes perilously close to the *felix culpa* argument. But it demonstrates Barth's awareness of God's original purpose. Barth's sense of this original purpose and his centring of the atonement remain in permanent tension in vol. IV/1 and throughout the *Church Dogmatics*: and the latter always gets the upper hand. Thus at vol. IV/1, 47–48 he says, 'In Jesus Christ we do not have to do with a second and subsequent, but the first and original content of the will of God, before and above which there is no other will – either hidden or revealed in some other way.' Which sounds like an entire endorsement of the view that the incarnation was God's original purpose, regardless of the fall. But just a few lines earlier, he has said, 'What takes place is Jesus Christ, in the historical event of the atonement accomplished by him in time, is not simply one history among others, and not simply the reaction of God against human sin. It stands at the heart of the Christian message and the Christian faith because here God maintains and fulfils his Word as it was spoken at the very first.' There is only one way to hold these two statements together – and that is to affirm the *felix culpa* argument and suggest that God in some way from the very beginning willed sin and evil in order to construe so great a redemption. Which, apart from impinging on God's sovereignty, is morally intolerable. David Bentley Hart, in his *The Beauty of the Infinite*, 165 (talking of Robert Jenson), shares my judgement:

> If God's identity is constituted in his triumph over evil, then evil belongs eternally to his identity, and his goodness is not goodness as such but a reaction, an activity that requires the goad of evil to come into full being. . . . All of history *is* this identity: every painful death of a child, every casual act of brutality, all war, famine, pestilence, disease, murder . . . all are moments in the identity of God.
>
> (Italics original, second ellipsis original)

around the fall, and in the end Barth's account of God's desire to be with us proves to be inextricable from the fall.[32]

The displacement of God's being with us in favour of God's being for us (notwithstanding Barth himself being untroubled by the transition, indeed seeing the two as inseparable if not indistinguishable) is deeply problematic. But it by no means invalidates Barth's contribution to incarnational theology – even in the midst of his account of redemption. Thus in the course of asserting Christ's obedience, and how that obedience was an inner-Trinitarian event, Barth makes a number of significant claims that advance an incarnational perspective equally well. First, he characteristically insists on the narrative of Jesus as the way we come to know the character of God: 'He is the history of God with [humankind] and the history of [humankind] with God.'[33] Second, Barth maintains that the atonement is revealed as history, and 'takes precedence over all other history', because it discloses the true meaning of all other history.[34] Moreover, third, Jesus does not alter or cease to be divine when he faces the full horror of the cross. 'God shows himself to be the great and true God in the fact that he can and will let his grace bear this cost.'[35]

In other words, if we see Jesus in humility and lowliness, that is truly the way God is. We may have notions of what divinity entails – attributes like supreme, absolute, non-worldly – but these notions have to be modified in relation to what we see displayed in Jesus.

Hart regards this as a reason to reject the supralapsarian understanding of the incarnation 'in its depressing Lutheran and Calvinist form' (164). I do not, because I do not locate God's identity in this 'triumph over evil'.

[32] Elements of with keep peeping through the swathe of for. For example, Barth reasserts his sense of the full sweep of God's purpose from creation to consummation: God participates in our being, which enables us to participate in God's being in the eschaton (*Church Dogmatics*, vol. IV/1, 13–14). Rather ironically in view of my project in this book, Barth concludes his treatment of God with us by saying he has surveyed 'almost everything that needs to be said about "God with us"' (vol. IV/1. 16). I beg to disagree.

[33] Barth, *Church Dogmatics*, vol. IV/1, 158.

[34] Barth, *Church Dogmatics*, vol. IV/1, 158.

[35] Barth, *Church Dogmatics*, vol. IV/1, 159.

Incarnation and passion do not mean that God suffers 'any change, any diminution, any transformation into something else. ... Who God is and what it is to be divine is something we have to learn where God has revealed himself and his nature.'[36] If we learn something in Christ that challenges what we thought we knew about God, it is the latter that needs to change. This is because what is revealed (revelation) and the one who does the revealing (the revealer) are the same thing. Jesus is the good news and the one bringing the good news. Revelation is not a partial affair, as if God were handing out morsels rather than the whole meal. There is no God other than the God revealed in Jesus: 'We have to follow the New Testament in understanding the presence and action of God in Jesus Christ as the most proper and direct and immediate presence and action of the one true God in the sphere of human and world history.'[37]

These Christocentric assertions apply just as fully to a truly incarnational theology as to what we might call a partly incarnational theology – one that emphasises incarnation and has an eschatological shape, yet switches from incarnation to redemption, from with to for, at the crucial juncture. My contention is that being with is the character of Jesus, the nature of his ministry, and the history of humankind with God and God with humankind; likewise that the history of God's being with us is the history in relation to which all other history has its meaning unveiled. ('Surely the Lord is in this place—and I did not know it! Gen 28:16.) Again, being with us, even (especially) in its ultimate form on the cross, is, far from being a diminution of the character or attributes of God, the definitive display of them. The revelation and the revealer are the same thing: God is being with, and revelation is of God being with – never as an abstraction, but always God being with God or some aspect of creation. Thus many of Barth's most telling and far-reaching claims apply equally well if not better to a truly incarnational theology.

36 Barth, *Church Dogmatics*, vol. IV/1, 179, 186.
37 Barth, *Church Dogmatics*, vol. IV/1, 198.

THEOLOGICAL ANTHROPOLOGY

A similar paradox emerges in relation to God's covenant partner, human beings. For Barth, Jesus is the true human: all other human beings find their identity as they relate to him. The appropriate relationship is faith and obedience. True humanity lives a theocentric life. Human beings have no inherent integrity: their lives are characterised by their relationships with God and one another. The human being 'thanks God for his grace by knowing him as God, by obeying him, by calling on him as God, by enjoying freedom from him and to him'.[38] While a somewhat limited outline of what it means to be with God, this identifies that there is a real encounter and relationship involved. Humans exist to participate with God in covenant relationship with Jesus. Human history is fundamentally the history of that covenant.

To discover what it means to be a human being existing in covenant relation to God, Barth characteristically looks to the life of Jesus. It seems that Jesus is a person with others. He does not hold aloof from them, or refuse to be like them: 'If we see him alone, we do not see him at all. If we see him, we see with and around him in ever-widening circles his disciples, the people, his enemies and the countless millions who have not yet heard his name. We see him … belonging to each and every one of them.'[39] And yet it turns out that the with is only in the service of the for. This account may engage the language of participation and partnership, but it quickly morphs into that of representation and substitution. It becomes a clear articulation of Jesus as a person-for-others. Jesus is understood as a person available and willing to support, aid, and transform those he meets.

> What interests him, and does so exclusively, is [human beings], other [people] as such, who need him and are referred to him for

[38] Karl Barth, *Church Dogmatics*, vol. III/2, trans H. Knight et al., ed. G. W. Bromiley and T. F. Torrance (Edinburgh: T & T Clark, 1960), 203.

[39] Barth, *Church Dogmatics*, vol. III/2, 216.

> help and deliverance. Other [people] are the object of the saving work in the accomplishment of which he himself exists. It is for their sake that he takes the place of God in the cosmos. Their deliverance is the defence of the divine glory for which he comes. It is to them that the Word and grace of God apply, and therefore his mission, which is not laid upon him, or added to his human reality, but to which he exclusively owes his human reality as he breathes and lives – the will of God which is his meat to do [cf. Jn 4:34]. From the very first, in the very fact that he is a [human being], Jesus is not without [other people], but to them and with them and for them. He is sent and ordained by God to be their Deliverer. Nothing else? No, really nothing else.[40]

Barth here makes a tantalising reference to the fact that from the first Jesus is with humankind. But that togetherness and mutual participation is immediately and overwhelmingly supplanted by the way Jesus' presence is characterised: humanity is constantly a problem and Jesus is the invariable solution. There is no simple enjoyment – there is only a constant working-for provision of help and deliverance. 'Nothing else? No, really nothing else': this explicitly and comprehensively rules out the open-ended and mutually emerging nature of with, in favour of the predetermined and narrow character of for. God's relationship to creation is a perpetual love-offering, not a mutual sharing. This is indeed a relationship: but of a particular kind, in which one party is dominant and always setting the terms, while the other party has a set of circumscribed responses. And all this helping and delivering points to the crucial moment. The being of Jesus for humankind means that

> He interposes himself for them, that he gives himself to them, that he puts himself in their place, that he makes their state and fate his own cause, so that it is no longer theirs but his, conducted by him in his own name and on his own responsibility. And in this respect

[40] Barth, *Church Dogmatics*, vol. III/2, 208–09.

> we have to remember that so long as the cause of [human beings] was in their own hands it was a lost cause. Their judgement was just and destruction inevitable, so that anyone taking their place had necessarily to fall under this judgement and suffer this destruction. In his interposition for them the [person] Jesus thus had to sacrifice himself in this cause for others.[41]

Here we see that the being-for-others expressed in the previous quotation is channelled into the definitive moment of working-for-others, which is the cross. At the crucial moment, humankind, aside from Jesus, plays no positive role. Jesus interposes himself for humanity. This is not just about what happened once on the cross. This is something that continues to take place as Christ meets human beings in the midst of their concrete reality. He is constantly 'the Representative and Bearer of all the alien guilt and punishment transferred from them to him'.[42] It is a perpetual act of substitution. Indeed, 'The whole witness and revelation of the [person] Jesus in time, the whole point of his life and existence, is that within the cosmos there should be declared as good news and operative as saving power the fact that God himself is for [humankind] and is [its] Covenant-partner. God interposes himself for [it], sharing [its] plight and making himself responsible for [its] life and joy and glory.'[43]

So much is clear. So why do I lament that Barth falls so comprehensively on the side of for, not just in his notion of substitution and representation in the face of sin and death, but also in his notion of the nature of human discipleship in imitation of Christ? Because Barth himself lays down, in this same passage, a principle fundamental to him, but one that speaks bleakly of divine and human destiny. This is it: 'There is freedom in God, but no caprice. ... There is nothing arbitrary or accidental but in which God is true to himself. ... God repeats in this relationship *ad extra* (outside himself) a relationship

41 Barth, *Church Dogmatics*, vol. III/2, 212.
42 Barth, *Church Dogmatics*, vol. III/2, 208–09.
43 Barth, *Church Dogmatics*, vol. III/2, 217.

proper to himself in his inner divine essence.'[44] But how can this be eternally? If Barth's whole notion of election and creation is eschatologically shaped, surely he must be attending to what everlasting life for humankind (and the rest of creation) with God must be like? And surely this everlasting life cannot be one of perpetual condescension and interposition? It must surely be one of participation and partnership, of mystery, delight and enjoyment.

Barth has articulated the very principle (he calls it 'the last and supreme step') by which his whole model becomes problematic. His very next words explain why:

> Even in his inner divine being there is relationship. ... There is in him a co-existence, co-inherence and reciprocity. ... He is in himself the one who loves eternally, the one who is eternally loved, and eternal love ... And it is this relationship in the inner divine being which is repeated and reflected in God's eternal covenant with [humankind] as revealed and operative in time in the humanity of Jesus.[45]

Once again, the revealer is the revelation. Barth's description of the Trinity, which is all about reciprocity, contradicts his account of Jesus' representation and substitution, where there is no reciprocity to be seen.[46] And yet Barth's 'last and supreme step' would fit perfectly if he were to alter his governing preposition from 'for' to 'with'. His account of election and creation is profoundly incarnationally shaped – until it becomes clear it is all in the service of for. But the eschatological perspective proves that for is not a sustainable model

[44] Barth, *Church Dogmatics*, vol. III/2, 218.

[45] Barth, *Church Dogmatics*, vol. III/2, 218–19.

[46] Further evidence of this emerges at the point where Barth insists that our notion of deity must adjust to the Christ we see on the cross. He does a somersault to argue that the Son is obedient to the Father – which he says does not jeopardise the unity and equality of Father and Son because obedience is inherent in being begotten of the Father. None of this would be necessary if Barth described salvation and the cross as the endurance of with rather than the performance of for. See Barth, *Church Dogmatics*, vol. IV/1, 197–204.

eternally. The only sustainable eternal destiny is with. With is the logic of eschatology – and of election, incarnation, creation and theological anthropology also. Barth has established an entire Christological framework that stumbles at the point he proclaims *for* instead of discovering *with*.

The consequences of Barth's failure to articulate a true notion of with become fully apparent when he offers an account of our eschatological hope. Human history is identified with Christ before time began and will be preserved after time concludes. Time is thus 'an intermezzo'.[47] But after time there is no more interaction between God and humankind: our history is preserved, but not our agency. Resurrection is not a continuation or restoration of life, but a preservation of the life lived. Time is the stage on which God interacts with humankind and human beings interact with one another. But there will come a moment when all these interactions are in the past. There is no continuation – even eschatologically. There is eternity, in which we may share – but not interact. 'The gift of the eschaton is the continuation of eternity's embrace, being that in the eschaton the object of the embrace no longer is the living life, but the life lived. … God will still relate to the creature, but the creature will no longer relate to God.'[48] The creature is history.

For Barth, Christ's resurrection and ascension are a lifting of the veil: they do not entail a continuation of his embodied life but a revelation to those in time of what his life meant.[49] Resurrection,

[47] This phrase is from Edwin Chr. van Driel, *Incarnation Anyway*, 106. I owe the analysis of time and eternity in these two paragraphs to his discussion in *Incarnation Anyway*, 105–18.

[48] Van Driel, *Incarnation Anyway*, 114. Van Driel notes (114 n. 107) that there are a handful of places where Barth describes the eschatological future of the creature as an active interaction with its creator. But he points out that 'They cannot be explained within Barth's ontological framework of time and eternity. If the creature's eschatological future is not the continuation of its temporal life but only the preservation of the life lived, there can be no further interaction between Creator and the creature as an active subject. Barth himself does not register this discrepancy' (114–15).

[49] Barth, *Church Dogmatics*, vol. IV/2, 132–33.

ascension and Christ's return do not inaugurate a new era in time and space – they anticipate eternity in time. It is a monumental anti-climax. After immense, elaborate and absorbing exploration of God's purpose, of the relation of Trinity, incarnation, election and creation, and after the extensive account of Christ's suffering as our representative and substitute, the salvation secured is indescribably thin. All this could be rectified if only Barth had a richer account of the genuine, profound, creative, generative and joyous eschatological interaction of humankind with God, one another and the renewed creation.[50]

EVIL, SIN AND DEATH

When Barth sets out to describe the force that constantly seeks to enlist humankind in its opposition to the purpose of God, he insists he is going to do so in his characteristic manner: his account will, he says, be Christological. 'How do we know that nothingness really exists, and does so in such a way, in such radical superiority, that it cannot be legitimately incorporated into any philosophical system, that we must not try to treat it as one element in the world among others?'[51] The answer is from the knowledge of Jesus. Accordingly, we witness that

> The Word became a creature which had fallen under the sway of a possessive and domineering alien, and was therefore itself alienated from its Creator and itself, unable to recover or retrace its way home … because it was betrayed and haphazardly subjected to a determination inimical to its creation in wisdom and mercy. … The Word became … a lost creature.[52]

[50] For a more detailed critique of Barth's eschatology, see Nathan Hitchcock, *Karl Barth and the Resurrection of the Flesh: The Loss of the Body in Participatory Eschatology* (Eugene, OR: Pickwick Publications, 2013).

[51] Karl Barth, *Church Dogmatics*, vol. III/3, trans. G. W. Bromiley and R. J. Ehrlich, ed. G. W. Bromiley and T. F. Torrance (Edinburgh: T & T Clark, 1961), 303.

[52] Barth, *Church Dogmatics*, vol. III/3, 303–04.

Is this indeed the way the gospels portray Jesus' journey to the cross? On the contrary, they seem distinctively devoid of such florid and amplified description. They talk simply of betrayal, denial and desertion, perversion of justice, persecution by oppressors and perpetration of ruthless execution. It is not clear that Barth's account of nothingness is as Christological as he claims.

When Barth becomes more specific, the Christological context surfaces more convincingly. Sin is the concrete form of nothingness – the way humanity makes nothingness its own act, achievement and guilt, thereby offending God, but just as much disturbing, injuring and destroying itself. Death is the intolerable, life-destroying thing to which all suffering hastens as its goal, annihilating creaturely existence, thereby discrediting and disclaiming the creator. Evil is something wholly anomalous that threatens and imperils this existence, and is radically opposed to creation and the creator. Barth roots this Christologically by describing Jesus' miracles and acts as conquests of evil, sin and death. 'He not only forgives the sins of [human beings]; he also removes the source of their suffering.'[53] This brings Barth to a definition of nothingness derived retrospectively from a Christus Victor understanding of the resurrection.

> Nothingness is the past, the ancient menace, danger and destruction, the ancient non-being which obscured and defaced the divine creation of God but which is consigned to the past in Jesus Christ, in whose death it has received its deserts, being destroyed with this consummation of the positive will of God ... Because Jesus is Victor, nothingness is routed and extirpated. ... It is that from whose influence, dominion and power the relationship between Creator and creature was absolutely set free in Jesus Christ, so that it is no longer involved in their relationship as a third factor.[54]

[53] Barth, *Church Dogmatics*, vol. III/3, 311.
[54] Barth, *Church Dogmatics*, vol. III/3, 363.

There are three problems with this account – each equally challenging.[55] Problem one is that this is so far to the extreme end of for that it portrays a Jesus and a Trinity almost unrecognisable from the character of the God who creates to dwell with the creation in relationship and mutual joy. This is a warrior, a pugilist, a destroyer, a crusader – one in whom the end justifies the means. Can one say of this description that the revealer is the revelation? Jesus appears to step out of character to destroy the destroyer, then to find sabbath rest having completed his work. Which yields problem two: evil, sin and death seem to be very much around us. For all Barth's commanding retrospective account of nothingness as that which Christ overcame, it looks as malevolent as ever. If the whole shape of the incarnation is determined by God's decision to overcome nothingness, how can the incarnation be asserted as valid, with creation apparently as submerged as it ever was? This is of course a test for all atonement accounts; but particularly for Barth, who grounds his before the foundation of the world. And problem three both reiterates the criticism levelled earlier and opens the way to a resolution – far-reaching, transformative, but nonetheless a resolution. Could not – should not – the account of evil, sin and death, of all that opposes God's purpose, be configured, not just retrospectively from Jesus' encounter with such forces, but as much or more from the point of view of God's eschatological purpose? In other words, if God's ultimate purpose is to be with us and for us to be with ourselves, one another and the new creation, 'nothingness' is all that inhibits such relationships – unfortunately, through mischance; clumsily, through muddle; or maliciously, through malign, evil, intent. That which opposes God's

[55] Van Driel offers a carefully argued fourth problem. He notes that, for Barth, 'all of what is not God necessarily lapses into evil unless God incorporates it into God's own being. . . . Creational life is governed by entropy' (*Incarnation Anyway*, 122). Van Driel suggests that this insight demonstrates why nothingness exists, why there is sin, and what eschatology means: all makes sense when one realises that, without God, the dynamic of creational entropy drains life away. But Barth never explains why this is so, or why God did not create humankind immediately incorporated into the divine being (van Driel, *Incarnation Anyway*, 124, 129).

purpose is that which undermines being with, through dismantling trust, or precludes it, through death and discord, or poisons it, through evil and lies.

Such an account addresses the three problems in Barth's description of overcoming nothingness. It does not deny that evil, sin and death are still around, because it eschews the language of victory and conquest; instead it rests on the conviction that Christ in his cross is with us – and with God – even in the most separating, alienating, annihilating of circumstances. It is this withness that God embodied in the incarnation, sought in creation and will finally herald in the eschaton. It is this quality of being with that truly characterises the Trinity and determines the story of God. These insights will be drawn together in Chapter 10 below.

OTHER PERSPECTIVES

Focus on the primacy of Christ and the theological priority of the incarnation does not end with Barth. A series of renowned theologians in the generation immediately following him made explicit reference to these ideas, although none has attempted to make them the cornerstone of a theological system.

Within the Roman Catholic tradition, Karl Rahner sees no conflict with such a position and the magisterium: 'In the Catholic Church it is freely permitted to see the Incarnation first of all, in God's primary intention, as the summit and height of the divine plan of creation, and not primarily and in the first place as the act of a mere restoration of a divine order destroyed by the sins of mankind, an order which God had conceived in itself without any Incarnation.'[56] Rahner elaborates on this view to envisage what a focus on the incarnation might entail:

[56] Karl Rahner, 'Christology within an Evolutionary View of the World', in *Theological Investigations*, vol. 5, trans. Karl-H. Kruger (Baltimore: Helicon, 1966), 185.

> Seen from God's side, the Incarnation is the means for the whole self-communication of God to the realm of created spiritual persons, while in the perspective of created realities, the Incarnation is the goal and summit of creation. The mystery of Jesus Christ consists in his really standing on both sides of the line that divides God from his creature in the purely natural order of creation.[57]

Here Rahner encapsulates the full sense of how Jesus is fully human as well as fully divine. Hans Urs von Balthasar takes the argument back to its origin: 'It was in view of [the Incarnate Son] that the venture of having any such thing as a world and world history could be made at all; in view of him and his Church that such a thing as the creation of man and woman could take place (Eph 5:31–32).'[58] Neither theologian takes the implication of these insights significantly further.[59]

The Reformed theologian Jürgen Moltmann insists that Christology is more than the presupposition for soteriology. He contrasts the incarnation perceived as an emergency measure with one that belongs to the eternally self-communicating love of God itself. The 'emergency measure' expresses the saving will of God outwards; it leaves God's own nature untouched. Moltmann makes a telling observation.

> Once the incarnate Son of God has achieved the reconciliation of the world with God, he himself becomes superfluous. … This is already inherent in the concept of the mediator; otherwise the mediator would stand in the way of what he mediates. Once

[57] Karl Rahner SJ, *Mary, Mother of the Lord: Theological Meditations*, trans. W. J. O'Hara (New York: Herder and Herder, 1964), 12.

[58] Hans Urs von Balthasar, *A Theology of History* (New York: Sheed and Ward, 1963), 62.

[59] For further Catholic treatments see Hans Kung, *Justification: The Doctrine of Karl Barth and a Catholic Reflection* (Philadelphia: Westminster, 1964), 288–301, and Michael Schmauss, *Dogma*, vol. 1: *God in Revelation* (New York: Sheed and Ward, 1968), 47–52.

> creation has been redeemed, purified from sin and liberated from death, the God-man no longer has any place in it.'[60]

By contrast, Moltmann argues, the notion of incarnation envisaged from eternity means its intention coincides with the formation of the world. Creation represents the external framework and preparation for the Son's incarnation. Then, somewhat like Isaak Dorner, Moltmann diverts into a notion of necessity, considering the nature of love and how love seeks to be beside the beloved and to enable those beloved to be eternally beside themselves. He concludes with an Eastern assertion that the incarnation took place for the sake of perfecting creation.[61]

Most significantly, the American Lutheran Robert Jenson articulates the heart of the matter: 'God's history with us is decisively shaped by our betrayal of the "with us".'[62] This judgement names the complexity of the divine–human relationship in terms that perfectly fit the language of my project. Jenson eventually lands by refusing to abstract from the actual incarnation: like Barth, he perceives that

[60] Jürgen Moltmann, *The Trinity and the Kingdom: The Doctrine of God*, trans. Margaret Kohl (London: SCM, 1981), 115. Moltmann repeats these arguments in his *The Crucified God: The Cross of Christ as the Foundation and Criticism of Christian Theology*, trans. R. A. Wilson and John Bowden (London: SCM, 1974), 256–66. There he particularly criticises Dorothy Sölle's notion of Christ as our representative. 'If representation is to preserve the longing for identity and is not to destroy it, it must not become replacement. The representative must keep open the place of the one he represents and retreat when the latter himself occupies the place. . . . Representation cannot possibly be conceived in personal terms without provisionality and temporariness' (262).

[61] The German Lutheran theologian Wolfhart Pannenberg proceeds in broadly similar terms. He says,

> The incarnation is the integrating centre of the world's historical order, which is grounded in the Logos and will find its perfect form only in the eschatological future of the world's consummation and transformation into the kingdom of God in his creation. Therefore the incarnation cannot be an external appendix to creation nor a mere reaction of the Creator to Adam's sin. From the very first it is the crown of the world order, the supreme concretion of the active presence of the Logos in creation.
> Systematic Theology, *vol. 2, trans. Geoffrey Bromiley (Grand Rapids, MI: Eerdmans, 1994), 64*

[62] Robert Jenson, *Systematic Theology*, vol. 1: *The Triune God* (New York: Oxford University Press, 1997), 72.

> the goal of God's path is just what does in fact happen with Jesus the Christ, and sin and evil belong to God's intent precisely – but only – as they appear in Jesus' victory over them. So a mystery of suffering, of an interplay between created realities and evil, must belong to the plot of God's history with us and to the character of its crisis and fulfilment.[63]

It seems the well of abstraction and counterfactual speculation has run dry. But Jenson recognises that a project of the kind undertaken in this book is a genuine prospect. 'The consequences of deciding that the Incarnation is neither an emergency measure nor construable apart from our sin, that precisely the gospel of forgiveness is not an afterthought, are, of course, extreme. Usual assumptions about the content of God's eternal will, about his relation to sin and evil, and about the relation between creaturehood and death must be rethought.'[64] Exactly. Hence the next part of this book.

Finally, Kathryn Tanner proposes a notion of God as the ultimate gift-giver.[65] God embarks on a programme of communicating goodness to the world: this eventually entails God's self-giving:

> God wants to give us the fulness of God's own life through the closest possible relationship with us that comes to completion in Christ. ... In order to give us the entire fulness of what God enjoys, God must give us God's very own life and not simply some created version of it. God cannot give us everything that God has to give by merely transforming human life itself into some created approximation of divinity. God must attach us, in all our frailty and finitude, to God.[66]

And this is what the incarnation does. Humanity becomes God's own. Through the incarnate Christ God gives boundless gifts to humanity:

[63] Jenson, *Systematic Theology*, vol. 1, 73–74.

[64] Jenson, *Systematic Theology*, vol. 1, 73.

[65] See Kathryn Tanner, *Jesus, Humanity and the Trinity: A Brief Systematic Theology* (Minneapolis, MN: Fortress Press, 2001) and *Christ the Key*.

[66] Tanner, *Christ the Key*, vii–viii.

thus humanity is saved, becoming one with Christ in faith and love. We are assumed by Christ, and Christ becomes the subject of our actions, just as the Son is the subject of Jesus' acts. Tanner compares our relationship with Christ to Christ's relation to the Father – 'a relationship of fellowship and correspondence of wills'.[67] She later expands this notion into an account of participation. She speaks of two ways we participate in God. On the one hand we simply derive our existence from and are shaped by God. On the other, through Christ, God gives us the gift of the divine image, and we make it our own. This gift is available to us from creation, but only Jesus enables us to receive it: it is no longer foreign to us. This is how the incarnation is the culmination of the original design of creation.[68] The cross is a paradigm of the pain and sin of human life that the incarnated Jesus redeems; it is not the principal means of that redemption.

Tanner's account is a suitable place to conclude our investigation of modern developments, since she goes a long way to providing what I have been seeking: a truly incarnational theology within a broadly Barthian shape. She commendably avoids both making the incarnation dependent on the fall, and giving a soteriological account that betrays Christ's incarnational nature. She also harnesses the Orthodox notion of participation to significant effect. But her version remains abstract – removed from the narrative of Jesus' actual life on earth – and this gives it few resources to develop any significant eschatological hope; which is where her proposal falls short.[69]

[67] Tanner, *Jesus, Humanity and the Trinity*, 57.

[68] Tanner, *Christ the Key*, 60.

[69] In his 'Sharing in Nature or Encountering a Person', Edwin Chr. van Driel contrasts Kathryn Tanner's Christology with my own. He concludes that, 'while Tanner's approach is better represented in both ancient and modern theological traditions, Wells' approach is constructively more fruitful' (194). He attributes the difference to Tanner's emphasis on sharing Christ's nature in contrast with my account of encountering Christ as a person. He also notes that Tanner's eschatological vision is very similar to Barth's, and outlines a criticism of Barth similar to my own criticism above.

GLEANINGS

While I have significant reservations about Barth's proposal, I have huge admiration for his Christocentric vision and its bearing on our subject. His immediate predecessors and successors also have significant insights to offer.

In relation to the **Trinity**, in God's inner divine being there is relationship. There is in God co-existence, co-inherence and reciprocity. Meanwhile God cannot be subject to a necessity or logic beyond God – even if that necessity is love. Being with us, even (especially) in its ultimate form on the cross is, far from being a diminution of the character or attributes of God, the definitive display of them. The Trinity repeats externally a relationship proper to itself in its inner divine essence.

As to **election**, God's decision is utterly free and yet completely loving. Because God is merciful, God identifies with human plight. Because God is patient, God allows the other to be different, separate, distinct. God's purpose is about glory and fellowship: the two are inextricable. If Jesus were simply the object of election, there would be no role for him after the incarnation had achieved its goal. But the incarnation is for its own sake: Jesus is therefore also the subject of election – the choosing agent, not simply the instructed instrument.

In regard to the **incarnation**, the decision to be united with humankind in Christ was part of God's gracious purpose from the very beginning. The covenant is part of that commitment. Jesus is the beginning and end of all things – there is no story of God before or after him. Jesus is the beginning of the story, the centre of the story and the end of the story. Thus Trinity, election and creation all converge on incarnation. God does not will to be God without us. God does wish not divine and human history to be separate, but causes them to take place as a common history. The narrative of Jesus is the principal and definitive way we come to know the character of God. Jesus does not alter or cease to be divine when he faces the full horror of the cross. The revealer is the revealed. The character of salvation must be entirely consistent with the form of incarnation: Jesus cannot flip from sharer to deliverer for one great substitutionary gesture. If the incarnation were simply for the sake of redemption, the redeemer would be supernumerary once redemption were gained.

Meanwhile **creation** derives its goodness from its future. Its joy is its destiny. It will not be divinised, but it will find its place eternally with God. God meets the world not in indifference or enmity but in love. God's desire for fellowship is the basis for the world's existence.

The identity of **humanity** is found in relation to Jesus. Human beings in general, and Jesus in particular, are the witness to God's glory and the object of God's love. Humans exist to participate with God in covenant relationship with Jesus. Human history is fundamentally the history of that covenant. God's history with us is decisively shaped by our betrayal of the 'with us'.

As regards **evil, sin and death**, sin cannot be an instrument God uses for some ulterior end. Evil is part of the universe, but was not part of God's original purpose. It is part of existence, but does not intrude into God's essence. Any incarnational theology will have to wrestle with the degree to which evil, sin and death are integral to the identity of humankind and the creation. Any account of salvation must recognise that the demise of evil, sin and death since Christ's resurrection is not evident. Renarrating God's story in a way that does not centre sin and the fall requires very significant adjustment.

Eschatology is the key to conceiving the incarnation correctly. An eternity that is not participatory, interactive, dynamic and unfolding is inconceivable as the outcome of Christ's suffering. The eschatological hope must reflect the transcendent difference-in-mutuality of the Trinity.

PART III Reconfiguring the Story

7 God

My quest is to perceive, ground and set forth a truly incarnational theology. In Part I I articulated and excavated principles, themes and dimensions for this quest. In Part II I gleaned wisdom from the three strands of theological investigation that have seen God's decision to be with us in Christ as the lens through which to perceive Christian theology. Here in Part III it is time to put to work the principles drawn from scripture in the light of the gleanings derived from tradition. I begin this chapter, as I shall the subsequent chapters in Part III, by reviewing the wisdom discerned in Part II.

What I gleaned from the tradition concerning God the Holy Trinity is this. The emphasis on the Trinity's ancient attributes such as omniscience, transcendence and immutability has tended to obscure more interpersonal dimensions of love, such as generosity, mercy, patience.[1] God seeks not just encounter but embrace. Love is at the centre of the universe, and its face is Christ – Christ beholding the Father and the Spirit, and Christ beholding creation. In God's inner divine being there is relationship.[2] There is in God co-existence, co-inherence and reciprocity. Meanwhile God cannot be subject to a necessity or logic beyond God – even if that necessity is love. God repeats externally a relationship proper to itself in the inner-

[1] 'This distinction between God and God based on the cross of Jesus Christ has destroyed the axiom of absoluteness, the axiom of apathy, and the axiom of immutability, all of which are unsuitable axioms for the Christian doctrine of God.' Eberhard Jüngel, *God as the Mystery of the World: On the Foundation of the Theology of the Crucified One in the Dispute between Theism and Atheism*, trans. Darrell L. Guder (Grand Rapids, MI: Eerdmans, 1983), 373.

[2] Nicholas Lash, in his *Believing Three Ways in One God: A Reading of the Apostles' Creed* (Notre Dame, IN: University of Notre Dame Press, 1993), 31, distinguishes between God and us. We *have* relationships, whereas God *is* the relations of the Trinity. God is relationship without remainder; we are not.

Trinitarian relations. It is out of these gleanings, matched with the principles, themes and dimensions of Part I, that I now articulate who God is, in the divine inter-relationships of the Trinity. The Trinity has a chapter on its own: only thus may I express my insistence that this is fundamentally a story about God, and that creation, human beings and their divine destiny must stand in the light of that priority. My concern is to withstand the anthropocentrism of so much theology, which centres human existence and need, rather than God's character and purpose, as the story's focal point.[3]

In embarking on this account of the Trinity, I recognise I may seem to be departing from the constraints theologians often regard as normative. For example, I do not quote a verse of scripture to accompany every bold assertion I make. (By contrast, one theologian states at the outset of his systematic theology, 'All aspects of the Lord's hypostatic being appear in Israel's scripture.'[4]) However, I do not believe I am offering unmoored abstract speculation: my method of identifying a path through scripture and tradition in Parts I and II guides my assertions here in Part III. According to Karl Barth, 'Everything that God does in time finds its antecedent in eternity.'[5] This cuts two ways. It means that no statement can be made about the Trinity that does not resonate with scripture, especially the account of the life, death and resurrection of Jesus. But it also means that when a statement accords with the Immanuel we behold in Jesus, a statement can confidently be made. This chapter makes confident statements about the Trinity that accord with the scriptural witness to Jesus Christ.[6]

[3] The following observation is typical. 'Maximus forbids the introduction of the aspect of time into Trinitarian theology in spite of the fact that one of the persons of the holy Trinity became incarnate in time. And yet, on the other hand he professes a Trinitarian preknowledge of what the incarnate Christ will be.' Thunberg, *Man and the Cosmos*, 78.

[4] Robert Jenson, *Systematic Theology*, vol. 1, 63. Jenson is seeking to deny that Christianity is an egregious departure from the faith of Israel.

[5] Barth, *Church Dogmatics*, vol. IV/1, 39.

[6] Rowan Williams, in his *On Christian Theology* (Oxford and Malden, MA: Blackwell, 2000), 177, says, 'If anthropomorphism is always perilously close in the kind of

THE TRINITY

There is something more profound than existence. This is where faith begins. Existence is finite; there is something that is not finite. Existence is fragile; there is something that is abiding. Existence is feckless; there is something perpetually trustworthy.

That something is essence. Essence is that which never comes to an end. Essence is forever. Essence is eternal. Conventionally existence and essence have been regarded as attributes of the same thing: existence is its 'whether' – whether it is actual, real, existent; essence is its 'what' – what it is, what it is like, what is most distinctive about it, how you would succinctly describe it. Thus in the usual configuration something can have an essence without having any existence: for example a minus number. But I mean something different by the word 'essence'. Essence is that which always was, and always shall be – whether or not there was, is or will be existence.[7]

My account of essence avoids some of the perennial problems with the usual configuration, in which creation is the beginning. Among these are problems are: How do we understand what the God who pronounced all things 'good' meant by 'good'? How do we reconcile the scriptural creation stories with the Big Bang and contemporary cosmology? Is there any way we can attribute intention to God's creation of the world? How do we avoid the incarnation

trinitarian pluralism which the life of Jesus seems to enjoin upon us, it is still finally deflected by the recognition that the "essential" or "immanent" Trinity can finally be characterised only as that which makes this life (and death and resurrection) possible and intelligible.' Again, my intention here is to do exactly what Rowan Williams is asking for – to provide an ontology that makes Jesus' life, death and resurrection intelligible: no more – and no less. Williams adds, 'We do not begin with the trinitarian God and ask how he can be such, but with the world of particulars, cross, empty tomb, forgiven and believing apostles, asking, "How can this be?"' (178). Hence the shape of this book, which starts with the particulars in Chapters 2 and 3.

[7] For a more conventional account, see Jenson, *Systematic Theology*, vol. 1, 207–18. I recognise that in this chapter an ambiguity surfaces on occasion about how to speak of time before creation. But whether or not one can clearly employ a temporal term like 'before', one can certainly speak of priority in God and in our apprehension of God.

becoming dependent on the fall, and thus rendering the story and God's action sin-centric, instrumentalising Christ for a human purpose? The notion of essence, as described and assumed in this book, avoids those problems. It enables an account of the Trinity that is not dependent on creation and humankind – as offered in this chapter. It can accommodate a gradual creation, emerging as cosmology describes, rather than requiring a rapid one with humankind appearing near the beginning of the story.[8] It is explicit about God's intention: to be with us in Christ in existence and always beyond existence. And it can make sense of the eschaton as something other than the significant improvement of humankind's experience of creation. Hard as it is to imagine essence, it is harder to conceive of how the Trinity and creation can share existence.

In the realm of essence there are many qualities to which existence can only aspire, and some kind of philosophical account is needed of what those are. There is, first of all, permanence. Permanence may immediately be contrasted with transience. But more subtly, permanence may find other contrasts. Permanence is the opposite of violence, evil, deception. Nothing bad lasts forever. The story that evil tells is not only false; it is too short. They are, in a significant way, the same thing. Permanence out-endures evil. A second quality of essence is depth. Foundations secure a house – but they only go down so far, and an earthquake can shake them. Roots secure a tree – but they too are limited, and a hurricane can uproot them. The depth of essence is never-ending. Depth may usually contrast with shallowness. But depth may also be set alongside misunderstanding. When two parties seek to excavate a misunderstanding, there is a mutual digging-back to a word with two meanings, a history with different degrees of significance, an instruction with hidden ambiguity. Depth goes beneath all these excavations to the point where there is coherence, comfort, confidence. Depth goes

[8] For an account of a gradual creation see John Haught, *God after Einstein: What's Really Going On in the Universe?* (New Haven, CT: Yale University Press, 2022).

below misunderstanding. A third quality of essence is trust. Trust may quickly be contrasted with suspicion. Suspicion puts together what is not known with what is not right, and each amplifies the other. But suspicion is just one symptom of something larger: and that larger thing is fear. Fear conflagrates powerlessness with imagination, fuelled by danger, proximity and suspicion. Trust does not obliterate fear; it withstands it. That capacity to withstand anything cultivates trust. Trust alone signals predictability, sameness, even boredom. But trust is never alone in essence. It is always alongside. In the alongside lies its dynamism.

What permanence, depth and trust together constitute is truth. Essence is synonymous with all three, but most of all with what they comprise together – and that is truth. Truth, like permanence, outlasts; like depth, comprehends; like trust, withstands. Existence is permeated by evil, misunderstanding and fear; essence is pervaded by truth. It is almost impossible to conceive of any existence that is not characterised by evil, misunderstanding and fear, the exploitation of which constitutes much of the dynamic of society. But there is something more real than evil, misunderstanding and fear – and that is essence. Essence is not an attribute of everyone or everything: it is the ultimate reality on which all things depend. Existence is contingent; essence is constant. To imagine essence is to suspend all the finitude, fragility and fecklessness of existence, and enter a realm of permanence, depth, trust and truth.

Thus the conviction of essence is the first step of faith. The second step is to recognise that essence is personal. Permanence, depth, trust and truth are characteristics of essence, more real than existence: but they are simply the substructure of something more dynamic, interactive and relational. We seldom need to speak of essence because instead we speak of God. The step made by faith is not so much to say, there is essence, beyond and more real than – though embracing – existence, or even that that essence is God, but to say that God fills essence. There is no essence besides God. Nothing besides God lasts forever – unless, as we shall see, at God's behest.

Certainly nothing lasts forever besides God that God does not inspire and uphold. There is nothing in essence that is not God; or at least godly.

But as soon as we say 'God', we immediately say 'Trinity'. It is indeed doubtful whether we should ever say 'God' without saying either the name of one person of the Trinity or simply invoking the Trinity as a whole. Calling on the name 'God' without either seeking one of the three persons, or the Trinity as a whole, is always in danger either of forgetting or suppressing the way God is always three, or treating the first person of the Trinity, traditionally known as the Father, as if 'God' were its synonym. A lingering deism or unitarianism or, at least, subordinationism is likely to be the result. The persons of the Trinity coinhere: they are utterly with (hence 'co-') yet mutually in (hence '-inhere').[9] Thus essence is utter and mutual relationship. There is no something-more-profound – something more permanent, deep, trustworthy and ultimately true – than relationship. There is no citadel to which one can squirrel away the fruits of relationship somewhere safe, locked, protected, guarded and hidden. There is only relationship. The relationship of the three persons of the Trinity is that citadel. There is no essence without relationship: the relationship of the three persons of the Trinity permeates the whole of essence; there is nothing besides. Yet in return, there is no relationship – no utter, mutual and effervescent relationship – that does not have some glimpse of essence. In the words of the ancient anthem, *Ubi caritas et amor, Deus ibi est*: where charity and love are, God is present.

[9] David Bentley Hart, in his *The Beauty of the Infinite*, 179–81, describes the difference in the Trinity and its significance for the church in terms that correspond to these. Referring to John 17, he is encouraged 'to see in the communality and interdependency of the church, the peaceful participation of Christians in one body, a true if vastly inexact image of how God is forever a God dwelling in and with, a God who takes delight and is truly at peace'. He goes on to point out that 'The motion of divine love shows self-contained singularity to be a faction of thought, for even in the "instant" of origin there is the otherness of manifestation: knowledge and love.' Hart then speak of the God 'who "others" himself in himself and contains and surrenders otherness as infinite music, infinite discourse'.

Thus at the heart of all things there is community and communion. Community, because the three persons are identified by their unity, while retaining their integrity; communion, because their difference only enhances their sublime mutuality. The three persons are defined by their relationship to each other. The reason why it is hard to find a more contemporary name for the Father is that the Father is not identified by a function (Creator) or by a sentiment, however profound (Lover), but by a relationship: the Father is the Father of the Son. Jesus makes this clear when he prays 'Our Father', and encourages disciples to do the same. The Spirit is not simply a quality that amplifies the relationship between the Father and the Son (the love between them), but is a person in its own right, in an equal, but different, relationship with the Father and the Son.

Each of the relationships within the Trinity has its own character.[10] There is an integrity to the relationship between the Father and the Son that is not entirely encompassed in the incarnation of the Son. This is articulated most characteristically in the great prayer of John 17. Jesus prays, 'Father, the hour has come; glorify your Son so that the Son may glorify you ... Glorify me in your own presence with the glory that I had in your presence before the world existed' (Jn 17:1, 5). Jesus later articulates the connection between the Father–Son relationship and God's whole intention for creation, incarnation and eschaton: 'As you, Father, are in me and I am in you, may they also be in us' (Jn 17:21). While the incarnation is in the heart of the Trinity before the foundation of the world, the fact that essence is prior to and in every way outside creation means that, to misquote Arius, there was when it was not. There was no creation without incarnation: but there was Trinity without incarnation. Just as there will be essence

[10] 'God is what happens between Jesus and his Father in their Spirit.' Jenson, *Systematic Theology*, vol. 1, 221. I still wonder whether Jenson's notion of the Holy Spirit is fully personal in the way the Father and the Son are. I hear my teacher James Mackey saying, 'The Holy Spirit is always dressed in hand-me-downs.' Jenson adds two further lapidary epigrams: 'God is the event of the world's transformation by Jesus' love, the same love to which the world owes its existence ... God might have been the God he is without this world to happen to' (vol. 1, 221).

after creation – after existence – so there was Trinity before existence. But there was no existence without incarnation. Incarnation names the moment the effervescence of essence spills over into existence. The relationship of Father and Son is that of care without control, tenderness without sentimentality, love without possessiveness, gentleness without impatience, relish without rush, ferocity without fear, truth without cruelty, embrace without exclusivity.

The relationship between Son and Spirit is not restricted to the sending of the Spirit at Easter and Pentecost, or to the Spirit's role in making the Son known in church and world. It is a true partnership, expressed in Jesus' words at the Last Supper: 'If I do not go away, the Advocate will not come to you; but if I go, I will send him to you' (Jn 16:7). It is a relationship of mutuality without competition, reciprocity without reproach, challenge without criticism, encouragement without patronisation, aspiration without inhibition, inspiration without reserve, effervescence without loss, attention without flinching, playfulness without triviality. When it comes to the activity of the Spirit in creation it becomes the epitome of a partnership that remains entirely complementary and never lapses into competition. But the relationship between Son and Spirit has its own integrity, short of any engagement with creation. God is content to be with God: the persons of the Trinity delight in the relations they have with one another beyond any relation the Trinity has with creation, still less humankind.

The relationship between the Father and the Spirit, while deeply characterised by the creativity of bringing all things into being together with the Son, and animating and sanctifying all things in anticipation of the eschaton, likewise has its own validity and expression beyond interacting with creation. Jesus outlines the relationship, again at the Last Supper: 'I will ask the Father, and he will give you another Advocate, to be with you for ever ... The Advocate, the Holy Spirit, whom the Father will send in my name, will teach you everything, and remind you of all that I have said to you' (Jn 14:16, 26). It is one of respect without attenuation, indwelling without infesting, firing without damaging, enlivening without exhausting, replenishing without emptying, enthralling without exaggerating, adoring without idolising, cherishing without smothering. It is not the same as the relationship that the Spirit has with the Son, or the Father has with the Son: but it is of the same permanence, depth, trust and truth.

I have dwelt upon the bilateral relations of the persons of the Trinity because I want to enrich our understanding of the qualities of *with* that they share together even before we speak of their relationship as a Trinity and then before we speak of how the Trinity interacts with creation. This is partly about ensuring creation knows its place: the inner drama of essence is, will be and always has been the principal and overarching drama, in relation to which the drama of God's relation with creation, and still more creation's drama with itself, must take its subsidiary place. The point is, being with is not an admirable quality that the Trinity identifies and affirms in creation: it is the distinctive and definitive characteristic of what it means for the persons of the Trinity to relate to each other. It is the abundant life in all its fullness which the Son embodies (Jn 10:10) and into which the Spirit draws all creation (Rom 8:14–17).

THE TRINITY BEING WITH THE TRINITY

The dimensions of being with are principally and originally portrayals of how the persons of the Trinity relate as a Trinity – as three persons in perfect unity.[11] The dimensions are attempts to characterise what that difference-in-unity precisely entails. But they are also characterisations of what it means to dwell with the Trinity in the realm of essence – to have been taken into eternal life and to find it both overwhelming and joyful, absorbing and enriching, transformational and in continuity with existence. Thus, *presence* means the three persons dwell together so thoroughly that they are a unity: as Jesus says, 'The Father and I are one' (Jn 10:30). Being present to one another means constant engagement, awareness, alertness, consciousness,

[11] This is how they were originally articulated in my *A Nazareth Manifesto*, 125–46.

appreciation. They are each present in one another's actions, but their perpetual readiness means there is never complete inaction. There is instead a continual offering and receiving, gesturing and understanding, seeing and perceiving. Sometimes theologians speak of 'three' as if three were a numeral – as if somehow divine attributes were divided evenly like a card player dealing three hands of cards. One can never talk of the Trinity without affirming the interrelationship that characterises the three persons. They are not separable from one another. Thus the incarnation cannot be an initiative the Son is left to undertake on his own.

Attention, as always, intensifies presence. Simone Weil taught her college students not to find the answer but to seek the problem. She argued that attention does not entail muscular effort: the performative 'frowning' attention of therapists' offices and business schools merely *displays* attention rather than truly *offers* it. True attention stands still rather than leans in: by being open to what arises rather than searching to find something, we reach a more mysterious dimension. What is required is what she calls 'negative effort': the cancelling of our desires, including the desire to impose meaning and structure prematurely. We do not seek, but wait; we do not concentrate, but dilate our minds. It resembles the difference between pity and compassion: pity seeks to help those in misfortune so as not to have to think about them any more; compassion identifies with afflicted people so that I feed them for the same reason I feed myself – because we are both hungry. We do not fully understand human beings by staring, or by commiserating with them; we must instead let go of our self and allow the other to grasp our full attention.[12] Thus

[12] See Simone Weil, 'Reflections on the Right Use of School Studies with a View to the Love of God', 1942, www.christclassical.com/wp-content/uploads/2016/09/Right-Use-of-School-Studies-Simone-Weil.pdf. See also Robert Zaretsky, *The Subversive Simone Weil: A Life in Five Ideas* (Chicago: University of Chicago Press, 2021) and his 'Simone Weil's Radical Conception of Attention', *Literary Hub*, 9 March 2021, lithub.com/simone-weils-radical-conception-of-attention.

the persons of the Trinity share not a therapy session but a constant process of unselfing.

Attention means not only interaction but interpretation. This is not simply relationship: it involves communication. When being is infinite there is always more to share, observe, discern and postulate. Attention develops its own language. Language is never the whole of interaction. For example, Albert Mehrabian, a researcher of body language, analysed the components of a face-to-face conversation. He found that communication is 55 per cent non-verbal, 38 per cent vocal and 7 per cent words only.[13] Body language, facial expressions such as a smile, eye contact and tone of voice count for a great deal. This is not to say the persons of the Trinity take their communication cues from twenty-first-century human beings, but simply to highlight how human interaction is more subtle and multivalent than it may at first appear: so how much more so for the persons of the Trinity. It is not the case that in the best communication, words are not necessary: instead, non-verbal dimensions of communication provide the context for verbal ones, and can modify a verbal message significantly. Thus the Word of God, the utterance of the Trinity and the person of Jesus, fully human and fully divine, is communicated in the context of the maximally attentive relations within the Trinity. Attention regards what is being said, what is not being said and what is being communicated in other ways.

Thus the interaction of the persons of the Trinity is analogous to a conversation. A conversation is an informal mode of interaction that can involve two or more parties, in this case three, in which each party seeks to build on and enrich the previous contribution, and each

[13] Albert Mehrabian, *Nonverbal Communication* (New Brunswick, NJ: Aldine Transaction, 1972). The anthropologist Ray Birdwhistell called nonverbal communication 'kinesics'. Birdwhistell analysed non-verbal communication between humans and estimated that most people speak for about ten minutes a day, and that the usual sentence takes 2.5 seconds. He also estimated that people can make and recognise 250,000 facial expressions. Allan and Barbara Pease, 'The Definitive Book of Body Language', *New York Times*, 24 September 2006, https://www.nytimes.com/2006/09/24/books/chapters/0924-1st-peas.html.

participant is considered an equal partner in forming a degree of wisdom, entertainment, enlightenment or sharing greater than the sum of its parts. This is what the persons of the Trinity are engaged in all the time. The secret is the combination of heightened attention without the urgency to pursue purpose: the three persons are cherished not for their usefulness but for their very selves, and the conversation is not attention-seeking but attention-offering.[14] Conversation entails language, and language is the most sophisticated form of communication.[15] Those who dwell with one another develop a language all their own, in which words take on their own meanings by association and allusion, generated by shared experience and memory. The Trinity has its own language, and through that language cultivates its own culture and community. The second person is known as the Word: but that cannot mean one word. It must mean the language and logic of the whole culture of the three persons together.

Mystery is at the heart of the Trinity. There are so many unknowns, like what began all things, and why there was a creation – let alone why there is evil. But even more significant is to recognise that the persons of the Trinity are to some degree a mystery to one another: a realisation that reinforces that a mystery is very different from a problem. A problem is always a negative, and the time it takes to solve it and move on is always a deficit, a setback – because life is perceived as an obstacle course and, even if one has little conception of where one is going, one certainly does not want to be held up. But a

[14] 'God is the divine interval of love's superabundance, of life, of the gift. In God is no inward, unrelated gaze, no stillness prior to relation, or suspended in dialectical relation to otherness; his gaze holds another ever in regard, for he is his own other.' Hart, *The Beauty of the Infinite*, 185–86.

[15] Herbert McCabe, in his *What Is Ethics All About?*, 74–75, describes language as a way of not being a prisoner of the sensuous life. 'The linguistic animal is the one that to some extent creates its own modes of response to the environment, its own modes of constituting a world, and to this extent is not their prisoner. … Actively sharing a common world is communication.' Later he again helpfully describes how human beings always reach beyond the language they have created, towards a future that, 'because the language does not yet exist, can only dimly be perceived' (90). We may project this insight onto the transition of the Trinity from delight to creation.

mystery defies the directionality of the problem-solving life; a mystery draws one into a whole new realm, where not all the rules seem the same, not all the characters are fully known, and not all the circumstances are predictable. Since the persons of the Trinity are fathomless, their perpetual conversation is not about solving a problem, but about being enfolded deeper and deeper into a mystery. There is no rush to resolve, no other thing to scurry ahead to, no sense of waste or delay or diversion: entering the mystery of one another is the Trinity's whole endeavour. The definition of a problem is an exercise of power and control; the recognition of a mystery is a ceding of both, and an entering into a different kind of relationship.

This discloses a benign notion of difference. Difference can evoke fear, suspicion, rivalry, anxiety, insecurity and thus conflict; but it can also provoke creativity and beget complementarity. The nature of the Trinity, three-in-one and one-in-three, is both a rebuttal of the false god of undifferentiated sameness and a definitive portrayal of difference as not conflict but peace. There can be no account of peace that settles for less than the dynamic diversity in unity of the Trinity. Peace cannot mean the suppression of distinctiveness or the dismantling of creativity: it must mean the weaving of discordant tunes into a previously undiscovered harmony. The differences within and among the three persons of the Trinity are a sign that mystery means that the endless new configurations of profoundly different yet boundlessly complementary, never settled but constantly intriguing, not mastered but perpetually fascinating perceptions each has of the other two. This is a sign that mystery can take tension right up to the dividing line where dynamic creativity parts company with destructive conflict.

To say that the persons of the Trinity *delight* in one another is to state perhaps the most obvious characteristic of their interaction. Earlier we saw that delight can refer to the exultant joy one takes in something or someone worthy of praise, but also the rich assets one finds in something or someone in whom it would be more common or more likely only to see deficits. While the latter is clearly less applicable to the interactions of the persons of the Trinity, the attitude of constantly looking for growth, development dynamism, and possibility, rather than assigning oneself the role of being the first to see the flaw, inadequacy, Achilles heel or potential contradiction is one exercised by the persons of the Trinity to the highest degree. What for human beings requires selfless effort, training and habituation, to the persons of the Trinity is a matter of course: each beholds the other in a spirit of perceiving abundance rather than seeking out scarcity, in rejoicing in fecundity rather than pinpointing defects, in celebrating new configurations rather than lamenting the loss of familiar patterns. When in 2 Samuel 6:14–22 David dances before the Lord, he exhibits the joy the persons of the Trinity share in the presence of one another; when Michal, daughter of Saul, looks out of the window and despises David in her heart, she turns delight into diminishment. The persons of the Trinity in their being with one another know no such diminishment; only joy. Like the recognition of mystery, delight is inherently non-violent: instead of coercing or exploiting deficit, it appreciates and validates assets. It is not looking to outwit, or dominate, but to build up and enhance.

It is, surely, in this delight that the beginnings of creation are to be found. We saw earlier in considering Bonaventure the significance of exemplarism, which perceives the fecundity of divine ideas, centred on the Word of God, as the template for all existence. This centres on the Father, unbegotten and effervescent, pouring forth like a fountain, and being the source of Son, the Holy Spirit and all that flows from them. We saw also how expressionism refers to the dynamics of bringing forth and generating, beginning with the Father generating the Son and the Spirit – the expression that is at the epicentre of all reality. We may here make a further distinction between self-expression and self-assertion. The first is a way of becoming vulnerable to others by offering not-yet-fully-formed gestures and ideas to be received, explored, evaluated and in some form returned. It is a generative form of communication, which turns intuitions into actions and gives impulses external form. The second is a form of domination that displaces communication and replaces it with control, by which, through fear of becoming vulnerable, we seek to fit others into our world.[16] Delight encourages and elicits the self-expression of the persons of the Trinity, in an endlessly generative and fertile celebration of vulnerability and creativity. It is not hard to see how this comes to issue in creation – and, given that Barth insists that the Word is the subject of the incarnation, to see that the second person is the key to the source of this most significant form of self-expression.

For the persons of the Trinity, *participation* means coinherence, or perichoresis. They are profoundly with one another, enfolded in a dance or embrace. The traditional processional language, in which the Father begets (Ps 2:7; Acts 13:33) and sends forth (Jn 3:16, 8:42) the Son, and, with the Son, sends forth the Spirit (Jn 15:26), might suggest both that the purposes of God outweigh the being of God, and that the ministry of each person for the other two prevails over their being with one another. But this is not so, because the eternal life with the Father without guilt or bitterness, into which the Son and the Spirit in the fullness of time usher the creation, is the entry of existence into essence – an essence that has hitherto been characterised entirely by with, having no trace of for. Moreover, as we resolved in Chapter 1, God's means and God's ends are identical: God ushers existence into essence by being with existence, not by working for it. It is participation at every stage. Participation among human beings and the creation is known as community; between humankind and God, it is known as communion. Eternal participation, as we saw in Chapter 4, entails both.

Partnership does not arise among the different persons of the Trinity until they begin to undertake their respective roles in relation to creation, incarnation and eschatology. While these roles are distinctive and definitive, it cannot be emphasised enough that the

[16] See McCabe, *What Is Ethics All About?*, 100. He adds, 'Colonialism, however mildly paternalistic ... , is almost the exact opposite of communication between two cultures.'

Trinity is not defined by its relationship to creation: it has an integrity before, beside and beyond creation. The Trinity is essence, not existence; existence is not necessary to the Trinity, but, once conceived, constitutes an irreversible commission and, in evoking the incarnation, activates a latent potentiality in the configuration of God. Thereupon, the Trinity's being with one another is never entirely detached from its purpose to be with creation, and the embodiment of that purpose in the incarnate Jesus. Covenant, community and communion – the three themes outlined in Chapter 2 above – name three forms that being with takes, each referring to a different but complementary aspect of the ways the persons of the Trinity are with creation. The Father's role is to beget and send: the focus of that role comes at Jesus' baptism, in the words, 'You are my Son, the Beloved; with you I am well pleased' (Lk 3:22). Here the quality of the inner-Trinitarian relationships, wherein each person is regarded by the other two as precious, honoured and loved, is exposed to public gaze (Isa 43:4). Likewise at the transfiguration, that sending is reaffirmed as the Father says, 'This is my Son, my Chosen; listen to him!' (Lk 9:35). Peter, James and John are invited into the inner-Trinitarian conversation, listening to Jesus as the Father and the Spirit have done from before the foundation of the world.

There is no incarnation of the Father or of the Holy Spirit. This may seem an unnecessary observation, but through it I note that this is indeed a partnership: the first and third persons of the Trinity have different roles to play. The Father, as we have seen, begets and sends the Son – while clothing the lilies of the field and feeding the sparrows (Mt 6:26–28). The Son embodies the Trinity's utter commitment to be with creation (Mt 28:20). The Spirit makes the Son present among friend and stranger, and empowers and equips the people of God to be with God and one another (Acts 9:4–6, 2:2–4). Here the persons of the Trinity work in partnership with one another in their most characteristic manner. The paradox is that their work is being with one another, humankind and the creation: their work and that work's final purpose are identical; which is different from the way the notion of 'work' is conventionally understood. Work is usually regarded as a somewhat burdensome undertaking whose value lies chiefly in the worthy goal it pursues. The Trinity's work is not like this. Its work and its purpose are the same. To reverse a familiar phrase, God's becoming is in being.[17] Here I remain true to the principle identified in Chapter 1 that God's means and God's ends are identical.

Enjoyment is the most poignant and comprehensive of the seven dimensions of being with, since it contains all the previous six. I need hardly say that the persons of the Trinity wholly enjoy one another with no thought to use; after all, Augustine says that the only thing we can enjoy is God – so could have no objection to saying the persons of the Trinity represent mutual enjoyment *par excellence*. While enjoyment is the most pertinent dimension of being with for describing the relation of the persons of the Trinity with one another, it is perhaps the hardest to imagine. That is because we have so little experience in human interaction of utter enjoyment, with no residue of use. Which is perhaps a way of saying we have no knowledge of human activity that is not impoverished by sin.[18] Can we imagine being with one another in a way that has no thought to transferability (relating the experience to a third party), preservation or creating an impression (taking a photograph), cultivating reputation or achieving some gain (hoping for an affirming compliment), deriving knowledge or personal pleasure, or confirming our status as an interesting and rewarding companion?

[17] Eberhard Jüngel, *God's Being Is in Becoming: The Trinitarian Being of God in the Theology of Karl Barth*, trans. John Webster (London: Bloomsbury, 2004). Strictly speaking, I should say, 'God's becoming is in being with.' Jüngel's title improvises on the phrase associated with Karl Barth, 'God's being is in act.' I would say, 'God's act is in being (with).'

[18] The philosopher of rhetoric Kenneth Burke puts this succinctly, and in terms pertinent to my argument and to traditional theology. 'If [people] were wholly and truly one substance', he says, 'absolute communication would be of [their] very essence.' See his *A Rhetoric of Motives* (New York: Prentice-Hall, 1950), 21, quoted in Marie Hochmuth, 'Kenneth Burke and the "New Rhetoric"', *Quarterly Journal of Speech*, 38/2 (1952), 133–44 at 137.

Enjoyment means being entirely present, leaving aside all thought or consideration of elsewhere, making no comparison to other experience or seeking to resolve any anomaly, perceiving only the capacity and potential and bracketing any deficit. It means being with to such an extent that we almost lose our sense of personal identity, matching our capabilities so they complement those of the other, and dispelling any inclination to harness this moment for any alternative or subsequent purpose. Perhaps the only human experience of such interaction is that of a baby ingenuously encountering another infant; and even then, by no means always, or even usually. Yet this is how the persons of the Trinity enjoy one another. Which is why it is so important to speak in detail of God before exploring God's purposes: because God is that which is wholly enfolded in enjoyment, and is entirely free of use. And this is the essence into which incarnation, creation and eschatology will introduce us. Which is why humankind needs to be converted from its mean absorption in the mechanisms and techniques of use.

Enjoyment has all the other-focus of love, without the possessiveness, the self-deception and the tendency to indulge in the experience of love aside from the object of love. Reflecting on Jesus' words to the scribes in Mark 12:29–31, identifying the greatest commandment as to love God with all your heart, soul, mind and strength, and to love your neighbour as yourself, the persons of the Trinity do all three of these: they love and enjoy God, neighbour and themselves. The significance of this is to downplay the zero-sum emphasis of many accounts of God's love: God's love is simply the persons of the Trinity extending to creation the inner-Trinitarian enjoyment they have of one another. It is thus God being God. The problem arises when it is suggested that God has any other disposition towards creation – as if for example justice were opposed to love. The mutual and utter enjoyment the persons of the Trinity have for one another is the template for what love means: it is not something creation can fully replicate, but it is the defining example of what love requires and provides. This love is already existent within the Trinity before creation: at a time when there is only being with, and no question of working for. Thus love should never become detached from this notion of enjoyment: it does not fundamentally lie in unequal gestures of sacrifice, but in mutual companionship and utter appreciation.[19]

In regard to the Trinity, we can speak of *glory* in only the first of the three senses identified in Chapter 3 – the all-sufficient wondrousness of the divine interactions and coinherence. Rather than attempt to fathom the full extent of this glory, which I have tried to portray in the foregoing account of the inner-Trinitarian interactions, this is the moment to pause and recognise that what we are describing is what is eternally permanent, deep, trustworthy and true: this is the ultimate gauge against which we evaluate all existence. Returning to the first point of difference from much conventional theology identified in Chapter 1, this is a story about God. And that means God momentarily disentangled from what becomes God's utter commitment to be with creation. Humankind's hubris and narcissism assumes this should always be a story about us. Even Gregory of Nazianzus' compelling phrase 'The unassumed is the unhealed'[20] is still locked into this anthropocentric configuration, in which everything is evaluated by whether it advances the salvation of humankind. Only if we let go of configuring God according to our needs, and begin allowing the shape of the Trinity to determine our understanding of all reality, can we begin to speak of the significance of God's glory.

This is, as argued by the third point of difference from much conventional theology named in Chapter 1, a story of abundance: the

[19] Likewise the problem of self-love is overcome if we love ourselves the way God loves us. This is the conclusion reached by Oliver O'Donovan, *The Problem of Self-Love in St Augustine* (Eugene, OR: Wipf and Stock, 2006). The alternative between egoism and altruism is ultimately a false one: speaking of God as loving (or sacrificial) is always in danger of tautology, for God is just being God.

[20] Gregory of Nazianzus, Epistle 101, 'The First Letter to Cledonius the Priest against Apollinarius', www.newadvent.org/fathers/3103a.htm, trans. Charles Gordon Browne and James Edward Swallow, Nicene and Post-Nicene Fathers, ser. 2, vol. 7, ed. Philip Schaff and Henry Wace (Buffalo, NY: Christian Literature Publishing Co., 1894), rev. and ed. Kevin Knight.

glory of the inner-Trinitarian relations is that of far too much love, joy, peace, patience, kindness, goodness, faithfulness, gentleness and self-control. Indeed, it is the effervescence of such fruits that brings about the incarnation and creation. It is also, as the third point of difference insists, about God's sovereignty and freedom. There is already a profound, fulfilling, eternal and absorbing story here, within the Trinity, without any significant mention yet of creation or humankind. God is not defined in relation to humankind: humankind is defined in relation to God. Glory is a characteristic of God: humankind gets to apprehend it only as humankind comes into relationship with God. There is no glory in humankind apart from God; because there is no humankind apart from God.

The final point of difference from conventional theology is the most important one: this is a story in which God's means are identical to God's ends. Unless we can gain an understanding of the essence of all things, the relationship that is the Trinity, we cannot fully grasp that God intends to extend relationship to creation. Neither can we recognise that the way God does so is through relationship, and the purpose of doing so is to form a definitive relationship through the incarnation of Jesus Christ. Nor can we perceive that the ultimate purpose of doing so is to bring all creation into relationship with the Trinity forever. Nor can we appreciate that there is no action of God that is not about being with and for the purpose of being with, because being with is the nature of the inner-Trinitarian relations that are the heart of all things, the essence beyond existence. If we did not comprehend the nature of the inner-Trinitarian relationship, and if we did not recognise that the incarnation of Jesus Christ was the earthly embodiment of the being with of the Trinity, then we would have no notion of why there was creation at all, and for what kind of eschatological fulfilment we were being prepared. The pieces of the theological jigsaw would be unconnected and incoherent. But once we perceive that God's means and God's ends are identical, we can appreciate the utter consistency between the original relationship of the three divine persons within the Trinity, the intention to be present to another and the creation of that other to which to be present, and the preparation of a glorious future in which that state of being with should be enjoyed by creation and by God in joyous companionship without end. There is no diversion, no detour, no dissembling, no deviation: all is God's constant character and consistent purpose to replicate the being with of the Trinity with another beyond the Trinity and the faithful pursuit of that purpose until time's end. That is glory.

8 God's Purpose

By separating God and God's purpose into two chapters, I may appear to be going against Karl Barth's principle that Jesus is the beginning and end of all things: that there is no story of God before or after Jesus, because Jesus is the beginning, the centre, and the end of the story. I maintain that, while insight into the inner-Trinitarian life of God does not come at the beginning of the story, either as told in the Bible or as experienced by Israel and the church, it is essential to treat who God fundamentally is before exploring who God is in relation to humankind and the creation. This is to preserve the principle that the story is always about God, and to diminish the degree to which the story invariably becomes about us.

To distinguish between Trinity and incarnation is somewhat artificial. But one benefit is that it does allow us to envisage incarnation, creation and eschatology as one great sweep; and, as our investigations into the tradition have shown in Part II, these are three doctrines best not kept far apart, provided one maintains, as I do, that the Trinity envisaged both being present in creation, and subsequently taking creation back into essence, at the same time as embarking on creation. While I thus regard incarnation, creation and eschatology as ultimately inseparable, in this chapter I treat them largely independently, to give each its due. But the treatment of incarnation ahead of creation makes the point that the latter is a consequence of the former. I should also say at this stage that I believe if one agrees with Karl Barth that Jesus is the subject as well as the object of election, and one insists that this is from beginning to end a story about God, then election ceases to have an identity as a doctrine separate from incarnation. There is little to be said about election that is not part of what is to be said about incarnation. So I do not offer a separate account of election here: although some might say this whole chapter is an account of election, if election is the moment the Trinity resolves to extend its love beyond itself, and the three themes discussed here are the outcomes of this primal decision.

Creation, or existence, refers to the activity of God in time. Infinity and eternity are characterised by Trinity and incarnation, rather than vice versa. Eternity and time are not opposites. Eternity is, like essence, a way of talking about the infinite qualitative difference between God and creation. In the incarnation and in creation God takes time into the Trinity in such a way that does not detract from God but instead provides the eschatological basis for an everlasting encounter between God, humankind and the whole creation. If it were not so, there would be no narrative in everlasting life, and consequently no true encounter. Thus eternity does not suppress time but out-narrates it, offering a more encompassing story that underlies it and completes it and identifies it and transfigures it.

INCARNATION

The gleanings from our investigation into the tradition yielded several conclusions regarding the incarnation. First, the incarnation is an expression of God's abundance. It is the moment when God's self-love and God's love for others become indistinguishable. The decision to be united with humankind in Christ was part of God's gracious purpose from the very beginning. This world was created as a theatre for this grand design. The incarnation reveals God's freedom to initiate and sustain relational presence regardless of human response. God does not wish divine and human history to be separate, but causes them to take place as a common history. God does not will to be God without us. Thus the incarnation is the final cause of creation, and human beings, in every aspect of their nature, were created to be in relationship with Christ – to apprehend him temporally and interact with him eternally.

Second, the incarnation is about the completion and fulfilment of humankind's original potential, which is to be brought face to face with God.[1] Divine life is salvific in its presence alone. That presence, because it is God, heals and saves.[2] The incarnation itself glorifies human nature, thereby revealing the divine desire to be with us – a desire that transcends any purpose to rescue us from the consequences of sin: after all, God being with us in Christ is not a consequence of the fall, but God's original intention.[3] It glorifies human nature because it reveals its original purpose and final destiny. In the incarnate Jesus the unity of all reality is brought to

[1] In *Summa contra gentiles*, 4.54.6, Thomas Aquinas grasps this, in a manner consistent with my argument in this book. God provides a way for human beings to achieve beatitude. Friendship is possible only between those who share a likeness – so to be our friend, God had to become human.

> Moreover, friendship is based on a certain equality, and consequently it would seem that those who are very unequal cannot be united in friendship. And so, that friendship between [humankind] and God might be more intimate, it was well for [humankind] that God should become [human] – since friendship between [human beings] and [other human beings] is natural – in order that by knowing a God made visible to us, we might be drawn to the love of things invisible.
>
> *On the Truth of the Catholic Faith*, trans. Charles J. O'Neil (Garden City, NY: Doubleday, 1957), 231, translation altered

God freely shares with us the love of the Trinitarian persons by becoming one of us, enabling a friendship whose purpose is 'the eschatological union between human beings and God that fulfils the teleological purpose of humanity's creation – and results in beatitude.' (Witt and Scandrett, *Mapping Atonement*, 108). This is not far from what I am advocating: there is little here that is about recovering from the fall, and rather more about fulfilling God's original purpose. This shows how simplistic it is to divide theologians into two camps according to their answers to the question about whether Christ's coming was a result of the fall.

[2] Perhaps the story that portrays this most explicitly is Jesus' encounter with the woman with haemorrhages in Luke 8:43–48. Purity proves more infectious than impurity, and Jesus heals without even making a conscious decision to do so. It is not a great leap to extrapolate from this story to perceive that the incarnation is not for the healing of the world, but yet the healing of the world is nonetheless a consequence of the incarnation.

[3] There is a simplicity in the incarnation's face-to-face encounter that runs counter to Kathryn Tanner's emphasis on incomprehensibility. 'Jesus is not the comprehensible stand-in for an incomprehensible divinity but the very exhibition of the incomprehensible divinity of the Word in a human form or medium. Jesus displays in his life what it means to be an incomprehensible image in the flesh of an incomprehensible God.' See her *Christ the Key*, 54–55. Tanner seems to me to overcomplicate the incarnation in her commendable desire not to domesticate God: there is a difference between appropriate awe (a suitable foundation for being with) and bewildered incomprehension.

consummation.[4] The incarnation is both the centripetal trajectory towards which everything points and the centrifugal detonation that catapults all things into existence. The incarnation is a historical event: we are not reliant on revelation alone, but can appreciate the incarnation in a way we are not able to perceive creation or eschaton.

Third, the simple narrative that Jesus came to save humankind from its sins does not tell the whole story. The incarnation tells a more encompassing story than that circumscribed by fall and redemption. In this larger story sin and evil do not play a determinative part, and while they remain significant, neither humankind nor God in Christ is defined in relation to them. Sin does not reach back to humanity's origin or forward to humanity's destiny. The incarnation was not a change of plan consequent upon the fall. God did not will sin and evil as a device to draw humanity into relationship through Christ. The narrative of existence is fundamentally about God and blessedness, not about us and sin.[5] The purpose of the incarnation is not to remove something bad; it is to facilitate a higher perfection.

[4] David Bentley Hart, in his *The Beauty of the Infinite*, 158, says,

> God does not even need us to be 'our' God; all we are, all we can ever become, is already infinitely and fully present in the inexhaustible beauty, liveliness, and 'virtue' of the Logos, where – as the infinitely perfect reflection of the divine essence that flows forth from the Father, fully enjoyed in the light of the Spirit – it is present already as responsiveness and communion. . . . Jesus of Nazareth . . . would have been or would be with or without a world.

This is as far as a notion of the priority of the incarnation can stretch.

[5] Thomas Aquinas explores how friendship with God means that all three persons of the Trinity indwell the believer. As human law should create friendship between human beings, divine law should establish friendship between human beings and God. *Summa theologiae*, 2/1.99.2; see Latin/English Edition of the Works of St Thomas Aquinas, vol. 16, trans. Laurence Shapcote, ed. John Mortensen and Enrique Alarcón (Lander, WY: Aquinas Institute for the Study of Sacred Doctrine, 2012), 274–75. In *Summa contra gentiles*, 4.21.3, Aquinas writes:

> Seeing then that by the Holy Spirit we are made lovers of God, and that every beloved object is in its lover as such, it follows that the Holy Spirit, the Father and the Son also dwell in us . . . Consequently, the effect of the Holy Spirit is that not only is God in us, but also that we are in God.
>
> *On the Truth of the Catholic Faith*, 122, translation altered

See also Witt and Scandrett, *Mapping Atonement*, 122.

Assuming the incarnation came about as a response to the fall is an absurdity, because it attributes the highest good of all to a defect. It also implies that a sinful world is much better than an unfallen world would have been. The story is about glory, not about rescue. If the incarnation were simply for the sake of redemption, the redeemer would be supernumerary once redemption were gained.

Fourth and finally, the character of salvation must be entirely consistent with the form of incarnation: Jesus cannot flip from sharer to deliverer for one great substitutionary gesture. That would break the seventh principle articulated in Chapter 1: God's means and God's ends are identical. The revealer is the revealed: there is utter consistency between the Trinity and the incarnate Christ. Jesus does not alter or cease to be divine when he faces the full horror of the cross. The narrative of Jesus is the principal and definitive way we come to know the character of God: thus there is no hidden God inconsistent with the God we meet in Jesus. If we want to know what God is like, we need to look at what is revealed to us in the incarnate Jesus: nothing we may finally eschatologically discover will be different in character from what has been displayed in his flesh.

These four sets of insights, regarding the reason for the incarnation, its relation to the eschaton, its independence from the fall and its relationship to Christ's passion and crucifixion, shape the exploration that follows.

I referred in Chapter 7 to the first two steps of faith: that beyond existence there is essence, and that essence is personal and relational. The third step is that essence wills to be in relationship beyond itself, with an other – not just a unified, modest, singular other but a vast, expansive, indescribable other. This is the desire that triggers the creation of all things – we would usually say universe, but 'all things' leaves open the possibility that this universe is but one of a number of universes, absurd as the nomenclature of that possibility may be. The point is, this desire, effervescent from the delight of the Trinitarian persons in each other, detonates what we now familiarly call the Big Bang – the concatenation of micro-events that cause the universe to expand into existence. This creation came to be because God wanted to be in relationship beyond God. 'Beyond God' entails existence. Incarnation is the choice through which existence comes into being.[6]

At this point there is a tremendous risk, one named in the title of this chapter. Hitherto (we have no notion of how or whether the inner-Trinitarian relations of essence translate into time) the Trinity has had no purpose. The three inner-Trinitarian persons have simply been with one another: there has been no work to do. But the emergence of purpose, and the transformation of essence from simply being with to working with consequent upon that transformation, threatens to change the character of God. Here it becomes vital that we recall the seventh principle articulated in Chapter 1: God's means and God's ends are identical. If God's character is not to change, God's way of bringing about that purpose must be entirely consistent with the nature of that purpose. Thus the incarnation is both the means and the end of God's purpose. God's ultimate purpose is for us to be with God: God achieves that purpose by being with us. The incarnation is God being with us: the eschaton is us being with God. While the coming of Christ takes place in time, the conception of the incarnation as the purpose of God, and the fulfilment of God's purpose in the eschaton, take place outside time. Nonetheless, all we need to know about them we learn from Jesus' life in first-century Palestine. 'Purpose' remains a risky term: but it need not be so if we continually recall that God's ends always coincide with God's means.[7]

[6] John Milbank refers to three impossibilities: (1) that anything should exist outside of God, who is replete being; (2) that creatures enjoying the absolute might reject the absolute in the name of something lesser; and (3) that redemption for a fault that would appear to be without redress (see his *Being Reconciled*,62–63). I concur that there are three, but I identify a slightly different three.

[7] Bruce McCormack's approach in his *The Humility of the Eternal Son* is illuminating here. He resists a notion of God abstracted from the gospel narrative of Jesus. He does not permit statements such as 'God cannot do or experience X', which restrict the import of a text to that compatible with the presupposed concept of God. Instead, he allows the concept of God to emerge through an account of what makes sense of the Christian confession that Jesus is Lord.

While the appearance of Jesus of Nazareth on the edge of the Roman Empire in the first century may seem impossibly obscure, the narrative of his life offers a series of signal moments of assembly that indicate how it constitutes the defining intersection of heaven and earth, essence and existence.[8] The birth narratives portray the coming together of various divergences (Lk 1–2). We espy the crossover between Zechariah's faithful service in the line of a thousand years of temple worship, and the coming of God's new story in Gabriel's announcement. We witness the intersection of God's grand purpose with the humble handmaiden in the annunciation to Mary. We recognise the coming together of a man, Joseph, and a woman, Mary, for trust and abundance where once a man and a woman conspired for suspicion and scarcity. We perceive the great movement of the peoples of the earth in the Roman census together with the very personal journey of Joseph and Mary. We witness the paradox of the Lord of glory being laid in a humble manger, there being no room in the inn. We see the meeting of the heavenly choir with the very earthy shepherds. This is an assemblage of all those whom Jesus has come to be with.

In Jesus' baptism and transfiguration, as we have witnessed in previous chapters, we are given profound disclosures of what it means for him to be utterly with the persons of the Trinity, yet equally with creation. One account deals with water, the other with light. One takes place at the Jordan, where Israel's settled period of being with God began, the other on a mountain, echoing the mountain where God's covenant with Moses was made. Both accounts involve words from the Father, invoking the language of Isaiah, 'This is my beloved Son', recalling the transformation of Israel in exile from assuming that God sought a relationship of working for to discovering God in a

[8] For a study in the obscurity of Jesus in relation to the transformation announced by the earliest Christians, see C. Kavin Rowe, *Christianity's Surprise: A Sure and Certain Hope* (Nashville, TN: Abingdon, 2020), especially 11–33.

relationship of being with.[9] The transfiguration account adds the announcement 'Listen to him!' (Mt 17:5), an instruction that invites disciples and readers to reflect on all that has been said and done in the gospel thus far. Through profound irony, in the transfiguration account we see the possibility of Peter, James and John being welcomed into the divine conversation in which Moses and Elijah already partake; yet they cannot cross over into that blessed state, and Peter foolishly searches for elements in Israel's history that might preserve the experience rather than allow it to engulf them. But Jesus then does four things that epitomise the incarnation (Mt 17:7). He comes to the three disciples. He touches them. Then he invites them to get up – while they are still frightened. Then he says, 'Do not be afraid.' The whole gospel is in this single verse: Jesus comes at Bethlehem and the Jordan; he touches, in teaching and healing; he lifts up, in passion and resurrection; and he empowers, at Easter and Pentecost.

In the temptation account, we are shown the three ways the incarnation could have gone wrong (Mt 4:1–11). The tempter offers the prospect of comfort: comfort not just as a means to an end, but as an end in itself – the ability to be independent of God, safe in a secure supply chain; the temptation of Israel in settled times. Then the tempter offers drama, the lure of attention, celebrity, the turning of the Father's delight into public acclaim – using what should be enjoyed. Finally the tempter offers control: a rapid way to relate to creation – but the complete betrayal of being with. It turns out that comfort is a detour on the way to being with God in a sustained relationship of mutual partnership over time. Drama is a distraction on the road to being with people in a way that draws them into true relationship. Control is a diversion on the path to patient interaction

[9] David Bentley Hart in his *The Beauty of the Infinite*, 168, describes the baptism scene as an icon, a crystallisation of the mystery of faith in one perfect image, manifesting the drama of salvation and the order of intradivine relations. Christ's descent into the waters is his being sent into creation from the Father, his emergence from the river is his resurrection and ascension, and the descent of the dove is Pentecost and the sending of the Spirit on the Son.

that yields a more profound pattern of being with. The temptation narrative demonstrates the depth to which God's means and God's ends are identical, and how easy it would be to slip from this consistency to achieve similar ends by nefarious means.

In Jesus' encounter with the Samaritan woman at the well, Jesus speaks of her five husbands, referring to the five kinds of foreign peoples that worshiped idols in Samaria (2 Kings 17) and the one who is not her husband, a sly reference to Rome. The archetypal scene by the well presents Jesus as the woman's seventh husband. The woman discovers the place to worship: the point is not to identify the correct mountain, but instead to be with Jesus. She leaves her water jar, the symbol of her degradation, because now she has found living water: faith, truth, testimony, transformation and reconciliation. The story displays the effect of the incarnation – being with Jesus. Jesus is the seventh husband who delivers the Samaritans from religious perversion and political oppression. He is the fountain of life who delivers the sinner from daily humiliation and the marginalised from perpetual thirst. He is the true place of encounter that enables people to be with God face to face. He is the reconciling grace that makes enemies into friends. He offers a way of life that lifts the labour of humiliation off the woman's shoulders and brings her joy. He calls this well of salvation living water and this abundant harvest unknown food. Those who read this story discover that their unquenchable thirst is over and their gnawing hunger gone. This is what it means to be with Jesus.

The raising of Lazarus is similarly a paradigmatic story of how Jesus comes to be with us in the incarnation and what that being with entails (Jn 11:1–44). Jesus crosses three thresholds. He crosses into Judaea: this is like becoming incarnate. He crosses into Bethany, where he meets people's needs and speaks the truth. Martha and Mary are like Israel: they are not the whole world, but they are a microcosm of the whole world. Drawing close to them is a human way of drawing close to all creation. Then he crosses the threshold of life and death and comes to the tomb, where we see him with Lazarus in life and beyond life. Meanwhile the story shows us Jesus' full humanity. He loves Lazarus, Martha and Mary, so much that his body is convulsed with passion. He weeps. We also see Jesus' full divinity. Only God can raise Lazarus after four days in the tomb. Twice we hear the words 'Did I not tell you that if you believed you would see the glory of God?' This is from beginning to end a story about God. Jesus' profound physical and emotional reactions are not just the essence of his humanity but the essence of his divinity. He is bearing in his body the full weight of his relationship with the Father. This is an anticipation of the cross, and, like the cross, it is a prefigurement of resurrection. The human drama of emotion and surprise and horror and glory is a backdrop to the drama of Jesus' relationship with his Father. The whole story is a portrayal of the incarnation: Jesus being with Israel, being with those he loves, being with the Father.

Lest anyone imagine that being with presents a rosy portrayal of incarnation, the controversies that pepper the gospel accounts are also portrayals of what incarnation entails. When Jesus is approached by Pharisees and Herodians and asked whether it is lawful to pay taxes to Caesar, the question becomes one of whom he is with (Mt 22:15–22). The question is threatening, because the answer yes, which suggests he is with Caesar, looks like idolatry, while the answer no, which suggests he is with God, makes him ripe for charges of sedition that will lead to his execution. The Pharisees have made their choice – they are keeping the company of the Herodians, whose position depends on the rule of Rome. Jesus makes the question one of whom one is with. The irony in his words begs the question of whether there is anything on earth that is not God's. Jesus is wholly with God and wholly with creation. He is challenging others to be the same – and recognising the risk in doing so. His words may also constitute a challenge to Israel: to cultivate its own currency. That way the Jews might be relaxed about being with Caesar in unavoidable ways, but take pride in being with one another in more tangible ways. The overall point is that the conflicts in which Jesus is engaged are about whom he and his antagonists are called to be with. Being with is not just about mystery and delight: its social repercussions are about identity and belonging. Incarnation follows the same logic.

The Last Supper offers a definitive account of being with through first breaking bread and secondly washing feet. Jesus says, 'This is my body.' He is promising to be with his disciples after his death. He is saying, 'I was with Israel when it ate the first Passover and when it crossed from slavery to freedom.' He is noting that all the meals he has shared with the disciples – most obviously the mass feedings – have been moments of companionship when scarcity has turned to abundance and God has drawn close; and so this will always be one such too. He is anticipating that as the bread is broken so will his body be broken, and indicating that his broken body will be the sign that God will never break the commitment to be with them always. And he is saying that this is how it will be with us, with God and God's companions, in glory forever. This is what heaven will be like: because this is what the being with of the persons of the Trinity has always been like. Intimacy, provision, abundance; permanence, depth, trust, truth. The Eucharist will be your defining practice of being with God. Meanwhile in John 13:1–15 Jesus enacts the incarnation at the Last Supper. He gets down from the table – a table that represents his communionwith the Father and the Holy Spirit. He sets aside his robe of majesty. He dons the towel of humility. He washes feet, encountering the full extent of humankind's condition. He teaches; he asks a question; he commands. He utters prophetic words, and declares what being with him requires ('Unless I wash . . .'). Eventually he releases the towel, dons his robe of majesty again, and returns to the heavenly table. The foot-washing is thus the whole incarnation in miniature.

The gospels portray incarnation as Immanuel, God with us, in limitless ways, but I have chosen seven, since seven is the scriptural way to illustrate such a point; and I now offer one more, since Emmaus is itself the eighth meal in Luke's gospel, and since the post-resurrection appearances have a special quality of being with beyond death that we should not ignore (Lk 24:13–35). The story of the encounter with the disciples on the Emmaus road is the story of incarnation. 'They stood still, looking sad': this is human life, without God: bewildering, meaningless, hopeless. 'We had hoped': this is an encounter with the incarnate God, but one that does not yet make sense. 'Was it not necessary': the disciples hear the story again, in a way that envelops and embraces but does not deny or obscure their story. They begin to be swept up into a larger story. 'Stay with us': they lower their defences and realise they want to hear the whole story, to remain in this place. 'Then their eyes were opened': suddenly they realise that this small story of this conversation, this meal, is not just their story, but the story of everything, everyone, forever. 'Were not our hearts burning within us?' They go from this place with a mission to share this experience with everyone they meet. This provides the shape of the Eucharist. Disciples begin confused and crestfallen: gathering. They share their stories, in all their fragility: confession. They hear God's story: readings and sermon. They resolve to eat together: communion. Then their eyes are opened in the breaking of the bread. And they leave realising their hearts have been on fire. The incarnate Christ takes God's story and creation's story, like two halves of the bread, and his scarred hands break that bread, and God's story and creation's story are conjoined in his broken body. The two stories are henceforth one. This is incarnation.

CREATION

The traditional account, by which I mean the story that the incarnation came about to fix the result of the fall, offers no explicit motive for creation. It needs emphasising that I am proposing a very different story.

From the perspective of my argument, there are a number of problems with the familiar rendering. The conventional story has no significant link between creation and incarnation; neither does it have a specific connection between creation and eschaton. If there had been no fall, so the story usually goes, there would have been no need for either incarnation or eschaton. To cast things in terms of essence and existence, in the traditional story God brings existence into being, for no stated reason; if there had not been a fall, presumably creation and in due course humankind would have gone on perpetually in an Edenic state. Would there have been procreation? It is not clear. If there were no procreation, we seem to have an endless story with almost no plot. If there were procreation, there would seem to be a perpetual stream of new life, certainly for humankind, whose need for food, along with a similar need among animal life, would doubtless have meant some curtailment of life in the non-human world.[10] But if there were no death, a point would be reached where there could be no further life. Eventually the threshold would have had to be faced: leaving aside sin and evil, if there were no death, there could be no new life – without life being curtailed to a greater and greater degree. So there must always have been death: and death is not a result of the fall.[11]

All this means that the resolution of the human predicament cannot lie in existence alone. If there is a creation of existence out of essence, there must always have been an intention eventually to draw existence back into essence: even with the most generous, selfless, benevolent human and non-human life in creation we can possibly imagine, creation would eventually have become an enemy unto itself. Such is the nature of finitude when that finitude carries infinite expectations. It is asking inherently limited creation to fulfil an unlimited role that is not its purpose.

[10] Without death and decomposition, there would not even be soil. And what else would the tree of life have been growing in? I am grateful to Farley Lord for posing this last question.

[11] Whereas Augustine is unequivocal in understanding death as a result of the fall, Irenaeus' notion of a developing creation leaves more scope for conceiving of mortality predating the fall – even though Irenaeus himself does not suggest this. See Irenaeus, 'Selections from the Work against Heresies by Irenaeus, Bishop of Lyons: "The Refutation and Overthrow of the Knowledge Falsely So Called"', in Cyril C. Richardson, ed., *Early Christian Fathers* (New York: Touchstone, 1996), 387–91, and Augustine, *The City of God*, trans. Henry Bettenson (London: Penguin, 1984), 510–13 (book XIII, chapters 1–3).

Our investigation of the tradition, while it did not come to such a stark conclusion as the one I have described, nonetheless arrived at some corresponding gleanings. First, creation is made for Christ: the incarnation and creation are inextricable. The one makes no sense without the other. God's desire for fellowship is the basis for the world's existence. The creation is the setting for God being with something and someone other than God.[12] That relationship is the purpose of creation. Creation would not just be incomplete without Christ: it would be meaningless – deprived of its purpose. Creation is not an end in itself: it is teleological – ordered to the end of God's relationship with humankind in Christ.

Second, creation is not simply a function of a limited project. If relationship is the heart of all things, as we saw in the previous chapter, then being the setting for such relationship is a high calling. The dynamism, beauty, delicacy and resourcefulness of creation is fitting given the purpose it is called to serve. (In passing we may observe that failing to honour and be with the creation is problematic because disrespecting the setting for the divine–human relationship is a profound indication of disrespecting the divine–human relationship itself.) On the contrary, creation is like a beautiful song that God freely desires to sing into the vast spaces of the universe. It is the loving outflow of a loving God whose infinite dynamic goodness is shared in a limited dynamic way.

Third, creation derives its goodness from its future. Its joy is its destiny. It is from the outset eschatological, because it is ordered

[12] David Bentley Hart, in his *The Beauty of the Infinite*, 157–58, vividly expresses the non-necessity of creation: 'God does not require creation to "fecundate" his being . . . ; God and creation do not belong to an interdependent history of necessity because the Trinity is already infinitely sufficient, infinitely "diverse", infinitely at peace. . . . The absence of creation, the theater of the Trinity's economy, would in no way alter how God is God.' I am with Hart until the last sentence: while God's being is in no way inherently dependent on creation, the incarnation is God's determination that creation will have the opportunity to affect how God is God. The implications of this become clear in Chapter 10 below.

towards its completion.[13] It will not be divinised, but it will find its place eternally with God. Fourth, in the meantime, God has a tender care for creation. It may experience the effects of the fall, but it did not cause them. God meets the world not in indifference or enmity but in embrace. There is no being that was not made to be with God in Christ and that will not find its eternal place in God's company, and God upholds it as something that comes out of the effervescence of essence and will finally be with God forever.

So we have seen that creation is incarnational, because the purpose of creation is to be the theatre of God's relationship with humankind, a relationship that extends to and involves the wider creation as its setting and enhancement. But the creation is incarnational in another sense, as I now show by highlighting four episodes in the gospels. Creation is incarnational because Jesus demonstrates what creation is and where it belongs in the story of God.

The Fourth Gospel begins by locating the Word and creation together. It defies the assumption that the gospel begins with Jesus' nativity (or even his baptism) and relocates the start of the gospel to 'the beginning' – when the Word was with God. Either creation and incarnation coincide, or incarnation precedes creation. We are shown that the word 'with' is foundational – it is the first word to connect the Word to God, and it comes in the first verse of the gospel, a verse designed to echo the first verse of the Bible. The Word was the agent through which creation came into being. The leap therefore to say that all things came into being to be in relationship to God through him is not a great one: it is an implied one. 'In him was life' states explicitly that the one through whom all things came to be is the one in whom all life began (Jn 1:4). Jesus is the meaning of creation. The

[13] In his 'The End is the Beginning: Creation and Apocalyptic', in *Approaching the End: Eschatological Reflections on Church, Politics, and Life* (Grand Rapids, MI: Eerdmans, 2013), 3–21, Stanley Hauerwas articulates Karl Barth's notion of creation as eschatological: 'Creation is therefore not a timeless truth, but rather we know there was a beginning because we have seen the end. The end we have seen in Christ was the beginning, and the beginning Christ has inaugurated is the end of the beginning. Real time, eschatological time, is the life-time of Jesus Christ' (12).

passage portrays the relationship of Jesus to creation as the light without which there would be no life: to have creation without Jesus would be like dwelling perpetually in darkness. There follows another contrast: on the one hand his own people did not receive him; on the other, 'we have seen his glory' celebrates that this inhospitality was not universal (Jn 1:14). The four mentions of grace in the closing verses of John's prologue emphasise that both creation and the new creation in Jesus' coming are utter gifts of God, and inseparable from one another.

Matthew's first way of talking about creation is to speak of the virginal conception of Jesus. It is not just that Mary is the new Eve, through whose obedience the first Eve's disobedience comes to be unpicked. It is that Matthew begins both his gospel and the narrative of Jesus' birth with the same word: *genesis* (Mt 1:1, 18). The Bible starts with the story of creation which we call Genesis. The gospel begins with a story of creation which Matthew calls *genesis*. What genesis means is that the conception of Jesus is the beginning of all things. Not chronologically: but the conception of Jesus names the Trinity's effervescence from essence into existence, the Trinitarian persons' decision to love another beyond the Trinity, and God's concomitant decision never to be except to be with us in Christ. And that decision is the beginning of all creation, of all life, of everything that matters. Thus creation itself is a virgin birth, because it was creation from nothing, and it was brought about by the Holy Spirit. And the virgin birth is a new creation, indeed the original creation, because it too is brought about out of nothing, by the action of the Holy Spirit, although this time, gloriously, with a woman at the centre of God's action. Humankind has been brought out of nothing to be made for relationship with God, and Christ has made a home among humankind to unite our hearts with his. Creation is a virgin birth. The virgin birth is creation.

The gospels go on to portray how Jesus is at peace with creation – especially at moments when the creation itself seems not to be at peace, or at least not to be at peace with the needs and fears of humankind. The Old Testament is built around two beginnings, both of which involve water. The first is creation: the spirit broods over the waters. The abyss, chaos, is the profound sense of what existence would be without God. The second Old Testament beginning is the exodus, the parting of the Red Sea. For Israel this is a second birth, just as baptism comes to be for a new Christian. From then on creation and liberation become the two creative acts of God. One makes a world; the other makes a people. The crucible of the Old Testament is the exile in Babylon. Hungry and helpless, lost without temple, king and land, the children of Israel search their tradition for signs of hope. They need a new creation. This is the moment when Israel begins to understand that suffering may be part not only of its own experience, but also of God's, and that somehow this suffering of God may be an indication not only of God's unalterable decision to be with Israel, but also of the manner of Israel's recreation. This is the discovery on which the whole of the New Testament rests. What Israel realises in Babylon, as it assembles its stories in narrative shape and reflects on the God who turns out to be in exile as well as in the promised land, is that liberation is a creative act of the same God who creates. No gulf exists between the two. The two watery moments of creation and liberation arise from the same guiding hand. Liberation is not rescuing Israel from the hostile creation: it is restoring Israel to its blessed place in God's created order.

When Jesus is roused from sleep in Luke 8:22–25, this is the tradition Luke is assuming. The disciples are in a place very much like Israel was in Babylon: they have experienced Jesus as liberator, healing people from disease and releasing them from debt; but they are suddenly panic-stricken that this power does not stretch over creation, and does not reach to them. Just to make the connections unmistakable, the story concerns water – water in the form of chaos, the archetypal setting for the creation story. So when Jesus rises up and stills the storm, he synthesises the stories of creation and liberation, and inherits the legacy of the Old Testament. The disciples become a microcosm of Israel. Well may they say, 'Who is this? Who is this, that wind and sea obey him? Who is this, that figuratively meets Israel in its place of fear and doubt, the exile, portrayed in this story as the boat on rough seas, reminds Israel of its heritage in creation and liberation, and enacts a new creation and a new liberation before our very eyes? Who is this, if not God among us, the covenant between God and Israel made flesh, the word of creation become incarnate, the story of liberation made new?' The so-called nature miracle is an enacted parable of where Jesus stands in relation to incarceration and chaos.

One short and often neglected episode displays a great deal about incarnation and creation. In Luke 13:6–9, having discussed the demise of those whose Pilate had mixed with their sacrifices and those on whom the tower of Siloam fell, Jesus tells a story about manure and a fig tree that bears no fruit. Manure is a vital component of creation. Animal waste turns into fertiliser, which provides nutrients to aid the growth of vegetation, which in turn feeds animals. Jesus implies that the sad and unjust aspects of creation can become the manured soil out of which new life comes. They can be put to use to bring about new life and growth. The negativity of creation is transformed from waste into fuel. But Jesus' story is also about a tree. Jesus is the gardener who says, 'Give the tree of life a chance.' Jesus is the one who is lifted up on that tree, taking the manure of the world, the vile intention and the sad misfortune, into himself on the tree. Through his life and death, manure turns to fruit. And some while later, women come back to that place early in the morning to see whether the gardener has done his work. They witness what takes place when all the manure of the history of the world has been taken into that tree and transformed into the fruit of salvation. This is the renewal of creation in resurrection.

Indeed, the most explicit moment at which incarnation illumines creation in the gospels is the resurrection account in John 20:11–20. In elemental terms it presents a man and a woman in a garden. Just as Song of Songs portrays a man and a woman in a garden, narrates a secret rendezvous that we may think of as the close linkage of the divine and human natures in Jesus, and offers a series of references to fertility and growth, so the meeting of Jesus and Mary demonstrates what new creation entails.[14] Gardens are precious in the Middle East – hence the Arabic term for garden, which is 'paradise'. Paradise means flowing water in a desert, green shoots in dry ground, lush beauty in the midst of arid wastelands. Mary mistakes Jesus for the gardener; but he *is* the gardener. The resurrection narrative is a glimpse into paradise. Beginning meets end, creation meets completion. Resurrection reveals the last page of the story, and the first page of the story. The resurrection of Jesus is the end of the beginning and the beginning of the end. It is a profound affirmation of the physicality of creation: Jesus is resurrected as a physical body. It indicates that when existence is finally drawn into essence, that way of being will be physical too: the resurrection is a reaffirmation of the incarnation. Here we see the destiny for humankind: to be remade beyond death as people soaked in humanity yet immersed in God. Jesus' resurrection is not something for him alone. He shares it with Mary. The garden is telling us that resurrection is intimate, social and cosmic. The garden represents the whole non-human creation. Just as Adam and Eve were the focal point for the destiny and fall of all things, so this secret meeting between Jesus and Mary is the focal point for the resurrection of all things. Henceforth it is clear that the eschaton is not just the uniting of individual human beings with God: this is a truly social vision, including the renewed creation.

ESCHATOLOGY

Given the apparent inextricability of creation and fall, the great question is not why there was an incarnation – I have insisted that the notion of creation is meaningless without incarnation; no, the great

[14] Ellen F. Davis argues that Song of Songs imagines the healing of the three great ruptures that occurred in Eden: between man and woman, human and non-human creation, and humanity and God. See her *Proverbs, Ecclesiastes and the Song of Songs* (Louisville, KY: Westminster John Knox, 2000) and *Scripture, Culture and Agriculture: An Agrarian Reading of the Bible* (Cambridge: Cambridge University Press, 2009), 170.

question is why God established existence at all. Why did God not rather transfer directly to the eschaton without the diversion into creation and incarnation? This remains a question even after creation, because one assumes God will draw down the curtain of history if and when the prevalence of evil, sin and suffering is such that there is no reason to maintain creation; so, short of the eschaton, the question of when creation is 'worth it' never goes away. The purpose of this section of the chapter is to establish the relationship between incarnation and eschaton, the better to understand why the Trinity's desire to be with an other led to this kind of a story.

In our investigation into the tradition, broadly six themes were gleaned. First, the tension between eschaton as judgement and eschaton as fulfilment broadly corresponds to the difference between a story that concentrates on fallenness and one that focuses on finitude. In the former case the operative term is 'redemption'; in the latter case the story is one of the fulfilment of potential. We saw earlier that Western theologians have tended to tell the former story, while Eastern theology has tended to emphasise the latter.

Second, Orthodox theologians almost without exception make considerable play of the notion of deification, based on the divine exchange – whereby God in Christ becomes what we are, that we might become what God is. This commendably asserts that God's purpose is not limited to returning humanity to its condition prior to the fall, and instead focuses on its future destiny. Deification is primarily concerned with overcoming the problem of finitude and ensuring humankind enters eternity – what I call essence. Orthodox theologians invariably insist that deification does not break down the creator–creature distinction, and retains human identity, rather than perceiving humankind somehow to blend into the Trinity. But they tend to find it difficult to distinguish between the glory of being with God and the glory of God's essence itself. (The ambiguity is inherent in the notion of eternal life: an attribute of God, and yet a gift of God to created, and therefore limited, humankind.) In discussion I suggested that being with is a more helpful notion than deification, because it insists on togetherness and thus has no danger of getting into confusion of identities or blending into the divine. It also has a richer understanding of what it means for there to be activity and interaction in heaven, for there to be multiplicity and interrelationship among those dwelling there, between themselves and not just with God, and for the whole creation to be with God rather than simply for there to be a backdrop for the divine–human relationship. This takes creation beyond the notion of being a theatre into being itself an active partner in relationship. In short, being with turns deification from a two-dimensional encounter between humankind and God into a three-dimensional interplay where human beings are raised to life with God, one another and the renewed creation. Heaven must be participatory, interactive, dynamic and unfolding.

Third, while Orthodox theologians continue to emphasise the fulfilment of human potential, they have been closely tied to two historical experiences – a millennium of imperial rule, and a half-millennium of oppression. The result is that there is insufficient reflection on what kinds of authority most faithfully reflect the just social relations of heaven, and a danger that in emerging from being oppressed, Orthodoxy will revert quickly to models of authority that turn it from oppressed to oppressor. A further issue is that, with an underdeveloped eschatology of the wider creation, Orthodox theology has fewer resources with which to contribute to the revival of a theology of creation in the light of the climate emergency. This and the previous gleaning constitute the prevalence of the themes of covenant and community we explored in Chapter 2.

Fourth, and bearing in mind the comments at the beginning of the account of creation above, the incarnation is the key to correctly conceiving of eschatology, and eschatology is an indispensable requirement of the incarnation. We saw in the previous section of this chapter that an endless existence, without finitude, is inconceivable even without sin: creation would, in the end, become its own enemy simply by occupying all the space available, however much it dug into the earth or built into the sky. Not all challenging things are the result of the fall. Some are inevitable as soon as infinite expectations are placed on finite creatures. Death and birth are inseparable, and there could be no existence without mortality. Creation is thus God's opportunity to be with creatures and especially to be humankind's companion in existence; for that relationship to be permanent requires God to draw all creation into essence. This must all have been in God's original purpose, lest the relationship be lost; and it is inconceivable that the eternal Trinity would let anything in all existence be finally lost. So incarnation and eschaton are not consequent upon the fall, but are part of the prior purpose. The eschaton cannot be an extension of existence for a finite time, since that time would only be an extension of creation, not its fulfilment. The eschaton must be the transformation of creation from existence into essence. But this is not a return to essence pre-existence: it is the taking of existence into essence. Essence now has time, lest it be without narrative; yet it has no death, and thus no birth. Therefore each of the three epochs – pre-existence, existence and existence-in-essence – has its own distinctive character; and the second person of the Trinity is at the heart of all three. Incarnation is how we understand the purpose of creation – being with God: it is also how we come to imagine the quality of the eschaton – being with God in Christ, and being with one another and the renewed creation. Thus the incarnation is how we understand eschatology.

Fifth, the summit of creation is the communion of all persons with one another and with God. Thus covenant, community and creation are not just continuous features of scripture, not just key aspects of Jesus' incarnate ministry, but abiding characteristics of heaven. The Eucharist is not simply or even primarily an encounter with the paschal mystery; there would have been a Eucharist even without the fall, because it enacts God's companionship with us, initiated in the incarnation. The Eucharist portrays the life of heaven. This requires some explanation, particularly for those to whom the Eucharist is largely or wholly associated with Christ's death as an atoning sacrifice and his resurrection as conquest of death. The logic goes like this. Heaven is not static, individual, disembodied or merely intellectual or spiritual. It is not God's memory bank of our life in existence. Heaven is interactive, dynamic, sentient, corporate and communal. In the gospels and so in heaven, Jesus speaks of and practises the realm of God – the life of heaven – more in meals than in any other way. At the Last Supper he says, 'I have eagerly desired to eat this Passover with you before I suffer; for I tell you, I will not eat it until it is fulfilled in the kingdom of God' (Lk 22:15–16).[15]

Every meal is in some way an enactment of the heavenly banquet. And every feature of the Eucharist is constitutive of the life of heaven. The faithful join with the heavenly choir in song and praise. There is confession, because being free of sin does not mean being free of tension and misunderstanding and ingratitude. There is the word of God, because God's children continue to eat not just by bread alone but by every word that comes from the mouth of God. There may not be the reciting of the creed in the liturgical sense, but there is still a narrative shape to essence, lest it become static and predictable, and the celebration of the Holy Spirit's guidance through that narrative and Christ's place at its centre continues to characterise the feast. There may not be intercession in the earthly sense, since intercession is articulating the longing for earth to be more like heaven; but there is profound naming of truth and the continued perception of how the Holy Spirit has turned crisis into opportunity. The sharing of the peace is less a timely moment for reconciliation of differences than the glorious outpouring of differences now cast in wondrous, beauteous and harmonious effervescence. Thus what at the Last Supper and at all previous meals was an anticipation of food to be shared in plenty, at leisure and in peace, becomes in heaven a joyous sharing where each is more concerned for the other's well-being than for their

[15] I am grateful to Farley Lord for inviting me to reflect on the significance of Jesus instituting the Eucharist before his death and resurrection rather than after. It is a remembrance of his life – his incarnation – rather than a commemoration of his death. And it is an anticipation of his eternal life, and of our spending that life with him – rather than specifically an anticipation of the manner of his death.

own, and no one fills their own plate because they are more concerned to fill one another's, and the food never runs out and no one is exploited in its preparation. And at the end there is an almost endless prayer of thanksgiving and a tangible blessing but no dismissal, for there is no reason to leave, no oppressed to go and deliver and no stricken earth to heal.

Sixth, the eschatological hope must reflect the transcendent difference-in-mutuality of the Trinity. The story has three parts (not four). The first part is essence, the inner-Trinitarian relationship prior to creation. The second is the incarnation and its concomitant creation, including the presence of Jesus Christ physically on earth as part of that second part. Within this part are undoubtedly significant chapters, notably Israel, Christ and church; but what I mean by 'not four' is that the story does not change gear after the fall and become a different story, one of rescue rather than encounter. It is a continuous story of covenant, community and communion, centred on Christ. So the third part is heaven, the reversion from existence to essence, but this time embracing creation whose bond to the Trinity is the incarnate Christ, now risen, ascended and glorified. The model for what interactive, dynamic, sentient, corporate and communal life in heaven might be like must determinatively be the inner-Trinitarian relations – although Christ's earthly ministry also gives strong indications, as we shall now see.

Anticipation of the eschaton in the gospels is of broadly three kinds: apocalyptic description of the dramatic end times ('Brother will betray brother to death, and a father his child, and children will rise against parents and have them put to death; and you will be hated by all because of my name', Mk 13:12–13); fierce warnings about individual judgement, whether from John the Baptist ('You brood of vipers! Who warned you to flee from the wrath to come? . . . Even now the axe is lying at the root of the trees; every tree therefore that does not bear good fruit is cut down and thrown into the fire', Lk 3:7, 9) or from Jesus ('As for this worthless slave, throw him into the outer darkness, where there will be weeping and gnashing of teeth', Mt 25:30); and depictions of the life to come ('In the resurrection they neither marry nor are given in marriage, but are like angels in heaven', Mt 22:30).[16] Historically the imagination of the church, and to a great degree its theologians, has been diverted away from accounts of the life of heaven and has been unduly focused on who gets there. (This is a significant way in which theology has been drawn into anthropocentrism rather than theocentrism.) Thus in this account I will concentrate on the third kind of eschatological anticipation.[17]

In a defining parable, Jesus speaks of the hungry, the thirsty, the stranger, the naked, the sick and the prisoner, and what it means to be with people facing such hardship (Mt 25:31–46). The parable is defining not because of its vivid account of what happens to those who were not with such people (it is a parable – it is by nature vivid to the point of being lurid). The key to the parable is that Jesus himself was hungry in the wilderness, thirsty on the cross, a stranger when his own people received him not, naked when he was born in a stable and when he died in the sight of mockers, sick when he sweated great drops of blood and a prisoner at the mercy of the Sanhedrin and Pilate. Moreover the actions Jesus endorses are not radical transformations but acts that require presence and attention: offering food to a hungry person and drink to a thirsty person, welcome to the stranger and clothing to the naked, care (not healing) for a sick person and a visit

[16] Stanley Hauerwas helpfully offers a description that harmonises these three understandings:

> Eschatology indicates that the world, including ourselves, is storied. . . . Creation is the first movement in the story that . . . involves the election of Israel, kingship, sin, exile, and redemption. For . . . all the gospels, Jesus is the 'summing up' of the history of Israel so that Jew and Gentile alike can now live as God's people. . . . Apocalyptic language suffuses the story that Matthew tells because such dramatic language signals the difficult task that Matthew undertakes to help us discover how we must learn to see and live in the world under the lordship of Christ.
>
> *Matthew* (Grand Rapids, MI: Brazos, 2006), 38

[17] 'The eschatological proclamation needs the narrative of Jesus in order to *identify* the eschaton that is in fact proclaimed' (Jenson, *Systematic Theology*, vol. 1, 170). For Jenson, the eschaton is a future in fellowship with Jesus – what I would describe as the determinative part, but not the whole of the promise of being with.

(not release) to the prisoner. These are all gestures that require physical presence – being with. They are not solutions to overcome problems: they are acts of companionship to overcome isolation. They are saying, 'We will never leave you alone.' They are described as the ways we meet Jesus. They are also ways to encounter those with whom we shall share eternity. But crucially they portray the human predicament not as guilt or mortality but as isolation. Heaven is a dwelling place where no one is isolated, because discovering incarnation is being with people as they face adversity, not to fix that adversity (whereupon they may become isolated again) but to embody the fundamental companionship that the incarnation is originally and always about. Those who cross the boundary of isolation to meet whoever they find facing hardship thereby acknowledge that they themselves are hungry, thirsty, estranged, naked, sick and in prison – and that these gestures are ways to overcome not only the recipient's isolation but theirs as well. This is the life of heaven depicted in Jesus' ministry. This celebrated parable is not fundamentally one of judgement, but one that displays the realm of God on earth.

The feeding of the 5,000, which appears in all four gospels, is a paradigm of transformation that depicts several elements of eschatological anticipation. It has no trace of suggesting that grace requires human assent: the benevolence of Jesus is indiscriminate. It leaves no doubt that the human situation without the incarnation is bleak: 'They were like sheep without a shepherd' (Mk 6:34). It works through partnership with human agency: 'How many loaves have you? Go and see' (Mk 6:38). It builds on human assets rather than ignoring or obliterating them: 'When they had found out, they said, "Five, and two fish"' (Mk 6:38). It distinguishes between Jesus, who is with God and humankind and can dwell in heavenly ways in earthly settings, and the disciples, who dwell close to Jesus, and the crowd who are largely unaware but whose deepest needs are met: 'Taking the five loaves and the two fish, he looked up to heaven, and blessed and broke the loaves, and gave them to his disciples to set before the people; and he divided the two fish among them all. And all ate and were filled'

(Mk 6:41–42). And it affirms that, in the realm of God, we are experiencing the transformation from scarcity to abundance: 'and they took up twelve baskets full of broken pieces and of the fish' (Mk 6:43). It demonstrates that the Eucharist is not simply a discreet practice in which an individual believer may find communion with the crucified and risen Lord: it is a radical event that occurs in any circumstance in which the scarcity of disciples is overwhelmed by the abundance of the incarnate Christ, and the life of heaven is anticipated in transformed human relationships.

When in his reply to the Sadducees Jesus says, 'in the resurrection they neither marry nor are given in marriage, but are like angels in heaven' (Mt 22:30), he is not saying heaven will be less than earthly existence; he is saying it will be more. Marriage changes, because resurrection does not come about by our conceiving and rearing children and grandchildren. Resurrection is something God alone can give. Thus God transforms marriage, because marriage and bearing children cease to be necessary for human survival. And there is something better than marriage. In the words of Thomas Traherne,

> Suppose a curious and fair woman. Some have seen the beauties of heaven in such a person. It is a vain thing to say they loved too much. I dare say there are ten thousand beauties in that creature which they have not seen: They loved it not too much, but upon false causes. Nor so much upon false ones, as only upon some little ones. ... They love her perhaps, but do not love God more ... I dare confidently say that every person in the whole world ought to be beloved as much as this.[18]

The eschaton is an experience of overwhelming delight in each and every creature – not the scarcity of envy and jealousy and possessiveness and suspicion. This is what it means to be with one another and with the Trinity: like the angels indeed. It is not the end of a dynamic

[18] Thomas Traherne, *Centuries* 2:68, in *Selected Poems and Prose*, 214.

story, but the beginning of one that makes earthly existence seem flat and two-dimensional.

Finally, Jesus' first miracle in the Fourth Gospel depicts the joy of God's realm in similarly transformative terms. The evangelist signals its importance at beginning and end: 'On the third day' opens the story, and 'Jesus did this, the first of his signs, in Cana of Galilee, and revealed his glory; and his disciples believed in him' closes it (Jn 2:1, 11). The event takes place on the seventh day of a sequence that begins at John 1:19. Everything therefore announces that this is going to be the miracle that sums up the whole gospel. The key to the story is not the sharp interchange between Jesus and his mother. It is the triple contrast from existence to essence. The water of life is turned into the wine of eternal life. The ordinary wine is replaced by outstanding wine. And the shortfall of wine is transformed into an abundance of wine (Jn 2:10). In each of these ways, the story portrays the incarnate Jesus as the one through whom creation turns into heaven, and the flaws in existence are overwhelmed by the foretaste of essence. Now is eternal life.

9 God's Unfolding Purpose

Jesus Christ names the Trinity's defining purpose. The Holy Spirit names the Trinity's unfolding purpose. Hence the difference between Chapter 8, on Jesus, and this chapter, on the Holy Spirit. The Holy Spirit is always closely linked to Jesus. But the meaning of this link is this: we recognise as the work of the Holy Spirit the occasions when it anticipates or echoes the action of God in Christ. More vividly, Christ, along with the Father, sends the Spirit, to point to Christ, to make Christ present in creation, to foster the ways human beings are with Christ, to prepare the way for Christ's first and second comings. Hence this chapter explores Israel, church and God's realm as particular lenses through which we see that Christ-prefiguring, Christ-imitating and Christ-replicating action of the Holy Spirit. The purpose of this chapter is to articulate the continuous activity of the Holy Spirit in actions of bringing people into relationship with God – in their being with God, one another and the wider creation. Just as the distinctive ministry of the Father is in bringing all things to birth – Christ definitively, and thence the creation – so the characteristic ministry of the Holy Spirit lies in bringing things to life – and by life, I mean relationship, covenant, community, communion, infused with presence, attention and so on.

ISRAEL

The Holy Spirit is at work in the Old Testament as Israel is with God and God with Israel in ways that anticipate how God is with humankind and the creation in Christ. We have already in Chapter 2 perceived God being with Israel especially in covenant. Here we look at other ways besides law and faithfulness in which Israel practises what it means to be with God. Without attempting to be exhaustive, we may identify six such ways: in wisdom, companionship, praise, blessing, suffering and imitation.

Wisdom is a Spirit-inspired way of coming close to God. It requires many of the dimensions of being with – attention, mystery, delight, enjoyment. The most striking portrayal of wisdom in the Old Testament is in Proverbs 8. Here we find an invitation to the heart of all things – insight that's more valuable than wealth or possessions, truth that's the soul of life. Then we read a confident statement that wisdom orders the world, and a route to justice, good government, riches, honour, wealth and prosperity. Next we discover that wisdom brings understanding, skill and delight, turning the technical work of creation into an act of rejoicing. Last it becomes clear that wisdom is also the secret of happiness. The Holy Spirit locates this portrayal of wisdom alongside the account of wisdom offered in Philippians 2 ('Let the same mind be in you that was in Christ Jesus', Phil 2:5). There, in Christ, the wisdom of God in Christ involves being poured out, setting aside privileges and advantages, and becoming obedient to the point of death on a cross. Wisdom is a fully engaged, utterly selfless willingness to make one's life a blessing to others.

The Proverbial approach appreciates that life is beautiful; the Philippian perspective sees also that all is not as it should be, and wisdom lies in being with those who are most exposed to life's challenges. The Proverbial approach recognises that God wants all to flourish; the Philippian perspective suggests that means looking out for the well-being of one another. The Proverbial approach perceives a connection with the inner workings of the world; the Philippian perspective assumes that a relationship requires us to be vulnerable, to make ourselves subject to forces and outcomes and potential to be hurt and let down in ways beyond our control. The Proverbial approach sees creation as the principal window onto the purposes of God; the Philippian perspective sees two things more fundamental than creation – Christ's incarnation as one among us and his resurrection that prefigures the renewal of all things. Proverbial wisdom and the Philippian Jesus are both ways of articulating how

God relates to us. But they make different claims. For Proverbial wisdom, relating to us is an afterthought for God. Creation is primary; relationship is secondary. By contrast, from the Philippian perspective, relating is the essence of God: God is relationship; creation happens only because of a prior decision to relate to it as a way of deepening the relationship within God. Thus the Holy Spirit inspires Israel's wisdom and draws it to into a deeper relationship of being with embodied in Christ.

The Trinity isn't the best guess of Proverbial wisdom; it is the revelation of the God who, in Christ, turns upside down our quest for knowledge, comfort and security, and instead calls disciples to pour out their lives in gratitude, grace and imitation. The Holy Spirit guides disciples from the pithy epigrams of Proverbial wisdom towards the passionate dialogue and deep companionship out of which such wisdom arises. The Trinitarian God is not an answer, but a conversation: not a solution to a problem, but an invitation into a mystery. Believing is not having access to an explanation – it is being drawn into a dialogue that will never end. The Holy Spirit mediates the disciple's conversation with the Father; and Jesus is the language of that conversation.

A very different Old Testament portrayal of the work of the Holy Spirit comes in the description of companionship, such as that of David and Jonathan or, most vividly, Ruth and Naomi. Ruth refuses to return to her home country, despite Naomi's insistence, and instead binds herself to Naomi. The five things she says are an imitation of the covenant, located in the relationship of a foreign woman to her Israelite mother-in-law (Ruth 1:16–17). Where you go, I will go. Where you live, I will live. Your people will be my people. Your God will be my God. Where you die, I will die. It is a moment where the Holy Spirit echoes God's covenant with Israel and anticipates the embodiment of that covenant in Jesus. 'Where you go, I will go': God will be with Israel in Egypt and in Babylon; Jesus experiences every aspect of human existence. 'Where you live, I will live': God dwells with Israel; Jesus sets up his tent among God's people. 'Your people will be my people': God says to Israel, 'You are my people'; Jesus comes to be one among them. 'Your God will be my God': the Holy Spirit draws the gentiles into Israel's covenant. 'Where you die, I will die': there is no other purpose besides this covenant; neither Israel, nor God, is a means to some further end; this is not an instrumental relationship; Jesus is committed to Israel until the very end, to the point of death. The Holy Spirit is present, making this encounter a foretaste of the incarnation – a true embodiment of covenant, community and communion.

Some of the most intense examples of Israel being with God in anticipation of Jesus are to be found in the Psalms. What the Spirit embeds in Israel and evokes in Jesus is an intense form of being with, in which dialogue, directness and expectation combine in commitment and relentless trust. We could call it communion. (Dialogue, directness and expectation largely correspond to the being-with dimensions of attention, participation and partnership.) The two genres that most commonly recur in the Psalms and reflect this dialogue, directness and expectation are praise and lament. Israel exalts in God, celebrates God's wondrous deeds, affirms God's steadfast love and calls upon other nations to share in joy; in return Israel rejoices to inhabit covenant faithfulness. The whole Psalter can be read as a movement from obedience (Ps 1) to praise (Ps 150). Meanwhile Israel protests to God, describing how far its circumstances are from those God promised, and demands that God respond to uphold the covenant and dispel the forces of death. Praise, in which Israel is obedient to God's commands, exchanges roles with lament, wherein God is required to be forthcoming to Israel's demands: 'Save me O God, by your name ... Attend to me and answer me ... Deliver me from my enemies ... Rouse yourself, come to my help' (Ps 54:1, 55:1, 59:1, 4). Submissive praise and assertive lament display a dynamic relationship that runs through the Old Testament from Sinai onwards. Praise is a joyful and unreserved form of obedience; lament is a more profoundly relational, dialogical and interactive expression of Israel's submission to God.[1] The normative, but not universal pattern is for lament to give way to praise: this takes place in Psalms 13, 22, 30 and 107 – but not in Psalm 88.

In praise and lament we see the Holy Spirit inspiring and comforting in equal measure – giving voice, just as Romans 8:26–27 will put it, to those who seek a direct encounter with the Father: 'The Spirit helps us in our weakness; for we do not know how to pray as we ought, but that very Spirit intercedes with sighs too deep for words. And God, who searches the heart, knows what is the mind of the Spirit, because the Spirit intercedes for the saints according to the will of God.' Meanwhile Jesus adopts the same pattern of praise and lament: saying, 'Father, I thank you for having heard me' at the tomb of Lazarus, and 'Father, glorify your name' on Palm Sunday (Jn 11:41, 12:28), yet 'Abba, Father, for you all things are possible; remove this cup from me' in Gethsemane, and 'My God, my God, why have you forsaken me?' on the cross (Mk 14:46, 15:34). Here we see being with as in no sense a passive yielding but as a passionate and dynamic interaction, full of reproach, imprecation, wrestling and renewal.

The greatest challenge to Israel is how to be with the nations. This is being with put to its most demanding test prior to the cross. The Old Testament narrates how Israel's culture moved from nomadic to settled, its sustenance from herder to agriculturalist and its devotional focus from Sinai to Zion. While one can trace a broadening perception of the purposes of God, from those concentrated on Israel out to all the nations encompassed at Zion ('Say among the nations the Lord is king!', Ps 96:10), out further to the whole earth in the exile, the nations are involved from the very beginning ('In you all the families of the earth shall be blessed', Gen

[1] For this interplay between submissiveness and challenge, see Brueggemann, *Old Testament Theology*, 236–44. Brueggemann himself laments, 'It is of course unfortunate that very much church theology has misunderstood or neglected this dialogic component in obedience and has resulted in a flat and stultifying understanding that negates the openness, vitality, and hard work that belong to covenantal obedience' (239).

12:3, and the genealogies of Gen 9–11). Some would say God's choosing of Israel was always part of a larger plan beyond the covenant towards right action and justice.[2] But in truth the sense that God's covenant with Israel is for no purpose other than itself never goes away; and the tension remains in the New Testament. Perhaps the most startling sign of wider purpose comes in Exodus 12:32, where Pharaoh says to Moses and Aaron, 'Bring a blessing on me too!'; but it is also there in Naaman's search for a cure in 2 Kings 5. The prophets bring a clear sense that the nations are subject to judgement outside the covenant when they commit brutal acts (Am 1–2). God is capable of punishing nations and of using them to punish Israel (Isa 10:5–19, 14:24–27, 37:22–29, 47:6–7). Nebuchadnezzar falls from power and realises the true sovereignty, truth and justice of God (Dan 4:36–37). Most striking of all is the description of Cyrus as 'my messiah' through whom transformation will take place (Isa 45:1).[3]

Being with the nations is always complex for Israel in the Old Testament. But one can trace a strand back to the covenant with Noah in which God undertakes to be with the nations and all creation prior to the covenant with Abraham: 'I will remember my covenant that is between me and you and every living creature of all flesh; and the waters shall never again become a flood to destroy all flesh'

[2] Levenson, 'The Universal Horizon of Biblical Particularism', 149. That would seem to be the import of Psalm 24:1, 'The earth is the Lord's and all that is in it, the world, and those who live in it.'

[3] In this paragraph I am indebted to the breadth of compass of Walter Brueggemann, *Old Testament Theology*, 245–61. He extends the nations to include the whole creation at significant points.

> Whereas Lynn White has famously faulted the Bible as the basis of the abuse of creation, Cameron Wybrow has made it clear that it is Enlightenment rationality – the same Enlightenment rationality that has produced nation states – that caused the reification of 'nature' as a commodity to be used and exploited. As the nation state may exercise hubris over weaker neighbouring states, so the human agent in hubris has taken 'nature' to be a usable, inexhaustible resource for human explanation.
> *(257)*

For greater detail on Israel and the nations, see Walter Brueggemann, *Theology of the Old Testament: Testimony, Dispute, Advocacy* (Minneapolis, MN: Fortress, 1997), 492–527.

(Gen 9:15). And it is this covenant, transcending national identities, borders and ambitions, that the Holy Spirit engages at Pentecost, when it turns diverse languages, the source of confusion in Genesis 11, into a means of godly communication, and pours out blessing on all flesh. Pentecost is not a new kind of being with: it is the reassertion of a somewhat suppressed strand in the Old Testament tradition, in which the Holy Spirit brings life to the world through the good news emanating from Israel.

Perhaps the most significant development in relation to being with in the Old Testament is the way in Second Isaiah, and the exilic experience in general, the people of Israel come to perceive suffering not simply as something they petition God to remove, but as something they discover God shares with them. We have already highlighted the role of Daniel 3 in this regard. The other stand-out passage that points to God as fellow-sufferer is Isaiah 53. The beginning and end of the poem about the suffering servant state three things: this is a person who is disfigured, despised and rejected; whose story is misunderstood; and yet who is finally vindicated. The next two sections of the chiasmus affirm similar paradoxes: this person is close to God, yet God lets this person be crushed; though this is troubling, nonetheless the Lord will prevail through it; and the sufferer will emerge with wisdom and insight. The third chiastic section intensifies the mood of alienation and violence: it uses terms like despised, rejected, suffering, infirmity, oppressed, afflicted and slaughter. All of this sets up and exalts the central assertions of the middle section: he has borne our infirmities, was wounded for our transgressions, crushed for our iniquities; by his bruises we are healed. We like sheep have gone astray and turned to our own way. The Lord has laid on him the iniquity of us all: it turns out he was suffering for what others had done wrong. His suffering restores them. God has worked through this and blessed it all.

The passage displays the profound dignity of the rejected – a deeper identity than the desire merely to belong and be accepted. It demonstrates the truth that can surface when one resists the immediate impulse to remove pain. In this poem pain yields connectedness, patience and endurance. Suffering is isolating – but that is not all that can be said about it: it can also make a new community. We witness the worth of not simply resisting an unjust accusation, but of bearing another's grief, punishment and constraint. Despite being despised, the servant finds wisdom and grace in keeping silent and retaining dignity. The fact that suffering is demoralising and overwhelming is not in question; but this is not the last word. Here suffering can yield wisdom and recognition. These are profound insights that go against conventional wisdom and indicate the guidance of the Holy Spirit through the power of the poem. The poetry affirms the central paradox of the exile, that suffering need not always be isolating, but that it can build community, reaffirm covenant and deepen communion. Jesus must have known this passage well; it is hard to imagine he did not self-consciously inhabit it on his way to Golgotha. When Jesus shoulders the cross, he is embodying the words of Isaiah 53 – whether or not those words originally envisaged an individual suffering in this way.[4] The Holy Spirit guides Jesus to enter his passion perceiving it as the definitive time when he will draw closer than ever to humankind and creation and to the Father and the Spirit. Christians read the way of the cross back into Isaiah 53 because they have such confidence that, in the crucifixion, they draw closer to God than ever before – so they are convinced Isaiah 53 must have been such a moment for Israel. The cross is the epitome of alienation, yet the icon of being with. That is its paradox.

These insights are significant because the promise of working-for models of theology, ethics and mission is that they will remove suffering. Working for offers to dispense with the need for being with

[4] Walter Brueggemann, in his *Theology of the Old Testament*, 621, carefully nuances this kind of use of Old Testament materials: 'The Christian community has taken up the invitation given by the text, but it cannot monopolise the text nor its invitation to imaginative reuse. I suggest that the Christian appropriation of the promise, authoritative as it claims to be, stands alongside other uses, none of which can defeat or deny the other uses.'

by taking away human pain and limitation. It overpromises, of course. But its hubris is not the point here. What Isaiah 53 discloses is that to abolish suffering would be to obliterate some of the most profound dimensions of human experience, such as solidarity and wistful wisdom – dimensions that arise only in the context of being with one another in the face of deep distress; and, even more important, to abolish suffering would be to eliminate access to key aspects of the character of God, which only the cross fully displays. Being with does not glory, rejoice or in any way indulge in suffering; but its unique quality is that it is the only form of relating that transcends and truly goes beyond suffering.

The full mystery of the cross is anticipated in an unlikely place: Song of Songs 8:6, which reads, 'Set me as a seal upon your heart, as a seal upon your arm; for love is strong as death, passion fierce as the grave.' This has a fair claim to be the most significant verse in the Bible, because it sums up the question at the heart of Old and New Testaments: is love as strong as death – even stronger? Song of Songs is never simply about two lovers, but is always reflecting on the faithfulness of God and Israel at its most intimate and consuming.[5] The words 'Set me as a seal upon your heart' resonate with the covenants of Noah, Abraham, Moses and David. The words 'Set me as … a seal upon your arm' evoke with the image of a crucified man

[5] Ellen F. Davis, in her 'Reading the Song Iconographically', *Journal of Scriptural Reasoning*, 3/2 (August 2003), https://jsr.shanti.virginia.edu/back-issues/vol-3-no-2-august-2003-healing-words-the-song-of-songs-and-the-path-of-love/reading-the-song-iconographically/, describes three gardens: Eden, the temple and the garden of the Song of Songs:

> Pilgrimage to the Temple was conceived as a return to Eden, to life as it was meant to be, for a few days each year. But the story of the second garden, like the first, ends with exile. So I believe that the third garden of the lovers takes up the 'story line' that proceeds from the other two, and effects – or envisions – a resolution of the abiding problem of humanity's exile from the Garden of God.

The Song concerns the restoration of intimacy in relation to the three primary spheres of relationship: between God and humanity, between woman and man, and between human and non-human creation. Davis speaks of the Song as a series of icons – a departure from her description of it as a dream sequence in her earlier commentary. See also Davis, *Proverbs, Ecclesiastes, and the Song of Songs*.

with his bare arms stretched out in agony. The question 'Is love stronger than death?' hovers over the exile, and hovers over Good Friday. The Bible is a long, textured, yet ultimately unwavering answer 'Yes.' Thus does the Holy Spirit dwell in the life of Israel and the pages of the Old Testament, and render in the New Testament new configurations of old questions and old truths. Jesus is God's defining purpose; the Holy Spirit is God's unfolding purpose – 'like the master of a household who brings out of his treasure what is new and what is old' (Mt 13:52).

Our review of the story of Israel in the Old Testament has yielded two linked claims. The first is that the way to discern the activity of the Holy Spirit in the story is to identify the manner in which it anticipates the pattern of the Trinity's activity as definitively displayed in the incarnate life of Jesus. We have described a number of instances in which we may perceive this pattern at work. The second claim is that we may trace the ways in which being with emerges as that definitive pattern, in the manner in which God and Israel relate to one another, in the role of the covenant and in the form in which Israel orders its life, understands its created environment and relates to the nations. The Holy Spirit is that which anticipates (or later, imitates) Jesus in drawing people into relationships of being with God, one another and the wider creation, in covenant, community and communion. This is God's unfolding purpose.

CHURCH

The church names the body of people that seeks to imitate Christ's embodiment of the Trinity's covenant, community and communion, and is thus guided by the Holy Spirit to be with God, one another and creation in anticipation of the way it will be with the Trinity forever.[6] Being church is modelling being with Christ. The church sits in

[6] Compare Robert Jenson's more sober understanding: 'The church is nothing other than an appropriate if beforehand unpredictable sidestep in the fulfilment of the Lord's promises to Israel.' See his *Systematic Theology*, vol. 2: *The Works of God* (New York: Oxford University Press, 1999), 171.

relation to five formative factors. There is, first, Jesus, whose life is the template for being with God. There is, second, Israel, which precedes church in notions of inhabiting covenant, community and communion with God. There is, third, the eschaton, in which all that has strayed far, sometimes very far, from communion with God will be brought back into a relationship as portrayed by Jesus – one of being with God, one another and the renewed creation. There is, fourth, the realm of God, understood as the appearance in and through the church, by the agency of the Holy Spirit, of echoes and signs of Christ's ministry and of the heavenly hope. And there is, fifth, slightly differently, the realm of God, understood as the appearance by the agency of the Holy Spirit of echoes and signs of Christ's ministry in the world beyond the church. The first and third of these have been addressed in Chapter 8, and the second earlier in this chapter. Thus I here treat the fourth of these, and in the next section the fifth.

The challenge for the church, in the light of these five constitutive elements, is paradoxically to remain in the present tense. The church is called to imitate Jesus – to be the body of Christ ('The one who believes in me will also do the works that I do', Jn 14:12): but it is not called to *get back* to Jesus, to repristinate all things to a first-century milieu, adopting the customs and dress of the first apostles. The church is called to be grafted into Israel, and to remain in warm and respectful relation to those contemporary representatives of ancient Israel that do not recognise Christ: but it is not called to adopt every aspect of Jewish law, nor to ascribe to itself the status of uniquely chosen people, particularly when understood in a narrow nationalistic sense. The church is called to live God's future now, by anticipating today the way we shall be with God forever: but it is not called to disinvest from the commitments or crises of today, as if they were of no account given God's coming realm. Instead, the way disciples practise what it means to be with one another, the stranger and the creation is precisely their response to their calling and their witness to all who have taken the freedom of God's patience not yet to believe. Being with precisely means presence, attention, mystery, delight, participation, partnership, enjoyment and glory; it does not mean taking one's eyes off the ways the Holy Spirit is manifest today because one is so preoccupied by the ways the Holy Spirit has made Christ known yesterday and will inaugurate Christ's final coming tomorrow. Being with primarily means embodying presence, attention, mystery and so on with Christ: for church is the body of people called to evidence what it means for the crucified, risen and ascended Christ to be with us through the Holy Spirit.

A brief, clear-eyed, unsentimental, contemporary account of church is in order. Church requires people. Lest that seem obvious, that means people who may have been battered or bruised by church, rejected because of what they believe or who they are, instrumentalised in a power struggle, antagonised by something too clumsy or superficial to inspire commitment. Such people come to realise that they can think, regret, ponder, ruminate and resent alone. But if they want to do something in the world – to transform, overturn, uphold, resist or vindicate – they need to do it together. Then there is diversity. In a healthy community everyone finds that the things about them that had elsewhere been seen as deficits are here discovered as assets. Elsewhere some were dismissed as shy: here they become people who pay attention to detail and enjoy keeping records. Elsewhere they were overlooked as wheelchair-users: here they are cherished as tellers of stories and dreamers of dreams. Elsewhere they were marginalised as argumentative troublemakers: here they are admired as ones who challenge oppression and direct the community's attention to the forgotten and neglected. There is no ideal church. There is no church other than the one made up of ordinary people. The motto is 'Strive to be the best church you can be – don't become a failed version of another church.' Each person that makes up that community has their own story, their own strong and tender areas, their own imagination and ideas. The church that emerges is a result of the people and stories that constitute it.

Race, sexuality, gender, nationality – these identities, sometimes regarded as a threat to the status quo and thus as the pretext for persecution and exclusion, are often about digging down to find a 'true self', distinct from other people or groups or ways of being. When named by a third party they can become, or inherently be, a method of othering, alienating, excluding or devaluing. When proudly identified by a self they can be a form of finding, asserting, cherishing or affirming.[7] But church has in the end a different notion of identity. It recognises there is an important conversation about where each is coming from, not least to understand and address how frequently people can be ostracised, and be located by others that are diminishing. But the real conversation is not about where each is separately coming from. It is about where all are together going. When church is a story about where people are coming from, it gets mired in debates about sin and the fall and whether God intended it this way or whether all have themselves to blame and if some are more to blame than others. Church is fundamentally a story about where people are going – a society that lasts forever, has a place for everybody, is shaped by truth and justice and peace, is about the flourishing of every living being, where suffering is no more. Church is a dynamic present that today embodies the hope and practises the life of God's future – as mirror, foretaste, arrow, down payment and pledge.

Then church requires organisation. In Acts, this involves the sharing of possessions and the distribution of food. Organisation can simply mean a group of people that have neither the close relationships of an association nor the historic credibility and status of an institution. But an organisation is a group of people who have got organised: they have called in favours, used their contacts, drawn on their experience, sought extra training, pooled their skills, raised awareness, advertised widely, raised funds, experimented with their programme, started to envision the future and planned a critical path to getting there. Organising means discovering that, despite feeling

[7] For a lucid analysis that locates the contemporary absorption in identity in Jean-Jacques Rousseau's delineation of a true self distinct from our presenting self, see Francis Fukuyama, *Identity: Contemporary Identity Politics and the Struggle for Recognition* (London: Profile, 2018).

few and isolated, a group can develop power through momentum, movement, management and muscle. Beyond that, church needs humility: people have been at this for 2,000 years. The chances that everyone before us got this totally wrong and a new movement is going to get it totally right are small. Plenty of predecessors were manipulative, cruel and smallminded. But doubtless the large majority were well-intentioned, kind and generous. Yet humility cuts both ways. In every generation church faces fresh challenges, some of which it has never faced before: this is how those who have been neglected or overlooked for generations finally get their moment, because theirs are the skills and experience that matter most now. A church that says, 'This is the way we've always done it' is really saying, 'We're going to go on doing it the same way regardless of whether it's working or not.' That is complacency and laziness masquerading as faithfulness.

The most important part of church is to live in no power but the Spirit's power. The Spirit decides if praxis is going to be a sandwich under the bridge with those sleeping outside or a high mass in a crowded cathedral with the great and the good clustered around. The Spirit decides if ministry is going to be a group of first-generation second-language children reading poems of freedom or a crowd of recovering addicts singing of finding dignity. The Spirit decides if mission is all the colours of the rainbow gathering round to proclaim joy or a pensioner in a flat clinging on in bereavement and too stretched to fill the gas meter. Church tastes of humble bread, bread of trust, bread of truth, bread of toil; and it tastes of wine – wine of sacrifice, wine of suffering, wine of beauty, wine of glory. The only characteristic of church that matters is not wealth, size, power, numbers, grandeur or acclaim. It is whether church looks like Jesus: Jesus the tiny baby dependent on others for life; the young child longing to discuss truth in the temple; the growing adult spending thirty years being with the people of Nazareth before venturing to baptism at the Jordan; the resilient prophet in the desert resisting temptation; the astonishing Nazarene in the synagogue proclaiming jubilee; the transformative preacher saying, 'Blessed are the poor'; the mother hen embracing the outcast and the unloved; the lamb of God led to the slaughter, betrayed by his own, scorned by the powerful, forgiving his persecutors, raised from the dead. God sends the Holy Spirit to give the church everything it needs to look like Jesus: covenant, community, communion – in short, the constituents of being with.

Perhaps the most instructive gospel passage in relation to church is the parable of the talents. The talents look like natural abilities or great wealth; but they turn out to represent the Holy Spirit. The Holy Spirit is the talent Jesus leaves the church for the time until he returns. This parable is telling us that, in giving us the Holy Spirit, Jesus has left the church all the gifts it needs for the time between his first coming and his second. If the church does not enjoy those gifts, it will be found wanting. Success means imitating Jesus. Those who were given multiple of Jesus' gifts and put them to work looked like Jesus. Those gifts are scripture, sacraments, prayer and preaching, among others. Jesus is a boundlessly generous benefactor who goes away and gives us far more than we want or need to imitate him in his absence. Jesus proclaims what he means by church and God's realm. Church is the way Jesus works through the ministry of those who follow him, and God's realm is the way Jesus works in spite of the indifference and rejection of the world and the many failures of the church. Beyond the Holy Spirit, the talents also represent Jesus: in sending Jesus, the Father did not bury the Trinity's love for creation in a hole dug in the ground; instead, the Father took that love to market, to face the risks, sufferings and dangers of relationship and encounter. The five talents are, in the end, the incarnation – God risking everything to be with us: the five more talents are, in the end, Jesus' resurrection – the proof that we will be with God forever. The parable demonstrates how the Holy Spirit equips the church to live in the strength of Jesus' incarnation and anticipate the life of God's realm.

The Acts of the Apostles proliferates with accounts of how the Holy Spirit does exactly this. We may survey five such narratives, beginning with Pentecost (Acts 2:1–21). Pentecost does not abolish diversity: it does not result in everyone speaking the same language. It does not require all living in their own country and preserving an ideal of racial, linguistic or ideological purity. At Pentecost all speak their own language but hear others as if they were hearing their own language. So the joy and gift of diversity is preserved, but the misunderstanding and mistrust are gone. Pentecost demonstrates how God acts: not through terror, cruelty, destruction, division, but through unseen yet subversive wind, electric yet creative fire, the creation of relationship, understanding, joy and hope. Pentecost displays what politics looks like. Politics begins and ends with networks, neighbourhoods, relationships and communities: it is fundamentally about empowerment. Jesus said to his disciples as he left them, 'Stay in the city and you will be clothed with power from on high' (Lk 24:49). The Holy Spirit clothes ordinary fisherfolk with power to do unbelievable things.

Pentecost is a second resurrection. The closed doors of the gathering-place are like the closed tomb of the burial place. Pentecost demonstrates how the Holy Spirit overcomes adversity and discouragement: not through might, not through punishment, not through fear, not through power: God the Father sends the Son to disclose the secret of the universe – and sends the Spirit to turn that secret into wind and fire: rushing wind to send disciples out of closed doors and through barred windows and spread the world over. Tongues of fire turn disciples into living flames of love, give them words of gentleness, wisdom and truth, burn away their fear and distraction and forgetfulness and feel their hearts burning within them. Pentecost is a whole theology of revelation and transformation. Jesus is the full glory of God looking humankind full in the face and the utter fragility of humankind looking God full in the face. Jesus' cross is the utter manifestation of God shouldering the consequences of humankind's failure and folly. Jesus' resurrection is God bursting open the everlasting glory of eternal life. But the Acts narrative shows that the disciples still would not act on these discoveries. So the Holy

Spirit empowers disciples to do so. Even at this moment there is no question of working for: the Holy Spirit is with the disciples in wind and fire – but it is the disciples themselves that speak and witness.

A second moment in Acts where the Spirit equips the church to imitate Jesus' incarnation and anticipate the God's realm is in relation to the new community (Acts 2:43–47, 4:32–35). These are depictions of *koinōnia*, the Spirit-led community of being with inspired and made possible by Christ. The central of the seven activities described in Acts 2 is breaking bread. The list affirms the practice of worship ('spent much time in the temple ... praising God'), and this is a clear nod towards eucharistic celebration; but it is set in the context of a wider communion of goods and a wider community of those in need. This echoes Jesus' feedings of the multitudes and transformative meals. It also resonates with the understanding of covenant in Deuteronomy 15:4: 'There will be no one in need among you.' Thus covenant, community and communion converge in the conclusion to the account of Pentecost. The account also has an eschatological flavour: the common people in Jerusalem who called for Jesus to be crucified now seem to be united in one heart and mind around the sending of his Spirit; and the temple, so recently denounced as a den of robbers, is now a place of constant gathering for the new community of faith. These transformations are surely indications of the Spirit's work on a wider canvas than simply the direct outcomes of Pentecost.[8] Nevertheless, these two passages are rousing portrayals of a rarefied experience of being with that follows the model of Jesus and is directed by the Holy Spirit. The church has found its ideal character.

A third way the Holy Spirit enables the early church to embody Jesus is through the story of Stephen (Acts 6–7). At the Last Supper, Jesus tells his disciples what it means to be a Christian. He says, 'The one who believes in me will also do the works that I do and, in fact,

[8] They also offer an account of the Spirit's work in salvation much more extensive than convicting the believer of the salvific effect of Christ's death on the cross.

will do greater works than these' (Jn 14:12). These words suggest three stages of faith: believing in Jesus, doing what Jesus does, and doing greater things than Jesus. The account of Stephen addresses that mysterious third agenda. Stephen feeds the hungry: he turns being a Christian into concrete acts of love. Beautiful and surprising things start happening around him: for him, being a Christian means people should look at your life and see traces of grace, perceiving that you have a peace, presence, power and purpose that draw them towards God. Stephen faces opposition: for him, being a Christian means that influential people dislike what he is doing and what he is saying and what is happening around him. Stephen tells the story of God, of Israel and of Jesus: how Jesus is the heart of God, how God has tried every possible way of being close to humankind and will never let humanity go. For Stephen, being a Christian means to be grafted into the story of Israel and Jesus – to be a living witness, to tell the story of Jesus in word and deed, a story that makes no sense without Jesus. Finally, Stephen sees the glory. He gazes into heaven and sees 'the glory of God and Jesus standing at the right hand of God' (Acts 7:55). To see the glory he has to be ready to die as Jesus died. His witness maps the paradigm of how the Spirit will henceforth guide the church.

Stephen dies surrounded by the Jerusalem Council. Jesus is surrounded by the Jerusalem Council. Stephen dies filled with the Holy Spirit. Jesus is filled with the Holy Spirit. Stephen dies having been dragged out of the city. Jesus is led out of the city. As Stephen dies, he prays, 'Lord Jesus, receive my spirit' (Acts 7:59). As Jesus dies, he prays, 'Father, into your hands I commend my spirit' (Lk 23:46). Stephen prays, 'Lord, do not hold this sin against them' (Acts 7:60). Jesus prays, 'Father, forgive them; for they do not know what they are doing' (Lk 23:34). To be with Jesus is to face death, filled with the Spirit. This is what the story of Stephen declares about what it is to see the glory, and what it is to be with Jesus through the Spirit.

A fourth account through which the Spirit demonstrates that church means being with God in Christ is the conversion of Paul (Acts 9:1–20). Conversion has many critics. Some say Christianity is about discipline, resilience, faithfulness, restoration, failures, companions, growth and learning to walk through all weathers. It is not about one moment that solves and settles everything and does all the work for you. Others argue that conversion is a way of centring one's own experience, rather than God's grace. It colludes with the anthropocentrism that considers all that matters is one's own flourishing and one's own eternal life. A related criticism is that such focus on the self invariably obscures what faith entails for social relationships. Some also see conversion as a tactic of cultural imperialism, by which people are manipulated and coerced into adopting a faith position with which they do not truly feel comfortable by those who are using religion as a form of power, and who perceive somewhat rigid notions of what conformity entails. But Paul's conversion affirms why conversion remains key to a notion of being with Christ through the Spirit.

In Paul's life Christianity is a priceless blessing and a profound good. Through faith in what God has done it heals the wounds of his past. Through hope in what God will do it dismantles his anxiety about the future. Through the transformation of his past through faith and his future through hope it enables him to love in the present. This is not the thoughtless imposition of an imperialistic agenda: it is the humble sharing of deep truth. It is not shouting, 'You have to believe this to belong.' It is saying, 'Try this, it actually works.' Paul's conversion affirms a fundamental trust in the notion of change. Change is in the character of creation, and sometimes situations and people can change for the better. Conversion is the name for the way a person's heart and soul and actions can change for good when they encounter the embrace of God's ever-loving arms. This is what happens to Paul.

Paul's conversion demonstrates a truth at the heart of Christianity: out of the deepest hostility, the greatest good can come. Out of the exile came Israel's new insight that the God that they thought was *for* them was actually something much better – a God that was *with* them. Out of the horror of the cross and the tomb came Christ's glorious resurrection. Out of the threat-breathing, plot-calculating life of Saul of Tarsus came the Apostle Paul who brought Christianity to the gentiles. Through conversion, the Holy Spirit takes the world, society and every believer and turns the worst in each of them into the principal instruments of God's realm and channels of Christ's peace. It turns out in this story that the two people who are crucial to Paul's new discipleship are Ananias, who lays hands on Paul in Damascus, and Judas, in whose house in Damascus Paul stays. There is an irony in these two names. Ananias is the name of the most unfaithful of the early Christians, who withholds his money from the fellowship of faith (Acts 5:1–6). Judas is the name of the one who betrayed Jesus. In those two names Luke conveys the power of transformation at the heart of the Christian faith.

The Jerusalem Council (Acts 15) offers a paradigm of how the Holy Spirit guides the church when it faces inevitable disputes. Disputes are not presented as a sign of poor faith or of one party being manifestly in the wrong: the chapter ends with a double irony that Paul, who himself not only has a chequered history, but has also just argued for grace at Jerusalem, finds himself so opposed to working with John, called Mark, on account of his unreliability in Pamphylia that he countenances a split with Barnabas (Acts 15:37–40). The overall structure of the passage is a question of whom Jesus is calling the church to be with, and how the Holy Spirit directs believers to perceive whom Jesus is with that they may be so too. The crucial intervention comes when Peter reminds the council that it is through the grace of Jesus Christ that each of them comes to belong to the church – and it is that same grace that is drawing uncircumcised believers. Moreover these uncircumcised believers have received the Holy Spirit, just as Peter and the council have (Acts 15:8–11). The overall argument is that Christ is freely bestowing the blessings of being with God, and the Holy Spirit is alerting the church to perceive that its role is not to hamper the Spirit's activity and Christ's impulse and example. It is not the church's role to guard the text of scripture so fiercely that it inhibits the Holy Spirit from acting in ways that celebrate the ministry of Christ.[9] The grace of God in Christ caused the foundation of the world through the Trinity's desire to be with us in Christ. That same grace will eventually reach all humankind (Isa 2:1–4). The church's role is to imitate and celebrate it, not to inhibit and circumscribe it. This is what it means for the Spirit to 'guide the church into all truth' (Jn 16:13). [10]

GOD'S REALM

The realm (or kingdom) of God is the anticipation in existence of the drawing of creation into essence, in which the pattern of Christ's ministry is evoked by the work of the Holy Spirit in and beyond the church. In this section we shall concentrate on the 'beyond'.

Just as we saw the parable of the talents characterise church, so here we may see the healing of the paralysed man identify the realm of God (Mk 2:1–12). The context is that of defining Israel's predicament. Does Israel (represented by the paralysed man) need cleansing of the demon Rome, or are its problems not so much external as internal, and does it therefore need forgiveness? The four stretcher-bearers break through the barrier constituted by the roof – thereby modelling exactly what Jesus has done, breaking through the barrier between God and humanity, coming down from heaven to earth – moving from

[9] See Willie James Jennings, *Acts: A Theological Commentary on the Bible* (Louisville, KY: Westminster John Knox, 2017). Luke Timothy Johnson, in his *The Acts of the Apostles* (Collegeville, MN: Liturgical Press, 1992), 271, says, 'The text of Scripture does not dictate how God should act. Rather, God's actions dictate how we should understand the text of Scripture.'

[10] Willie James Jennings draws out the profound contemporary resonances of these conclusions. He speaks of special, cultural and desperate segregation. The issue of whom God is with inevitably implies the issue of whom we are called to be with. Noting Acts 15, he insists,

> Difference is best maintained, maintained in its life-giving realities, through communion with others. Only in life shared, joined, and exchanged in desire of being made permanent, can differences emerge in their deepest beauty – as invitations to the expansion of life and love. The Gentiles learn of Israel's story, enter its prayer life, learn its songs and in turn bring into Israel a world of difference that expands the contours of its life with God, and all of this through Jesus Christ, the bringer of life.
>
> *Acts*, 147

essence into existence, as I have described it. It is a gesture that resonates with Jesus because he recognises himself in it. It is thus a gesture in which we may perceive the Holy Spirit at work. It is a manifestation of the realm of God.

When in Tiananmen Square in Beijing in 1989 a man stood still while four tanks rumbled mercilessly towards him, he made a gesture of the realm of God, since Jesus stood still before the rumbling power of Roman oppression and the Jerusalem authorities' plotting, and Jesus faced a hostile regime by riding into Jerusalem on a donkey. When on 9/11 at the Twin Towers firefighters clambered up the stairs while thousands hurtled downwards to save their lives, they made gestures of the realm of God, since Jesus too put his life at stake to be with humankind to the very end, and described his ministry as like that of the good shepherd who left the ninety-nine to look for the one that was lost. When on board the passenger ferry *Herald of Free Enterprise* in Zeebrugge harbour in 1987 a man lay between two broken corridors and made himself a human bridge at the cost of his own life so that others could walk over him to safety, he made a gesture of the realm of God, since Jesus too laid down his body in mercy and love while others fled for their lives. When in Northern Ireland in 1987 Gordon Wilson forgave the IRA for killing his daughter Marie in the bombing at Enniskillen, he made a gesture of the realm of God, since Jesus too at the moment of his death asked his Father to forgive unsanctioned killing, and insisted that if we do not forgive we cannot expect forgiveness. When in Pennsylvania in 2006 in Amish Bart Township, members of the community reached out to and embraced the widow of the man who had shot and killed ten girls aged six to thirteen in their one-room schoolhouse, they made a gesture of the realm of God, because Jesus too taught us to pray 'forgive us … as we forgive those'. These people made gestures of the realm of God because, by the agency of the Holy Spirit, their actions resembled the ministry of Jesus. That work is not fundamentally about whether the person or movement involved is a Christian, or whether it is undertaken in explicit desire to imitate Christ. The common factors are the work of the Spirit, which blows where it wills, and the resemblance of the outcome to the ministry of Christ. That is how God's unfolding purpose comes about – sometimes through the church, sometimes beyond the church, sometimes despite the church.

The point is not to be confident that the church can accurately identify the motives and meanings of every gesture of any person or group of people in the world, particularly when the story is in motion. It is to recognise the teleology of being with – that there is an integrity and validity to being with that is not limited to whether the participants are Christians or not but expands to whether the Holy Spirit is at work or not and whether the activity echoes or imitates Jesus or not. The fruit of the Spirit is 'love, joy, peace, patience, kindness, generosity, faithfulness, gentleness, and self-control' (Gal 5:22–23). These are qualities that contribute to covenant, community and communion – that make possible the practices and exhibit the dimensions of being with. Where they are found, the Spirit is at work. The Holy Spirit makes the Jesus of yesterday and the Jesus of forever present today in time-honoured and surprising ways. The time-honoured ways are in the sacraments of baptism and Eucharist, in the practice of personal and corporate prayer, in the contemplation of scripture and in gestures of mercy, courage and grace. The surprising ways are in the generosity of a stranger, in the apparent catastrophe that turns out for the best and in the Spirit's habit of working through the most surprising people.

A neglected but crucial passage in highlighting the work of the Holy Spirit in this dispersed yet Christocentric way is the genealogy in Matthew (Mt 1:1–16). God works through Tamar (Gen 38), Rahab (Josh 2), Ruth, and Bathsheba (2 Sam 11–12; 1 Kings 1). Each of them is an outsider to what is understood as 'God's people', yet each plays a vital role in the way the Holy Spirit construes the incarnation. In analogous ways the Holy Spirit draws forth individuals and communities to model and advance God's realm: the significance of such actions may not be visible or recognised in this generation, and may not surface for generations to come; but just as the conclusion of the genealogy in Christ shows the underlying teleology of the work of the Spirit, so that work continues to point to Christ in his embodiment in Galilee or his everlasting presence in eternity. Hence the expression 'It is better to fail in a cause that will finally succeed than to succeed in a cause that will finally fail.' The Spirit's work and God's realm in general is one that is teleologically perceived and eschatologically ordered.[11] The ascended Christ seeks to gather up to himself all things in heaven and earth (Eph 1:10), and thus any act of so unifying, assembling joy from diversity and finding truth through difference is an anticipation and imitation of Christ's ascended role. If in God's realm nothing is wasted (Jn 6:13) and all are reincorporated into the story, the Spirit's activity of shaping that realm begins from the moment of creation.

Acts 10.44–48 is a story of surprise. Peter is telling gentiles that God shows no partiality. Then the Holy Spirit falls upon everybody listening. There follows some controversy over the proper sequence of events: should one believe before one becomes a Christian – and does one then receive the Spirit? Or can one receive first and then believe and subsequently become? The story seems clearly to be encouraging the church not to get stuck on the sequence. The Holy Spirit runs on its own timetable. The Acts of the Apostles narrates a series of encounters with people, each of which challenges what the church assumes the Holy Spirit can or cannot do. The Ethiopian eunuch is a

[11] Edwin Chr. van Driel intriguingly rephrases the question 'Why does God delay the eschaton so long after the resurrection and ascension?' into the somewhat different 'Why did God start so early?' 'Here we are, still in the midst of history, and we already taste and see a transformation that was promised only for the end. . . . The surprise of resurrection, ascension and Pentecost is that the eschaton has moved from the future into the present.' Edwin Chr. van Driel, '"What Is Jesus Doing?" – Christological Thoughts for an Anxious Church and Tired Pastors', in Edwin Chr. van Driel, ed., *What Is Jesus Doing? God's Activity in the Life and Work of the Church* (Downers Grove: IVP Academic, 2020), 1–23 at 13. Van Driel suggests thus that God is making us participants in preparing the ground for and foreshadowing the eschaton – though he is careful to emphasise that the eschaton will still contain many surprises, and much that we thought would 'make the cut' will not. But his key point is that this means that 'in the Lord our works were not in vain' (15).

gentile man whose mutilation seems to contravene the stricture of Deuteronomy 23:1. Yet the Spirit leads him into belonging. Then Saul, a Pharisaic persecutor of Christians, comes to belong. Then Cornelius, a Roman commander, who was both a gentile and a member of an army that kept the Jews from restoring God's promise: he too comes to belong. The only issue is whether the church can keep up with the Holy Spirit. The Acts of the Apostles is not just a narrative of the Holy Spirit's sudden and unpredictable awakenings. It is also a story of the slow formation of a *koinōnia* of Jew and gentile, slave and free, men and women, oppressor and oppressed: of the slow becoming of the body of Christ out of a people who had known many dividing walls of hostility. The Holy Spirit is about receiving, but also about becoming. It is also about believing – but not only about believing. It is about offering epiphanies of the realm of God in neglected, forgotten, unheralded and forsaken places, through and among oppressed, rejected, unseen and undervalued people.

The Holy Spirit makes Jesus present, and makes present everything he achieved and represented. This happens in established ways. But the church has an assumption and a suspicion that constantly need disrupting. The assumption is that the Holy Spirit is under the church's control. The suspicion is that God is in short supply. The Holy Spirit interrupts both the assumption and the suspicion. The Holy Spirit does not simply work in the believer's heart from the moment of conversion: the Holy Spirit is at work in every living person all the time, fostering the paths that lead to peace, the practices of being with, the reconciling gestures that repair the world. The Holy Spirit is all the time and in every way seeking to stir imaginations and change hearts and move souls to be in utter relationship. Church is the definitive way the Spirit is at work in the world. Christians have repeatedly assumed that this meant that God was working only through the church and not in any other way. But that is to be too inflated in one's notion of the church and too limited in one's understanding of how the Spirit works. The Spirit constantly sends the church strangers, who turn out to be angels, and who humble the church by enabling it to recall that it is not coterminous with God's realm. But as we have just seen, the work of the Spirit is by no means limited to the life of the church.

God's realm is not simply about occasional surprises and epiphanies. It can be about genuine common efforts to do social good that go across boundaries of religion, class and culture. It is alive, for example, when initiatives are made to enable people with disabilities to get in and join in so all their gifts can enable an organisation truly to flourish. To achieve such a goal requires collaboration with people inside and outside an organisation to make a workplace that anticipates heaven, where diversity is a source of life, opportunity is in the air, and the partnership dimension of being with is tangible. Such activity is the Holy Spirit making God's realm visible in ways that reflect Jesus' pattern of empowerment and inclusion. God's realm is alive in a neighbourhood where there has been knife crime and gangs are moving in – when the local imam and rabbi say, 'Let us act together on this', and a few weeks later there is a homework after-school club with wi-fi access that meets at a different religious building each day of the week, and young people get to know more about each other's life and worship. Such places and moments when things happen and people come together are like church, and sometimes better than church, but are not church – yet they offer a glimpse of heaven. This is the Holy Spirit revealing and displaying God's realm.[12]

[12] Rowan Williams describes what being with means in 'realm of God' terms, in the kind of encounter through which I am suggesting the Holy Spirit acts, in this case not so much in reconciliation or response to hardship, but in facing the truth.

> How do you learn to confront the fact, say, of racism in British society? Not by information, not by words. They produce the kind of pain we cannot handle, and we take refuge in ideological denial of the facts of power in Britain. To confront both the suffering of the victims of racism and my own *de facto* involvement in and responsibility for this, without fantasising and self-lacerating guilt, requires *specific encounter and the possibility of its continuance*; not reconciliation, but a kind of *commitment without evasion*. The 'reading' of our situation in certain terms rests on existing small-scale transformations – and also, of course, assists in the creation of further transformation.
>
> *On Christian Theology*, 181, italics added

The scriptural book that strives most assiduously to perceive the realm of God is Revelation. In the final scenes of the book we may discern the characteristics of God's realm in both eschatological and contemporary perspective (Rev 21–22). John sees a new heaven and a new earth, and the holy city, the new Jerusalem, coming down out of heaven from God. The city has no temple, and is in perpetual light. Its gates are perpetually open. A river runs through it, and on either side of the river is the tree of life, whose leaves are for the healing of the nations. This tells us several things about God's ultimate purpose. A 'new earth' demonstrates that creation is a permanent part of God's vision, not a temporary theatre for humankind. The earth is not a means to an end. Embodiment is part of what will be taken up into essence. Relating to one another in our diversity and relating to the creation in its complexity is not going to pass away. A new 'Jerusalem' means that God's ultimate realm is in continuity with the Jewish people, with the covenant, with the temple, with the whole story of the chosen people before God. God neither extinguishes the earth to make a new world nor sidelines Israel to make the church. God has not forgotten the covenant. But the new Jerusalem has no temple: Jesus is present and worship is constant and reconciliation with God is complete; so there is no need for a temple. God has healed Jerusalem. Jerusalem is a city. The Bible is ambivalent about cities: but in God's realm all is incorporated. God brings the garden into the city: a river and the tree of life and twelve kinds of fruit and leaves on the tree. God doesn't wipe out the history of human interaction in the city. The tension between city and garden that runs through the Bible is resolved by the creation of a garden city.

This is how God's realm works. God does not destroy the earth: God makes the earth new. God does not reject Israel: God makes a new Jerusalem, but one that reflects the presence of Jesus. God does not choose between the garden and the city: God brings the garden

These notions of specific encounter and commitment without evasion are vivid portrayals of being with the stranger.

into the city. Here we see the Holy Spirit's work in opening up God's realm. Scarcity is replaced by abundance: God's light is permanent and sufficient. Preservation and exclusion are replaced by diversity: the tree of life produces twelve kinds of fruit. Fear and jealous protection are replaced by inclusion and welcome: the gates of the city never shut. Destruction of the rest of creation is replaced by harmony: the garden and the city are reunited. Nothing is ultimately discarded. Discarding and destroying are ruled out. The Holy Spirit works with what is, and through attention, mystery, delight and enjoyment, celebrates and renews: all is finally healed. Being with is a way, a truth and a life ultimately extended to everything.

10 God's Unbreakable Purpose

The purpose of this chapter is to draw together the whole argument of the book thus far to face the defining question that it must answer, and through that answer to unfurl the full significance of incarnational theology. The question is, what happens when God's purpose to be with us now and forever meets with a refusal? As we have seen, addressing the question of humankind's alienation from God, itself and the wider creation is not, from the point of view of incarnational theology, the central dynamic of Christianity, as it is in conventional accounts. But the utter with-ness of Jesus inevitably encounters the profound, widespread and powerful resistance to God's embrace: and the truth of God is thereby revealed as never before. Jesus does not 'come to die': yet in his death and resurrection he exposes the forces that oppose him and displays the dynamic that sent him and settles the only questions about existence and essence that ultimately matter.

The resources accumulated in the foregoing account have not been assembled simply to address the question of what happens when the tidal wave of God's desire to be with us meets with resistance, opposition and rejection. This interface is not the principal focus of incarnational theology, which is, as I have emphasised, about God, and is not preoccupied with human shortcomings and jeopardy. Nonetheless all that has been explored in the foregoing chapters becomes vital for understanding how God encounters hostility.

The issue of how God's will to be with us overcomes our opposition is generally known as the doctrine of the atonement. It should be now be clear why the notion of atonement sits uneasily within the account of God and God's purposes I have outlined above.[1] Existing theories of the atonement are problematic in regard to incarnational theology for a number of reasons. Such theories tend to contravene the theocentric principle by placing human guilt and mortality, and consequently sin, evil and death, in the centre of the story. They are inclined to downplay covenant by airbrushing Israel out of the story: Israel's only significant role is as a failed attempt to redeem humankind. (The blame is attributed to Israel, not to God.) It is a tendency of these approaches to undervalue community by focusing largely or entirely on humankind rather than the wider creation. These theories can pay so much attention to overcoming individual guilt that in most cases they have no notion of any engagement with, participation in or transformation of society as a whole. Such theories tend to impoverish communion by concentrating on the rescue of individual human beings, with little or no account of what kind of eternal life they are destined for, other than that it is not damnation. They can be inclined to theorise in such a way that downplays or eradicates mystery.

Atonement theories sometimes contravene God's sovereignty and freedom by making God subject to a notion of justice or honour, thus allowing the metaphor to control the true author of the story. One consequence of this is that they can fail to align God's means and God's ends, distorting the character of God by, for example, opposing the Father to the Son in some scheme of egregious punishment. In regard to the gospels, they can tend to disregard Jesus' life and resurrection and concentrate solely on his death, making unclear what is the significance of the one who went to the cross. Atonement theories are generally preoccupied with a working-for model of God's activity that not only obscures God's purpose to be with, but almost perceives working for as God's assigned role, in ways that make any transition to other forms of relationship in eternity

[1] In short, atonement belongs to the inner arch of a story that begins with the fall and concludes with the cross – whereas the story of incarnational theology belongs to the outer arch of a story that begins with the Trinity and ends with heaven. See Andrew Louth's image of the two arches in Chapter 4 above.

unachievable – since in eternal life there is no working for to do. And if that were not enough, such theories tend to pay little or no attention to the fact that, for all their drama and conviction, the world seems as full of sin and evil as ever, suffering abides despite human efforts to suppress it, and death has not lost its dominion: in short, if the aim was to reverse the effects of the fall, those effects appear to be still in full swing.

To name all these shortcomings is not to say that every account of atonement is prone to all of them; but to recognise that, by regarding the incarnation as subsequent upon the fall, every atonement account is likely to find itself in one or several of these unsatisfactory places. In short, atonement theories strive to address one problem but invariably end up creating several others. None of which is to deny that the cross of Christ is pivotal to understanding who Jesus is and how God is with us. But one can perceive this only if one lets go of a goal Jesus needs to achieve and stops trying to fit the events of his passion into a preconceived (or foreordained) model of what salvation is and requires. The account of Jesus' passion, death, resurrection and ascension offered in this chapter begins with no such preconceived model. Yet the cross is at least as significant in the account below as in any atonement theory.[2]

PASSION AND CRUCIFIXION

The narrative of the Trinity is the overarching story of everything – and the centre of the passion story. It is characterised by three persons being with one another in utter and mutual relationship. This is the relationship whose generativity and effervescence brought about incarnation and creation: this is the relationship into which the

[2] This is a subtler point than it may appear. Robert Jenson, in his *Systematic Theology*, vol. 1, 179, points out that his account of Jesus decentres the cross, in a way he finds also in Pannenberg, Moltmann and Kasper. If I decentre the cross, I do so by insisting that the cross can be considered only in close relation to and continuity with the whole sweep of God being with us as described in this book – something most atonement theories signally fail to do.

Trinity will one day draw the whole of existence. The purpose of this Trinity is to extend to creation the quality of being with that belongs to its inner-Trinitarian relationships. Then there is Jesus. Jesus is the way the Trinity extends its purpose of being with to humankind and the creation. Jesus models what being with entails in every aspect of his conception (Mary being with the Holy Spirit), birth (the Holy Family being with shepherds, magi, and the heavenly host) and ministry (being with the disciples, the crowds and the authorities). All the while he is with the Father and the Holy Spirit, as his periodic conversations and withdrawals for prayer indicate.[3]

We may consider the other characters in Jesus' passion in three groups. First there are the disciples, whose lives are punctuated by moments of revelation ('You are the Messiah', Mt 16:16), devotion ('Let us also go, that we may die with him', Jn 11:16), self-absorption ('Grant us to sit, one at your right hand and one at your left, in your glory', Mk 10:37), forgetfulness ('How can one feed these [4,000] people with bread here in the desert?', Mk 8:4), duplicity ('He kept the common purse and used to steal what was put into it', Jn 12:6) and vainglory ('Though all become deserters because of you, I will never desert you', Mt 26:33). Alongside them are an assortment of those

[3] Bruce L. McCormack, in his *The Humility of the Eternal Son*, 104–05, refers to Karl Barth's 'Christological objectivism', by which

> What is accomplished by God in Jesus Christ is the reality of reconciliation and redemption, not merely its possibility – a possibility to be made actual later by the work of the Spirit. No, the work of the Spirit in awakening an individual to faith and obedience does not make Christ's work effective; it simply brings Christ's work in its efficacy to conscious awareness so that the individual is redirected, reoriented to a future of which they had been unaware'

What I am proposing here is a corresponding kind of objectivism – an objectivism of Christ's being with us, which is valid even though, in his profound isolation on the cross, we are not with him. McCormack points out that this is how Barth manages to combine divine passibility with divine immutability: 'God does nothing in Christ that is not already contained in what God is essentially; God is the experiencing subject in Christ of nothing that is not anticipated in what God is essentially. God is, therefore, not changed when God suffers in Christ on our behalf' (105). This sounds marvellous, but to say this requires sin to be an inherent part of the story of God – which is too high a price to pay.

integral to Jesus' circle, such as Mary Magdalene, those drawn into the story, like Simon of Cyrene and even the criminal whom Jesus says will today be with him in paradise, and those mysteriously in the background, like the man who ran off without his linen cloth (Mk 14:51–52). Second there are those who conspired against Jesus or colluded in his execution. These include the chief priests, the elders, scribes and Sanhedrin, Herod Antipas and Judas, together with the crowd gathered for the festival. Along with these are the bystanders who hurl ironic abuse at the crucified Jesus, and the closet supporters Joseph of Arimathaea and Nicodemus. Third there are the Romans: Pilate, the procedural bureaucrat exposed by the question 'What is truth?', the soldiers dragooned to whip and crucify and the ones moved by something deeper: Pilate's wife, and the centurion at the foot of the cross.

Among the many poignant moments in the passion account, we may at this stage consider three. In Gethsemane, Jesus says, 'Abba, Father, for you all things are possible; remove this cup from me; yet, not what I want, but what you want' (Mk 14:36). Jesus is immersed in the utter with-ness of the inner-Trinitarian relations. These are his principal conversation partners. He has come to Jerusalem and not walked away from what looks set to be a violent confrontation with only one outcome for him. He displays his complete humanity in being daunted by what lies in store, and his full divinity by engaging conversation within the Trinity. This is the moment perhaps above all others when we see him utterly with both God and humankind. The question is, can he continue to be completely with both the Trinity and humankind, given what he is facing? This is the dynamic at the heart of the passion account. The gospels have portrayed Jesus being utterly with both God and humankind to this point: that is the demonstration of God's purpose. But can it continue, in the face of betrayal, denial, desertion, scheming, hatred, cruelty, violence and torture? The immediately subsequent event – Jesus finding the disciples asleep (Mk 14:37–41) – is not propitious. If Jesus can no longer be with humankind, the whole divine purpose, inhabited by the

Trinity, set in motion in creation, embodied in incarnation and set to be completed in the eschaton – that whole divine purpose will be discredited, undermined, evacuated. For the divine purpose to be opposed *by humankind* is not new; but for the divine purpose to be abandoned *by God* is confounding. Yet this is what Jesus is weighing in his mind and heart in Gethsemane. Meanwhile if Jesus can no longer be with God, the consequences are more devastating still. The Trinity is no longer the Trinity: the rupture between Father and Son cleaves the utter communion of with and creates a chasm of indescribable catastrophe. Thus Jesus' agony in Gethsemane, and throughout the passion, is not just the conflict between his divine and human natures but his anguish in trying to be with the Father while still being with humankind and the creation.

When Jesus stands before Pilate, he is asked if he is the king of the Jews. Jesus replies, 'My kingdom is not from this world' (Jn 18:36). Again we have a conversation, in which this time Jesus is fully human, standing bedraggled before Pilate, yet fully God, speaking about the essence he shares with the Father and the Holy Spirit, and how existence, in this case the tortured land of Israel, under Roman occupation, was far from resembling that heavenly realm. Here we see a stage beyond Gethsemane. If Gethsemane posed the question 'Can Jesus continue to be with both humankind and the Trinity in the face of threats and hostility?', Pilate's trial portrays how far apart those two realities are: the one a realm where Jesus is delighted in and enjoyed, the other where he is tossed from one threatened leader to another nervous one, each looking to dispose of him as effectively as possible. To be at the mercy of such leaders is to dwell in a reality where truth has ceased to exist. Thus Jesus exposes how far creation in general and humankind in particular have strayed from the utterly mutual enjoyment of the persons of the Trinity. The forces that condemn Jesus represent the antithesis of *with*. It would be hard not to hear Jesus' words as a wistful desire to rest in the simplicity of being with the Trinity without the demands and agony of being with creation and in particular humankind. But this only enriches our understanding of the challenge Jesus undertakes in being with both – a challenge getting sharper as he enters further into his passion.

When Jesus is nailed to the cross, he says, 'Father, forgive them; for they do not know what they are doing' (Lk 23:34). Our eyes are inevitably drawn to the complex and heavily laden word 'forgive'. But that would be to miss the fact that Jesus is again having an inner-Trinitarian conversation. He is uttering a prayer to the Father. Jesus does not say '*I* forgive *you*.' He says, '*Father*, forgive *them*.' How can he forgive, when he's being mercilessly executed? He is calling on the Father to do what he cannot do. In his greatest moment of suffering, as he begins his sojourn on the cross, he takes refuge in being with the Father and cannot bear to be in conversation with the bystanders, the leaders, the soldiers or those crucified beside him. Meanwhile some are culpably incapable of being with him at his hour of greatest need: the disciples have betrayed, denied and fled. Luke is providing a comprehensive account of human failure – as if it were a painting where everyone's expressions were frozen in time. Some actively sought Jesus' death; some went along with it; some were under orders or threats; some watched; some ran away; some mocked. It is the full range of human reaction: no one escapes. All of them are part of the word 'them'.[4] In different ways, none of them know what they are doing. Practically no one – not the disciples, not the crowd, not those he has healed or forgiven – is able to be with Jesus, even as he is losing his life to be with them.

Here, on the cross, we have an agonising contrast between being with and being without. Jesus is the epitome of being with – but the forces arrayed against him are the embodiment of all that inhibits that condition. He beholds, face to face, the nature of sin. Sin is being intentionally without God, living as if you are your own god, using God for your own purposes or turning something inferior into your god, constructing a whole world around your own divinity or the divinity of what you have chosen to regard as your god, telling a false

[4] 'God was with us, with us his enemies. . . . He was with us as one of us. His word became flesh of our flesh, blood of our blood.' Barth, *Church Dogmatics*, vol. I/1, 115.

story to locate you in the right and justify your actions. Pilate's god is the Roman Empire, maybe the Emperor himself, maybe simply a stable system of domination and rewards in which Pilate has achieved seniority, and is focused on keeping it. The god of the members of the Sanhedrin is their own survival in the dangerous conditions of the occupation, and their privileged status as legitimisers of Roman authority.[5] But that sin crosses over into evil when it turns palpable falsehood into fake truth: thus the chief priests say, 'We have no king but the emperor' (Jn 18:15). This is being intentionally without God.

If sin is being intentionally without God, suffering is being without comfort. Jesus experiences profound suffering on the cross. It is not the only, or the greatest, of the being-withouts; but it is profound, nonetheless. What sustains us through suffering? Food and drink; but Jesus is offered vinegar. Companionship; but Jesus is completely isolated. The hope that it will pass; but Jesus knows he will not be taken down from the cross until he is dead. Solidarity; but his disciples have fled. Fundamentally, the comfort of the second person of the Trinity comes from the third person of the Trinity, the Holy Spirit, the comforter, who makes the Father present to the Son: but not here; not now – at least we have no testimony to tell us so. There is naught for Jesus' comfort. There is only open-ended suffering: physical, mental, emotional, spiritual. If suffering is being without comfort, death is being without everything. It is being without breath – with no signs of life, no vital energy – crossing over from the animate to the inanimate – creation without spark. It is being without connectedness, with no sense of anyone or anything else, no with, no together, no senses. It is being without consciousness, without any mental faculty, without awareness, reflection, sense of self or others. It is being without a body, without physicality, without anything to recognise as oneself, without identity, without history, without future, without even the

[5] 'He died as three times excluded: by the Jewish law of its tribal nation; by the Roman universal law of empire; by the democratic rule of the mob.' Milbank, *Being Reconciled*, 96. We might add a fourth – excluded by his disciples.

present.[6] It is utterly not being – yet not 'not having-been', but 'having been but utterly no longer being'.

But the greatest isolation is beyond even those. It is expressed in Jesus' cry of dereliction: 'My God, my God, why have you forsaken me?' (Mk 15:34). This is being without the Father, and thus being not-God – being without the with that is the very essence of God.[7] If one could speculate what is in Jesus' mind at this moment, perhaps it could be the cascade of Old Testament testimony that promises God will never leave Israel. 'It is the Lord your God who goes with you. He will not fail you or forsake you' (Deut 31:6). Sentiments almost identical to this are found twenty-five times in the Old Testament.[8] Yet at this most significant of all moments, it seems the Father is not with Jesus.[9] The import of this separation is so great that we need to pause and take stock of all its dimensions.

We should spell out what it means for the Trinity that has become incarnate and created to embody being with, then to find it is not with itself. The covenant is between God and humankind: no one has contemplated that God could be an insecure covenant partner on account of the Trinity not being with itself. How can there be communion if the Trinity is not itself in communion? Here the eight

6 'Death is not really an event. It is eventless, a non-event.' Jüngel, *God as the Mystery of the World*, 363.

7 'In this event God allows the world and humanity to take part in the history of the inner life of [the] Godhead.' Barth, *Church Dogmatics*, vol. IV/1, 215.

8 The contrast is heightened when compared with the completeness expressed in the Fourth Gospel. 'Upon the cross, in the Gospel of John (which deliberately alludes in its opening verse to the opening verse of Genesis: "In the beginning"), he says "It is finished" or "It is perfected," with Pilate having said a few verses earlier, "Behold the human being" (John 19:30, 5).' See John Behr, 'From Adam to Christ: From Male and Female to Being Human', in Thomas Arentzen, Ashley M. Purpura and Aristotle Papanikolaou, eds., *Orthodox Tradition and Human Sexuality* (New York: Fordham University Press, 2022), 303–19 at 304–05.

9 As Kathryn Tanner points out, 'As Augustine himself maintains in his earlier books, the persons of the trinity are never without one another.' This observation makes the cry of dereliction even more poignant. See her *Christ the Key*, 5. Eberhard Jüngel in his *God as the Mystery of the World*, 361, makes a similar point: 'The special severity of Jesus' God-forsakenness on the cross is the experience of that God-forsakenness by an existence which derived wholly from God.'

dimensions of being with amplify the intensity of the drama. A separation between Father and Son evacuates *presence*, because Jesus at this moment evidently finds himself utterly alone. This is a moment when Jesus cannot reach the Father; nor can the Father reach Jesus. It empties *attention*, since for the first time the Father and the Son seem to have lost sight of each other. It has no *delight*, because this has become a scene of total deficit, with no redeeming feature (with the exception in different accounts of the good thief and the moved centurion, and perhaps Mary and the beloved disciple), no silver lining. It most obviously has no *participation*, because the foundational with of the Father–Son relationship has gone. It lacks all *partnership*, because any sense that Jesus has that each person of the Trinity has a key role to play in the embodiment of God's purpose disappears in the single word 'forsaken'. And there is no *enjoyment*, because enjoyment celebrates that which lasts forever – and this is the moment when it seems nothing does, even those relationships whose nature is to be forever. *Glory* has departed: there is darkness over the earth (Mk 15:33) – but no *shekinah*, no cloud of the Father's presence. There is only one aspect of the breadth of being with as articulated in this book that this moment does not disrupt. What alone abides is *mystery*: a notion that may expand into this most acute of all crises. Mystery alone embraces even this most horrifying eventuality. It is mystery that, of all the dimensions of being with, at this tremulous moment offers some hope. But before speaking of hope, we need to name the three kinds of terror Jesus' cry of dereliction evokes.

In the first place it takes the Trinity into unknown territory. Being with is what the Trinity *is* – what essence is. The Father, Son and Spirit have no identity detached from one another. God is *one*: there is no notion, either outside God, or more seriously within God, of what being not-one could possibly mean. There can be attenuation of with – on a human level, lovers can argue, lose their tempers, be furious, even walk out on each other, even though deep down they know they are bound to each other in faithfulness, care for their common concerns and affection, let alone desire. But Christ's cry of dereliction is not an attenuation of with – it is separation, detachment, fissure, rupture, division. There is no suggestion that the Father is separated from the Spirit, and the bond that both the Father and the Son share with the Spirit is what is keeping the Trinity from disintegration at this moment. But the Father and the Son are not with each other. We do not know what this means for the Trinity: neither does the Trinity. It is unimaginably bleak.[10]

In this light, Jesus' words 'Father, into your hands I commend my spirit' (Lk 23:46) are particularly intriguing. Rather as his words 'Woman, here is your son' and 'Here is your mother' (Jn 19:26–27) are often seen as creating the church, we may take the reference to the Father in the context of the spirit (or Spirit[11]) as a commendation to the Father that the Spirit will ensure that the Trinity does not disintegrate in the face of the death of Jesus and of the (temporary) separation of the Father and the Son.[12] It begs the question, did Jesus know, at his moment of death, that he would be raised on the third day? The predictions of the passion are eager to assure us that he did. But the witness of the cross, particularly the bleakness of the cry of dereliction, seems to contradict those predictions. We may at least say that, as in Gethsemane, so on the cross, any confidence that Jesus had that the Father and the Spirit would see him through his trials seems to

[10] It is important to note that what I am describing here is not *kenosis*, the self-emptying of the Son, nor patri-passianism, the suffering of the Father – two themes much explored in the tradition. This is about a rupture within the profound being with relations of the Trinity. To use a phrase from Sergei Bulgakov, this is the metaphysical Golgotha underlying the historical Golgotha.

[11] The Greek word is *pneũmá*, which is the word used for the Holy Spirit.

[12] My point that the Spirit upholds both the Father and the Son at this moment has some similarities to the argument of Eberhard Jüngel in his *God as the Mystery of the World*, 368. Jüngel cites the notion of the *vinculum caritatis*, which preserves the unity of Father and Son despite their separation, although he does not suggest as I do that it is precisely the Holy Spirit that restores the relationship of Father and Son at the resurrection. Augustine's notion, also known as *vinculum amoris*, is found in Athanasius, Basil of Caesarea and Gregory of Nazianzus. See David Williams, *Vinculum amoris: A Theology of the Holy Spirit* (Bloomington, IN: iUniverse, 2004), 15–18. See also Bruce L. McCormack's account of Jüngel in his *The Humility of the Eternal Son*, 162–77. Jüngel's account of the cross, though in some respects like mine, heavily emphasises the event of crucifixion as God-forsakenness according to the Jewish law.

have become faint if not obscured altogether. Indeed we cannot face the true extent to which Jesus on the cross is with us unless we are prepared to face the reality that he experienced utter abandonment by both those around him and the Father. Luke's portrayal, by which we can perceive he is not abandoned by the Spirit, helps us understand how the Trinity's integrity is profoundly jeopardised, with indescribably catastrophic potential consequences, yet how the Spirit finds a way to be with both the Father and the Son, and in doing so, points the way to how this greatest of all crises will come to be resolved over the course of this most holy of weekends. The cross in the heart of God is indeed there, but that cross is a sign of how profound is the Trinity's commitment to be with us and how much it cost God and how close that commitment brought God to unimaginable calamity.[13]

In the second place Jesus' forsakenness jeopardises not just existence, but essence. This is not just a catastrophic problem for creation; it is an unthinkable disaster for that which lies beyond creation – God's purpose to draw all things into essence to dwell with the Trinity forever. How can this happen if there is no Trinity? How can the Father or the Spirit uphold creation without the ministry of the Son? It seems everything is lost. There is no precedent for a fissure in the Trinity, and thus no template for how such a rupture could be healed – if at all. When theologians have spoken about the 'crucified God' they have tended to suggest that the suffering of the Son impacts the Father and the Spirit also, such that there is a cross in the heart of God; and then there have been debates about whether this elevates suffering too much, making it permanent, even eternal, in a way that undermines key convictions about the Trinity. But less energy has gone where perhaps it needs to go: to reflect on how this puncture in the coinherence of the Father and the Son can possibly be repaired –

[13] 'There was a cross in the heart of God before there was one planted on the green hill in Jerusalem. And now that the cross of wood has been taken down, the one in the heart of God abides, and it will remain so long as there is one sinful soul for whom to suffer.' Charles Allen Dinsmore, *Atonement in Literature and Life* (Boston: Mifflin and Co., 1906) 232, quoted in D. M. Baillie, *God Was in Christ: An Essay on Incarnation and Atonement* (London and Boston: Faber and Faber, 1986), 194. For further reflections see my *A Cross in the Heart of God*.

how being without the one who in essence one is with can be transformed; and even more pressing, what it means for existence and essence to continue when the ground of their being is disrupted and damaged so searingly. Essence is forever, and the Trinity is coterminous with essence: but the Trinity is punctured, its inherent relationships severed. All things – all eternity – teeter over a precipice.

In the third place, it seems that the fissure in the Trinity creates a vacuum – a vacuum that evil and sin may fill. Have evil and sin prevailed? The factors that inhibit being with pervade the scriptural story and constantly lurk at the door. But nowhere else is there the shuddering possibility that they may become the predominant elements in existence. And if they gain such purchase in existence, could they even permeate into essence? Could the Trinity be not only damaged, but challenged, ontologically? To contemplate a separation between Father and Son begs the question of whether existence can continue if not upheld by the Trinity in all its diversity: the prospect of utter non-existence, of existence that comes to an end and is not translated into essence, is terrifying. But the scenario by which existence is given over to sin and in which evil casts its fake truth so broadly that no perception of the truth of God incarnate survives – this is perhaps an even worse horror, if such is possible. We are navigating the outer reaches of what can be contemplated.[14]

[14] Bruce McCormack, in his *The Humility of the Eternal Son*, 270–71, points out that there have seemed only two possible options for understanding the subject of Jesus' death in being abandoned by the Father. The first presupposes Chalcedon, so that the Christological subject is identified with the pre-existent Logos. Since this Logos spoken of by Chalcedon cannot suffer death in God-abandonment, Jesus functions as an independent subject. The second option is to follow Jürgen Moltmann and collapse the second person of the Trinity into the human subject Jesus. This entails a rift in the being of God, such that the Father is no longer the Father of the Son. McCormack proposes a third option. This is that the human Jesus experiences death in God-abandonment as the Spirit departs from his human consciousness, and thus he loses the presence of the Father to him. This is a human experience in the Logos that has an ontological effect. The Christological subject of this event is the God-human in his divine-human unity; neither Jesus alone nor the Son alone. I find this illuminating but elaborate to the point of being abstruse. It evidently depends on a rather different account of the Trinity from the one I offer in Chapter 7 above. It will be clear that my proposal is closest to the second option.

How has this happened? And what, exactly, has happened? Jesus asks a question; one that receives no answer. The question quotes the first verse of Psalm 22; but efforts to make this a triumphant statement by arguing that Psalm 22 begins in lament and curves upward to praise miss the point. The notion that Jesus, as he hangs on the cross, is uttering oblique but fulsome praise to the Father is absurd. The poignancy of the dialogue is that Jesus is still talking to the Father even at the very moment of his abandonment. This is the Trinitarian impulse – to understand everything in relation to the coinherence of the three persons, even as that coinherence is being clawed apart. This is the moment when the full extent of the risk of incarnation and the profound contingency of creation coincide. Jesus has a choice that the incarnation was supposed to overcome. The incarnation is Jesus being utterly in mutual relationship with the Father and the Spirit and yet at the same time utterly with humankind. Now he must choose whether to continue to be utterly with us or to withdraw into being utterly with the Father. He chooses us. Choosing us means facing a human death. By definition, death is something of which, when you enter into it, you do not know the outcome. In existence, death is the end of being, and the end of with. For Jesus, who in essence with the Father and the Spirit is perfect being, and utterly with, this is an indescribable contradiction. The paradox of the crucifixion is that Jesus undergoes the opposite of being with – complete separation and non-being – yet thereby affirms and demonstrates God's unbreakable commitment to being with us – whatever befall. He loves us to the end (Jn 13:1).

Meanwhile the Father also has a choice. The choice the Father faces is whether to let the Son be with us even to the point of death, or to insist that the integrity of the Trinity must prevail and refuse.[15] We need to dwell upon how poignant a choice this is. On the

[15] In his *The Crucified God*, 260, Jürgen Moltmann helpfully adds texture to this portrayal of the Father, and grasps the inner-Trinitarian character of what is taking place:

one hand the whole logic of incarnation and creation is at stake: the whole purpose of God. If the Father interrupts the process now (and the temptation narrative suggests a way this could happen – 'For it is written, "He will command his angels concerning you, to protect you" (Lk 4:10 – those angels could rescue Jesus from the cross), then the whole purpose of incarnation and creation will have failed: God will not be with humankind and creation – not now and, presumably, not forever. The whole logic of God in covenant, community and

> Jesus suffers dying in forsakenness, but not death itself; for [human beings] can no longer 'suffer' death, because suffering presupposes life. But the Father who abandons him and delivers him up suffers the death of the Son in the infinite grief of love. We cannot therefore say here in patri-passian terms that the Father also suffered and died. The suffering and dying of the Son, forsaken by the Father, is a different kind of suffering from the suffering of the Father in the death of the Son. Nor can the death of Jesus be understood in theopaschite terms as the 'death of God'. To understand what happened between Jesus and his God and Father on the cross, it is necessary to talk in trinitarian terms. The Son suffers dying, the Father suffers the death of the Son. The grief of the Father here is just as important as the death of the Son. The Fatherlessness of the Son is matched by the Sonlessness of the Father, and if God has constituted himself as the Father of Jesus Christ, then he also suffers the death of his Fatherhood in the death of the Son.

What Moltmann does not do is perceive the way this jeopardises the Trinity, nor see how only the Holy Spirit, the Spirit of the Father and the Son, can restore both Jesus and the relationship between Jesus and the Father. Instead, he tries to find community where there is only separation:

> This deep community of will between Jesus and his God and Father is now expressed precisely at the point of their deepest separation, in the godforsaken and accursed death of Jesus on the cross. If both historical godforsakenness and eschatological surrender can be seen in Christ's death on the cross, then this event contains community between Jesus and his Father in separation, and separation in community.
>
> *(260–61)*

Moltmann's introduction of eschatological surrender evades the real issue in this moment, which is the horror of the separation of Father and Son, and the question of how damaging this is and how it can possibly be rectified. It is quite probably with this passage in mind that David Bentley Hart, in his *The Beauty of the Infinite*, 157, refers to the 'loose, rhapsodic, paraenetic expostulations of Jürgen Moltmann'. Rowan Williams criticises Moltmann as 'weakening the force of the recognition that Jesus' suffering is humanly inflicted, through his concentration on the cross as the Father's giving-up of the Son, a transaction in a mythical rather than historical space'. *On Christian Theology*, 178. In my account in this chapter I avoid this criticism by insisting no transaction is taking place.

communion will suddenly halt. Being with as God's mode of interacting with existence will cease: what will follow it is unknown. God will move from faithful and constant to arbitrary and unpredictable. It goes so far against the character of the Trinity that it is almost impossible to contemplate. On the other hand, the cost of allowing Jesus to be with humankind to the point of death is immense. There is no conception of what a split in the Trinity means. There is no knowing what agony is involved when those who have been in such perfect communion and coinherence are torn from each other: one imagines physical metaphors like a hole in a boat causing it to ship gallons of water, or damage to a spacecraft leading to it leaking oxygen – metaphors that suggest the injury is catastrophic, irreparable, insurmountable.

This echoes the shuddering story of Jephthah's vow, by which he promised to sacrifice the first person to emerge from his house if he returned victorious from defeating the Ammonites – only to find that first person turned out to be his daughter (Judg 11:29–40). Here the Father has made a similar vow – to pursue the purpose of incarnation, creation and eschaton whatever befall; and it has come to this. Should Jephthah have broken his vow? Of course. Should the Father now break this solemn vow to adhere to the logic of incarnation? That is the unanswerable question Jesus' cry of dereliction poses. The Father keeps his vow. The Father lets Jesus be with us, whatever the cost to his being with the Father. God's purpose is unbreakable. Even if it threatens to break the Trinity. It is the choice at the centre of existence. It is perhaps an even bigger choice than the original choice never to be except to be with us in Christ – the choice that triggered creation and existence. It is bigger because without the first choice there would never have been existence. But without the second choice there might not even be essence. It is a choice beyond description. It is grace beyond grace. It is a demonstration that there is no God behind or beyond being with. Being with is the very soul of the Trinity: it knows no other way. It is not, in the end, a choice. It is God being

God. God being God means with. Here God stands: God can do no other.[16]

At this point we may pause to reflect on the principles set out in the first chapter. Whereupon we see that this is indeed a story about God.[17] What is at stake is not the destruction of evil: there is no evidence that this has come to pass.[18] Neither is this about taking away sin or paying some kind of debt or penalty for it: there is no transaction taking place. This is in every way at every stage about relationship. This is no arm's-length arrangement: unlike some atonement theories that see this as a task the Son assumes on behalf of the Trinity, this understanding engulfs the whole of the Trinity. No aspect of the Trinity is anything other than wholly engaged in this moment. This is not about destroying death: any destroying that is going on is, if anything, working in the other direction: Jesus and the Father are facing the full consequences of Jesus entering a world pervaded by evil, sin and death. There is no pre-existing agenda, no work plan, by which Jesus is commissioned to fix a list of things wrong with human existence or creation in general. There is no representative role taken up: there is no for in Jesus' death at all; only with. Jesus does not actively seek his death by crucifixion; he actively

[16] In his book *Atonement and Incarnation: An Essay in Universalism and Particularity* (Cambridge: Cambridge University Press, 1991), Vernon White distinguishes between *constitutive* models of atonement, which argue that Jesus, through some combination of his life, death and resurrection, uniquely creates a salvation available by no other route, and *illustrative* ones, which suggest that Jesus is the prime example of a salvation already universally available. My proposal is neither – not least because it does not set itself up as a doctrine of the atonement, since it rejects the premise that Jesus comes to reverse the fall, and thus, without denying the prevalence of sin and evil, eschews the language of salvation almost entirely. Nonetheless it meets the constitutive criteria White sets out.

[17] 'What happened on the cross was an event between God and God.' Moltmann, *The Crucified God*, 261.

[18] See the discussion in my *Humbler Faith, Bigger God: Finding a Faith to Live By* (Grand Rapids, MI: Eerdmans, and Norwich: Canterbury, 2022), 27–53, where I suggest that the two theological questions concerning sin and evil are: (1) If Jesus ascended to heaven having completed his work on earth, why is there still evil? and (2) If, in the fullness of time, God will vindicate the oppressed, why does God not do so now?

does not avoid the inevitable consequences of inhabiting the story of Israel as it finds itself infested by Roman domination. It is hard to imagine the story ending any other way than by allergic reaction: the world of occupation, informers, quislings, collaborators, flawed justice, exploitation, squalid survival, humiliating compromise – this world cannot tolerate the presence of Jesus. It regurgitates him. His death is not 'part of the plan'. But it is almost inevitable: and his predictions littered threefold in the synoptic gospels indicate he knew this all along.

This is a story about how God so loves the world, about how God's only son was sent (Jn 3:16): but not to fix a problem.[19] Instead, Jesus enters a mystery.[20] And the mystery is not ended when he dies. Jesus is not supernumerary after 'completing' his 'commission'. This is a relationship, not a transaction: an unbreakable covenant, not a

[19] I am aware that since I do not configure the story as one in which Jesus is the answer to God's need to fix the problem of sin that humankind has caused but cannot resolve, some may suggest I am adopting some version of Peter Abelard's 'moral influence' theory. This is several kinds of mistaken. In the first place, Abelard is wrongly (but frequently) characterised as rejecting 'objective' atonement theories in favour of his own 'subjective' approach by which Christ's example of obedient love for God inspires a corresponding obedient love in the believer. He does no such thing: he simply questions whether God had no other means besides Christ's death by which to redeem humankind. In the second place I repeatedly emphasise that what is happening in Christ's death is an ontological event within the Trinity, not simply or mainly any impression his death may leave on humankind. What I am questioning is why the whole gospel is conventionally understood as God's fixing of the sin problem. I am suggesting instead that engaging sin is part of the context of the incarnation, and not its pretext or purpose. On Abelard, see Witt and Scandrett, *Mapping Atonement*, 83–92. Witt and Scandrett commend Abelard and the Wesleys for their model of atonement as divine love because it (1) brings the whole story from creation to consummation into one narrative arc and (2) unifies Jesus' birth, life, death, resurrection and ascension to affirm Jesus as the revelation of divine love. While I have some sympathy for Abelard's notion that Christ came to unite humanity to God in love, and the two unities noted here accord with my strategy in this book, this approach is still locked into a notion of the incarnation being dependent on the fall, and I do not believe that its account of love is as rich as the purpose and dimensions of being with.

[20] T. F. Torrance insists there can be no 'theory' of the atonement: 'The innermost mystery of atonement and intercession remains mystery: it cannot be spelled out.' See his *Atonement: The Person and Work of Christ* (Downers Grove, IL: IVP Academic, 2009), 2. See also Witt and Scandrett, *Mapping Atonement*, 212–21.

short-term contract. Thus, to take our second principle, this is a story about Jesus. Just as the transfiguration shows that the incarnation is always a human story about conversation, conflict and controversy at the same time as being a divine story of covenant, community and communion, so the crucifixion is a human story of betrayal, denial and desertion at the same time as a divine story about constancy, faithfulness and unbreakable purpose. Jesus is at the centre of the story of incarnation, creation and eschaton, and Jesus is at the centre of the way that story is concentrated in his passion, death and resurrection.[21]

This is a story of abundance. That may seem paradoxical in the face of agony, isolation and death. But this is the heart of the Father's choice. To close down the story, to call a halt, to say 'The incarnation is a priceless gift, I cannot watch it being trampled and destroyed this way' – that would demonstrate that the story of God was ultimately one of scarcity. But the Father's decision to honour the original purpose, whatever befall, is the ultimate demonstration and confirmation of abundance. God is limitless. God will find a way. God does find a way. Nothing is impossible with this abundant God. There is always more. The resurrection is that astonishing more.

[21] Jürgen Moltmann, *The Crucified God*, 263, insists that by keeping us at the foot of the cross, this story avoids unitarianism and atheism:

> The doctrine of the Trinity is no longer an exorbitant and impractical speculation about God, but is nothing other than a shorter version of the passion narrative of Christ in its significance for the eschatological freedom of faith and the life of oppressed nature. It protects faith from both monotheism and atheism because it keeps believers at the cross. The content of the doctrine of the Trinity is the real cross of Christ himself. The form of the crucified Christ is the Trinity. . . . The concrete 'history of God' in the death of Jesus on the cross on Golgotha therefore contains within itself all the depths and abysses of human history and therefore can be understood as the history of history. . . . There is no suffering which in this history of God is not God's suffering; no death which has not been God's death in the history on Golgotha.

This is to abstract the elemental story of a man dying outside a city wall and make it the story of everything: yet without including even the resurrection. Though suggestive, this is surely inflated and distorted. As Rowan Williams says in his *On Christian Theology*, 111, 'A finished account of Christ as containing all meanings would make Christology non-eschatological.'

This is a story about God's sovereignty and freedom. God is not bound by external assumptions about honour or justice. God is not obliged to pay off a debt or take punishment for a crime. There are no arbitrary rules about who can be taken up into essence, and how God must facilitate the process, provided human beings cooperate. In God's utter freedom God chose to be with us through incarnation and creation, and through the eschaton to be with us forever. The full consequences of that decision, the full extent of the risk of incarnation, are vividly undergone in Jesus' crucifixion. The fact that the Father and the Son each have a choice to make is not an inhibition of their sovereignty or freedom: they are free to make those choices. Freedom is not freedom from having choices to make – it precisely is having the opportunity to make choices and not being subject to pre-ordained givens. God's choice to be with us in Christ is not a curtailment of God's freedom – it is an expression of the Trinity's inherent character, and thus a manifestation of God's freedom. That choice could be rescinded at any time – as we have seen in relation to the Father allowing the Son to choose to continue to be with us even as it meant death. God has that freedom; but such an exercise of freedom would go against God's inherent character. This, and not any curtailment of freedom, is the reason why the Father does not make that choice.

Most importantly, this is a story in which God's means and God's ends are identical. There is no metaphor at work, no necessity for God to adopt some technique or fulfil some demand. God does not conquer anything or defeat anyone, satisfy any requirement or substitute for any guilty party. God's end – God's purpose – is to be with us in Christ; in existence, and ultimately in essence. God's way of bringing this about – God's means – is simply to be with us in Christ. And that being with is unbreakable, even when it entails Christ facing agonising death, even when it means the Father and the Spirit beholding the Son face death, even when it involves a fissure between the Father and the Son. God never deviates from this unbreakable purpose; nothing changes the Trinity's inherent character. God remains with us in Christ, even when humankind expresses its greatest-ever aversion to that will to be with us, by exterminating the Christ who embodies it. The steadfast love of God never ceases; God's mercies never come to an end: great is God's faithfulness (Lam 3:22–23).

RESURRECTION AND ASCENSION

This is, of course, not the end of the story. The apocalyptic bleakness of Good Friday does not have the last word. The desolate battle-scene of Golgotha, of death, destruction and distress, will pass: Christ's appearing is as sure as the dawn; he will come to us like the showers, like the spring rains that water the earth (Hos 6:3). The Holy Spirit finds a way to remain with both the Father and the Son despite the fissure between them. The Holy Spirit finds a way still to be with Jesus, even though Jesus is dead, thereby indicating that the Spirit finds a way to be with each one of us, even when we are dead. Here is the other side of being with. We have seen how Jesus is with us, even to the extreme point where almost none of us are with him, in the most abiding, adhesive form of being with imaginable. Now we see how the Spirit is with Jesus, through and beyond his death, and their being with one another is so magnetic, so effervescent, so restorative, so healing, that it brings about the transformation we call the resurrection. We often say 'death could not hold him' – as if death were a positive entity with intentions and powers. What we perhaps should say is, death could not ultimately resist the dynamism of the Holy Spirit. The Holy Spirit's enduring, patient, animating, enlivening manner of being with drew Jesus back from death to new life.[22]

[22] Bruce McCormack's account is slightly different.

> That the eternal Son should be humble and obedient unto death means that death is not simply the end of human life in this world but an end of human life that the eternal Son experienced directly in order to 'relocate' it (hermeneutically and ontologically) from an event in this world to an event in the life of God; a 'relocation' through which the power of death to define the very meaning of 'finitude' is itself cancelled or annulled. In that this has taken place, death is no longer *the* defining feature of finite existence as known and experienced by us. By virtue of the fact that the eternal Son *lives* his death, that he exists in it, passes through it, and is raised

Behold the eight dimensions of being with at play here. The Holy Spirit is *present* in the tomb, where no one else could possibly be present, the boulder being rolled in front. The Holy Spirit gives the dead Jesus its whole *attention* – the whole attention of one who coinheres and is in utter relationship even beyond death. The Holy Spirit enters the *mystery* of Jesus' death and is undaunted by it – not because the Spirit has some formula or method practised a thousand times before elsewhere, but because this mystery calls upon the full depth and extent of the Trinity's with-ness – its limitless togetherness and utterly mutual interpenetration (*participation*) and sheer delight. Out of that *delight* the Holy Spirit finds so much abundance that abides amid such loss and desolation, and discovers there is still more than enough relationship, more than enough mutual receiving, more than enough instigating and initiating to enspirit Jesus once again. This is the *partnership* of the Trinity working in a whole new way, facing a whole new challenge, but each person of the Trinity still being true to its distinctive character – not least that Jesus cannot move like the Spirit can move, and the Father cannot reanimate the Son until the fissure between them is healed – which only the Spirit can do. Imagine the *enjoyment* as the risen Christ relishes the Holy Spirit like never before, and the rift with the Father is resolved, and Jesus can once again be with us with no damage to his being with the Trinity. This is unprecedented *glory*.

Again God's means and God's ends are identical. This is not a story about conquest or triumph. This is an account of the ultimate unbreakability of God's being with us in Christ. God does not destroy death: God outlasts death, out-narrates death, finds resources within the Trinity that infiltrate the tomb and animate the lifeless body and

> from it, death as the defining feature of 'finite' existence itself dies.
> It is *absolutely* delimited in being given its own absolute end. Finitude as proper to created being is itself transformed and, I would say, elevated.
>
> *The Humility of the Eternal Son*, 23–24, italics original

This is about as healthy as a 'for' account of Jesus' 'work' can be. I very much concur with the decentring of death as McCormack describes it. But I see the account I offer here as more holistic in its treatment of Jesus' resurrection and ascension.

restore the plaintive soul.[23] Jesus is raised to find a creation in which sin and evil are still evident: but one in which God's will and resolve to be with us always can never again be questioned. From the famous hymn the words 'conquering Son' and 'hymns of triumph sing' may be problematic; but the sentiment 'No more we doubt thee' shines brightly.[24]

Among the many resurrection narratives the gospels offer, the most compelling is the simplest: Jesus' encounter in the garden with

[23] Rowan Williams, in his *On Christian Theology*, 104–05, in seeking to articulate the limits of Christian claims in relation to Judaism and to other faiths, articulates this understated quality of the resurrection in quoting Jacques Pohier's *God – in Fragments*, trans. John Bowden (London: SCM, 1985), 294:

> The resurrection of Jesus Christ and the Pentecost of his Spirit do not mean that Jesus Christ is henceforward the answer to everything ... They indicate that God bears witness that the question raised by Jesus Christ is the one by which God manifests himself ... God does not show himself in Jesus Christ as being the totality of meaning. Jesus Christ does not manifest himself as being the totality of meaning. When they believe that this is nevertheless the case, Christians prevent meaning being found in the manifestation of God in Jesus Christ, which is not a manifestation of the significance of omnipotence. One could say, in a rough paraphrase of St. Paul: We do not have omnipotence of meaning; we do not proclaim to you the totality of meaning; we have nothing to proclaim but Jesus dead and risen; we have only this news which has no value as a response to everything or as the totality of meaning, but has value in itself.

In characteristic fashion, Williams calls this the revelation of a God 'who is authentically creator of a world because this God does not wish to be everything' (105). I am not saying Jesus is the totality of meaning. I am saying present and ultimate meaning and purpose are to be defined in relation to the Christ who, as cross and resurrection definitively show, will never not be with us.

[24] 'In Peter's paradigmatic sermon in Acts the Crucifixion appears as that which God *overcomes* by the salvific Resurrection: "This man ... you crucified ... but God raised him up."' Jenson, *Systematic Theology*, vol. 1, 180, italics original. Jenson encompasses the proposal I make in this chapter as follows.

> The Crucifixion put it up to the Father: Would he stand to this alleged Son ... who ... hosts publicans and sinners ... ? The Resurrection was the Father's Yes. We may say: that the Resurrection settled that the Crucifixion's sort of God is indeed the one God. The Crucifixion settled what sort of God it is who establishes his deity by the Resurrection.
>
> *(189)*

My answer is, 'A being-with sort of a God.' Crucially Jenson insists that this is an action of the divine and human nature simultaneously.

Mary Magdalene (Jn 20:11–20). She is discovering two things: Jesus, despite all, is with her; and his purpose is to bring her and all creation to be with him – which is why she cannot be allowed to cling to him. The depiction of a man and a woman in a garden explicitly returns us to the moment in Genesis 3 when human beings are depicted refusing God's offer to be with them, and jettisoning the opportunity to dwell in the perfection of being with God, one another and the creation in anticipation of doing so in the eschaton forever. In very brief, simple strokes, Jesus' encounter with Mary offers the deepest Easter truth. In this eternal image we have the conclusive statement that God, humanity and creation are ultimately inseparable. There is no future for God that is not wrapped up in humanity and the creation, and there is no destiny for humanity and the creation outside the hands and the arms of God. Being with is here to stay. Life remains complex and it continues to be lived on the edge of death. But Easter shows humankind that it will never be alone. There is no humanity that is not at the heart of God. And there is no God that is not utterly with humanity.

The difference between this theocentric account of Christ's passion, death and resurrection and the anthropocentric account is demonstrated in the ascension. In the anthropocentric account, where first Israel is called and then Jesus is sent to be the way God resolves the shortcomings of creation after the fall, the ascension has very little significance, besides completing the story of Jesus' ministry. But in the Christocentric account, ascension is much more important. To grasp this takes us back to the narrative identified in our study of the Eastern theologians. The Christocentric story, which should by now be familiar, goes like this. The Trinity dwelt in the glory of eternity, utterly sufficient in three-personed unity. Out of fathomless love, God resolved to be defined by relationship: not just the inner relationship of the three persons with one another, but outer relationship. Humankind is the name for the partner in that relationship. God's life was shaped to be in relationship with humankind, first by Jesus being both fully of God and fully of humankind, and second by the creation of the universe as the setting for that relationship. Israel was chosen as the people among whom God was to come among us in Christ.

This yields what we could depict as a pair of square brackets inside a pair of curved brackets. The first outer, curved bracket at the beginning of time is God's original decision never to be just content with the inner relations of the Trinity, but to resolve to be in relationship with a partner – humankind. The final outer, curved bracket at the very end of time is the moment when God turns that relationship from one with all the contingency and flaws and suffering and fragilities of being in time into a relationship that is forever: a moment we call heaven. Inside those two curved brackets is a pair of square brackets. The opening square bracket is Christ's annunciation and nativity: the moment Jesus' earthly life, the full relationship between God and humankind for which the universe was created, begins. The closing square bracket is Jesus' ascension. This is the moment when Jesus' earthly life ends. In other words, Ascension is the flipside of Christmas. And in the middle, between all those brackets, is the epicentre of God's story: Jesus' crucifixion and resurrection. The crucifixion plays out the logic of the first two brackets, that being with us whatever happened would stretch God's character and love and commitment to the very ultimate. The resurrection anticipates the logic of the last two brackets, that nothing can separate God from God, which we see played out in Christ's ascension, and that nothing can separate us from God, which we see confirmed on the last day and the entry-point to heaven. That is what it means to see Good Friday and Easter Day as a microcosm of the whole history of everything.

At Christmas, God's longing to be in relationship with us means that God in Christ becomes a true inhabitant of creation – still utterly God, but now fully dwelling in and with humanity. Then at Ascension, humanity reaches out from time-bound existence into the forever of God's eternal essence. At Christmas, because Christ is fully divine, we can trust that the whole character and heart of God is wrapped up in Jesus being among us. Jesus is God completely invested in relationship with humankind, without reserve. Meanwhile at Ascension, because Christ is fully human, he represents and embodies every single human being, every person that ever lived and ever will. When he is embraced into the whole of the Trinity, humankind is too. Christmas means God forever belongs with humankind. Ascension means humankind forever belongs with God. Christmas is God in Christ reaching out to humankind. Ascension is humankind in Christ reaching out to God. At Christmas, Jesus embarks on the central definitive embodiment of God's indelible relationship with us. At Ascension, Jesus disembarks from that definitive moment and brings humankind and creation with him into the heart of God. At Ascension, we discover that God takes humankind and the creation into forever: this makes Ascension a vital if neglected part of the gospel story. At Christmas, the whole of God reached out into unbreakable and eternal relationship with humankind, whatever the cost to God; and at Ascension, the whole of humanity and all creation reached out into unbreakable and eternal relationship with God, whatever the reluctance from humankind. This is a truly Christocentric account of the gospel story in general, and the ascension in particular.

After Jesus' ascension, the Holy Spirit makes Christ present in creation in ways that remain true to the manner in which Jesus was present as recorded in the gospels. Jesus' eschatological presence in essence is one in which he interacts with humankind and the restored creation as described in Chapter 8 above. There is a profound difference between the moment of Christ's ascension, in which he brings humankind into forever, and the period after his ascension, in which he interacts in eschatological ways with humankind and the creation. The difference is that of dynamism and narrative: once the path into essence has been opened up by the ascension, humankind can enjoy beyond death the full experience of being with the Trinity, which the limitations of created existence hitherto inhibited. The second coming of Christ is not a moment of opening out forever – that has been done in the ascension – but of sweeping the whole creation into that forever.

EVIL, SIN, SUFFERING AND DEATH

Where does this leave evil, sin, suffering and death? I have left this question to the end, precisely to ensure what Duns Scotus was so keen to emphasise, that this not be a sin-centric story determined by deficit. Let me clarify what the story told above means for sin and evil, before turning to suffering and death.

Sin and evil refer to those forces that inhibit being with – God's being with us, and our being with God, one another and the creation.[25] The story of Adam and Eve does not present itself as the quasi-historical explanation of why there is sin: for example, it offers no account of why the serpent tells a false story of God's purpose that presents it as constraint rather than freedom, and scarcity rather than abundance. Almost any interpreter of this narrative will infer beyond Eden to something Eden implies. The traditional implication is that existence came into being good, but early on became flawed – and that humankind was culpable in that. This account is difficult to reconcile with the story of the Big Bang and of evolution. The story I have told above does not require resistance to the stories of the Big Bang and of evolution. God is not in a hurry: the likelihood that the universe is 14.8 billion years old, and that human beings have occupied it for only a tiny fraction of that time (starting at what is sometimes known as five minutes to midnight, when existence is portrayed as a clock), is

[25] In their *Mapping Atonement*, 80, William G. Witt and Joel Scandrett make a helpful distinction between sin and sins. *Sin* refers to habitual human behaviour; notions of recapitulation and participation accordingly point to moral transformation, while victory language sees sin as a defeated enemy. *Sins* refer to wrongs enacted, which cause guilt and offence, and require forgiveness and accountability. Stanley Hauerwas makes a similar distinction in his '"Salvation Even in Sin": Learning to Speak Truthfully about Ourselves', in *Sanctify Them in the Truth: Holiness Exemplified* (Edinburgh: T & T Clark, 1997), 61–74 at 62, where he speaks about coming from a revivalist culture of weekly repentance from one's sins to a more sophisticated university milieu. 'We were reschooled to say the problem is not sins, but sin. … We are left quite unsure what it means for us to be saved, much less made holy. As a result, we lose the ability to tell the truth about our lives.' This resonates with my description below of sin as a false story.

not a problem to the story of God. But it is a problem to the traditional story of creation and fall. Where does the fall belong in a story in which most of the early running was made by astro- and geo-physical forces of immense magnitude and in which it is difficult to identify when human beings as we understand them first arose?

It is because of difficulties such as this that some theologians have come to portray the fall, or the flawed nature of creation, as concurrent with creation itself. Hence Karl Barth, who envisages a story in many respects like the one above, departs from such an account when it becomes clear that if Jesus is to become incarnate as the reconciler there must be sin and evil to be overcome and a profound division across which he can mediate. This comes at best dangerously close to the 'happy fault' notion that sees the fall as in some way God's intention in order to facilitate such a magnificent redemption: we saw earlier that Friedrich Schleiermacher takes such an approach. If the historical approach just mentioned runs into a factual problem, surely this intentional approach runs into a moral problem. The incarnation is an unqualified blessing – but in this account it brings with it an enormous and intolerable number of casualties. Untold suffering, distorted lives and indescribable atrocities seem to be incurred en route to so great a redemption. This seems utterly out of keeping with any recognisable portrayal of God.

An alternative approach sees evil and sin as pervasive, either more or less from the beginning from a fallen angel, in the manner of John Milton's *Paradise Lost*, or as arising from a maximal notion of what was lost in the fall. For example, Athanasius sees the fall as a moment of de-creation, wherein humankind turns from God to the most proximate alternative, the human body, thus idolatrously turning from grace to nature and substituting indulgence for transcendence. As a result, humankind loses incorruption and faces corruption and death. The trouble with such overwhelming accounts of the fall – expressed succinctly in the Calvinist phrase 'total depravity' – is that they so inflate the impact of evil and sin that it is hard to see how they will be anything other than perpetual adversaries.[26]

The story of being with suggests an alternative that does not have God creating sin and evil, does not simply take refuge in their inexplicable origin and their perpetuation through God's commitment to human free will, and does not verge on dualism. Staying with Adam and Eve and the serpent, it notes that this is a story, and a story about a false story – the serpent's false story that God has other purposes than being with Adam and Eve, that those undisclosed purposes are unfair and unjust, that they should not respect God's terms of engagement, and should go ahead and eat the fruit without fear of death. Thus they forfeit presence (in the garden), attention (from God), delight (in each other and the creation), participation (in the abundant coinherence of the Trinity), partnership (in enabling the garden to be fruitful), enjoyment (in the ability to enjoy all things, and to regard none simply as objects of use) and glory (in the wonder of God, and being with God, and the glistening of God's creation). Like Esau, they sacrifice their birthright for a mess of pottage. Like David, they have everything, but fixate on the one thing they cannot have, and thereby embark on a series of false stories that depart from the true story that God wants to be with them with no ulterior motive.

And this is the point that reveals why the Adam and Eve story is still so helpful to a notion of sin and evil, yet not in the way conventionally assumed. Their story is a story of how a false story ruins everything. Which is how sin works. Sin is a false story.[27] It is fundamentally a false story about God: the serpent says, 'You will not die'

[26] As tends to be the case with descriptions that work hard to take sin and evil seriously, sin and evil become so profound and so pervasive that they are almost more foundational than good or God; meanwhile it becomes hard to perceive that they can be overcome, even by the sacrifice of Christ.

[27] Speaking of Dante's *Divine Comedy*, Denys Turner, in his *Julian of Norwich, Theologian* (New Haven, CT: Yale University Press, 2011), 92, notes, 'Hell is the condition of those who do not repent of their stories, who refuse the offer of their revision by the divine love, and insist on living by means of the story that sin tells, the story of the attempt to achieve a self-made significance independently of the story of the divine love.'

(Gen 3:4), whereas God had said, 'In the day that you eat of it you shall die' (Gen 2:17).[28] But it is subsequently and consequently a false story about ourselves, one another and the creation. Sin tells a false story: no one will ever know, people do much worse things, I've done so many good things that I deserve a bit of licence, it doesn't really hurt anybody, I'm so overcome by desire that I can't help myself, one more won't do any harm, everyone does it, someone else will be glad to clear up, it's no one else's business but mine, I've got to look after number one, life's too short, what you don't know can't hurt you. All of these are false stories. What they have in common is that they are too short. They lack the authenticity of the original story and the destiny of the final story. What they also have in common is that they inhibit, undermine, dismantle, obstruct and poison being with. It is that teleological damage, rather than any intrinsic deontological flaw, that makes them sinful. What is false about these stories is that it is impossible to conceive of any circumstances in which the narrative they tell leads towards enhancing being with God, ourselves, one another or the creation. Instead, they put God, other people and creation on hold for as long as is required to fulfil their false telos – like a person saying, 'Hold on a second' before leaving a phone call for an indefinite period of time in order to pursue some other interest. Sin will never succeed in ultimately distorting the story: that is what we discover on the cross – that God being with us will never not be the nature and destiny of existence and ultimately essence. But sin is capable of interrupting and obscuring that story for short or long periods. Thus to sin is literally to have lost the plot.[29]

[28] Interestingly, Eve says, 'But God said, "You shall not eat of the fruit of the tree that is in the middle of the garden, nor shall you touch it, or you shall die"' (Gen 3:3). But in Genesis 2:17 God says nothing about touching the fruit. Which illustrates how sinisterly sin and evil may infiltrate even a conversation pursued in innocence, since memory is so seldom capable of rendering a true story. Eve is relying on Adam's memory, since according to the story Eve had not been created when God gave the injunction about the tree. So Adam is the first illustration of the link between a story being distorted on retelling and the way sin arises.

[29] 'Sin is how we exclude *ourselves* from reality by preferring to inhabit the self-destructive unreality of the story that sin tells, by refusing to allow ourselves to be

Sin is a false story – in particular a false story about God, that forgets or denies that God longs to be with us and that Jesus' passion and death have removed any doubt that God desires to be with us whatever befall and that Jesus' resurrection and ascension reveal his intention to take us into essence and be with us always and that Pentecost offers us in the meantime everything we need to be with God, one another and the creation.[30] Sin consequently is a false story about ourselves, that we do not belong in this story; about one another, that other people constitute threats to our being with rather than assets and companions; and about creation, that we can use it to create an alternative story rather than enjoy it as it belongs with us in the being with story. Where sin differs from evil is that sin is a false story about the real God – whereas evil is a truly malign story about a very different god, a story that substitutes destruction for flourishing, cruelty for tenderness, ruthlessness for mercy, chaos for companionship, and fear for hope.[31]

The risk of incarnation and creation is not just that humankind might reject the offer to be with God, but that the very way in which they receive that offer entails risk that it might be misconstrued. Another way to say this is that sin and evil are conventionally located in relation to theological anthropology, as facets of the complex and flawed nature of humankind. But they might better be located in

told by the story of compassion that the divine love tells. . . . It is an attempt to place a nothing at the heart of the real.' Turner, *Julian of Norwich, Theologian*, 98.

30 Thomas Aquinas notes the profound irony that humankind cannot even sin without depending on God's grace. See his *Summa theologiae*, 2/1.109.8–9, in Latin/English Edition of the Works of St Thomas Aquinas, vol. 16, 449–52.

31 The notion of sin as a false story escapes what Robert Williams calls the twin problems of sin in modernity. Problem one is that sin is not regarded as part of human nature, because humans are regarded as created good; problem two is that sin is inherited and inevitable, yet humans are presumed to have freedom and autonomy. (See Robert R. Williams, 'Sin and Evil', in Peter Hodgson and Robert King, eds., *Christian Theology: An Introduction to Its Traditions and Tasks* (London: SPCK, 1982), 168–95.) A false story is in the water of existence; human beings may steer their way through and beyond it by learning and being conformed to a true story, but false stories are still everywhere. Thus we may be held responsible for acting in accordance with them, but this does not inhibit our created goodness or our freedom and autonomy.

relation to revelation, because they are both perversions of the story by which human beings come to understand God's call to be with the Trinity, one another and the creation. We may think of four kinds of revelation. One is the apprehension of wonder, often beauty, in creation or in the configurations human endeavour can make of creation. A second is an immediate apprehension of a *mysterium tremendum et fascinans*, 'a gentle tide pervading the mind with a tranquil mood of deepest worship',[32] a heart strangely warmed or an awareness of absolute dependence. A third kind is scripture, more straightforwardly understood – the story of how God has been made known and been understood in the life of Israel, Jesus and the early church. And a fourth is when the story of scripture comes alive in sacrament, service, solitude or the stranger. Theological accounts of revelation tend to concentrate on the third kind. But what is unique about the third kind is that it is a story – and once God has committed the invitation to humankind to be with the Trinity to a story, that story can go in any number of directions, many of which become the pretext and justification for sin or evil. Baptism is the public recognition of the renunciation of a story of alienation and the declaration of having been grafted into a story of being with God. The Eucharist is the enactment of the true story of what it means to be with God.

Understanding sin and evil as false and perverse stories explains both why sin and evil have such power and why they ultimately do not exist.[33] Stories have immense power: when a soldier faces death for land, flag and nation, each of those commitments presupposes a story. When one tribe goes to war against another tribe, what causes conflict is a particular story about the past and an assumed or

[32] Rudolf Otto, *The Idea of the Holy: An Inquiry into the Non-Rational Factor in the Idea of the Divine and Its Relation to the Rational*, trans. John W. Harvey (London: Oxford University Press, 1928), 12.

[33] In his *Being Reconciled*, 22, John Milbank, inspired by Hannah Arendt, refers to 'that saddest of all the errors of evil (and of Satan) whereby it always imagines that it is yet more evil than it really is. For evil to be at all, it must still deploy and evoke some good, yet it would like to forget this: evil as positive is evil's own fondest illusion.'

imagined story about what is anticipated for the future. Such stories induce people to do brave, foolish, astounding or appalling things. Sometimes such stories are sinisterly crafted and intricately twisted, becoming part of an evil project to distort, misinform, discredit and destroy. Hence Jesus speaks of the devil as the 'father of lies' (Jn 8:44).[34] At other times such stories arise from misunderstanding, lack of information, impatience, deficiency of imagination and self-centredness: such are the sages of sin.[35] The point is, the channels that bring us revelation are the same channels that bring us false stories. So it is not that God 'allows' free will or 'plants' sin to enable a great redemption. It is that inextricable from the true story are a host of false stories, some harmless but many profoundly damaging and destructive: and sin and evil arise in and out of such false stories.

How then are sin and evil dispelled? Not by a substitutionary death, not by a triumphant resurrection, not by a transformative defeat. It is the church's calling to live, to perceive, to tell, to witness to and to celebrate the true story – the story of God's original desire to be with us.[36] Every telling, living or celebrating of this story is the church's attempt to dispel sin and evil.[37] The trouble with diverting from such an approach and seeking instead to destroy sin by

[34] Perhaps also the sin against the Holy Spirit (Mk 3:29) is the wilful distorting of God's story.

[35] 'The most terrible thing about the Holocaust was that *even this* event was brought about through a chain of seemingly "good reasons" – economic, cultural, scientific, peace-seeking – whose delusory appeal is unfortunately *not* alien to our common humanity.' Milbank, *Being Reconciled*, 55, italics original.

[36] John Milbank's profound reflections on forgiveness are illuminating precisely because in his description of gift-giving he comes very close to imitating the language of being with. He regards charity less as a performance than as a state of fraternal, friendly and harmonious co-existence; we may say, an underdeveloped notion of being with. (I say underdeveloped because I see it as embodying delight and partnership but not the other six dimensions.) He goes on to say, 'Charity is not an empty disposition . . . but the ontological bond between God and creatures . . . To forgive is to re-establish a reciprocity only possible as the attainment of a mysterious harmony through its participation in the divine infinite harmony.' See his *Being Reconciled*, 57.

[37] That is not to say that the only form of truthful (Spirit-inspired) form of living takes place within the church. The Spirit inspires many forms of life beyond the church, as we saw in Chapter 9. But the church names the community in which truthful

punishment or evil by killing is that in the service of the story it departs from the story. Thus it breaks one of the principles of the story – that God's means and God's ends are identical – and in so doing risks itself communicating a false story. In an ironic way it is a form of diverting from *with* to *for* – because in order to uphold the story, which is a story of with, it adopts a different mode of practice, pulling itself out of shape, in an attitude of for.[38] The church's aim is that its ends and its means should become as identical as God's. Pentecost gives the church everything it needs to be so; but the church is as prone as anyone else to fall into the sin of following a false story, and is not immune to the evil of embracing a truly perverse and distorted story, as the experience of the German Christians who backed Hitler shows.

Sin and evil will abide as long as creation, until the eschaton, because the cost of abolishing them would be the abolition of stories, and without stories, humankind would never learn the story of God. The question is, does the leaving-behind of sin and evil as malign features of existence mean there is no story in essence – that the eschaton has no narrative? Put another way, is it possible to have story without the possibility of false stories? Does there have to be a choice between static idyll and narrative complexity? This question must be left to mystery – but the answer lies in the exploration of the

living in accordance with the revelation of God's being with us in Christ is intentionally sought and specifically named.

[38] This was Bishop George Bell's argument in the House of Lords against the carpet-bombing of German cities by the Allies in the Second World War: in order to defeat Nazism, they had made themselves as bad as the Nazis.

> When a Minister of the Government speaks in exulting terms of a ruthless and destructive bombing of the German people; or quarters, supposed to be authoritative, contemplate the subjection of fifty German cities to the same terror as Hamburg (or Coventry) has suffered, or the wiping-out of Germany as an industrial unit; then we have real cause to grieve for a lowering of moral tone, and also to fear greatly for the future. … To bomb cities as cities, deliberately to attack civilians, quite irrespective of whether or not they are actively contributing to the war effort is a wrong deed, whether done by the Nazis or by ourselves.

Quoted in Ronald C. D. Jasper, *George Bell: Bishop of Chichester* (London: Oxford University Press, 1967), 276

Trinity itself, on which we embarked in Chapter 7. If the Trinity can have story without sin, we must hope it can make such a story in essence with us, too.

We turn finally to suffering and death. Death, as we have seen at the crucifixion, is the definition of being not-with; suffering may so profoundly isolate that it makes being with almost impossible – but it may in some cases enhance being with, or be transfigured. As we saw in Chapter 8, death is an unavoidable consequence of a finite creation. Eternal life is possible only in a condition of infinity: that is what essence is. It is God's purpose to bring humankind and the creation into essence; but in existence, there must be death. The ethic of being with is to perceive death not as a problem but as a mystery. As Jesus says, 'It is for God's glory, so that the Son of God may be glorified through it' (Jn 11:4). The horror of death was genuine even for Jesus, as his recorded words in Gethsemane and on the cross make clear. So while death is never something to be celebrated, still less acclaimed (there is no approximation to the 'happy fault' with which the Easter Exsultet upholds the fall), the horror of death is nothing of which to be ashamed. Death does after all take away every aspect of being with – oneself, one another, the creation. Just as the Holy Spirit was taken to its utmost in raising Jesus from the dead, we imagine that drawing each one of us from existence into essence is no small enterprise. Existence is an indescribable gift: the gifts of oneself, others, and creation each take far more than a lifetime to explore and enjoy. But it is not a permanent gift; perhaps it would not be the cause for such attention, delight and enjoyment if it were. The real question is not, does death bring all these things to an end? It manifestly does. The real question is, does God's being with us transcend death, and is with truly the most enduring feature of existence – indeed the presence of essence in existence and the part of existence that transfers into essence? The hope of Christianity is that it is and it does. Thus approaching death is not so much about postponing the inevitable for as long as possible, as if limitation were humankind's greatest predicament; it is about fostering relationships of with, learning to be with oneself and the creation, and thus preparing to focus one's whole being on being with God – and this in losing the whole world, as one does at death, nonetheless gaining true life with God (Mk 8:36).

Paul's approach to suffering is that of comparison: 'I consider that the sufferings of this present time are not worth comparing with the glory about to be revealed to us' (Rom 8:18). But his deeper reflection concerns the God of being with: 'I am convinced that neither death, nor life, nor angels, nor rulers, nor things present, nor things to come, nor powers, nor height, nor depth, nor anything else in all creation, will be able to separate us from the love of God in Christ Jesus our Lord' (Rom 8:38–39). We and God are ultimately inseparable: here is a succinct summary of the gospel of with. In Romans 8:28–39, Paul explores what it means for God and us to be inseparable. This requires a specific notion of good and a renewed understanding of God.

The specific notion of good, in the phrase 'all things work together for good', is entirely non-transactional. This is not a contract in which in return for blessings, comforts and security, human beings offer devotion, faithfulness and commitment. Instead, goodness is defined in a very particular way: it means being conformed to Christ. Paul's five verbs – foreknew, predestined, called, justified and glorified – are all Christocentric: 'predestined' is not about any absolute decree regarding ultimate destiny – it refers to being conformed to the image of Christ. God's purpose is to be with us in Christ, and as we are with Christ, we become more like him. God's purpose is thus to make us and remake us to look like Jesus. There is nothing here about comfort, security or other blessings. But there is a lot about suffering. Most of the things we tend to feel deprived of are things Jesus did not have: healthy family, long and happy life, rewarding job, loyal set of friends, warm home, wholesome partner or quiverful of offspring. Meanwhile Jesus was homeless, rejected, betrayed, tortured and executed. For Paul, these are signs that things are good – that we are being conformed to Christ.

The renewed understanding of God follows. Paul lists seventeen circumstances or contexts that could qualify our confidence in God being with us: hardship, distress, persecution, famine, nakedness, peril, sword, death, life, angels, rulers, things present, things to come, powers, height, depth, anything else in all creation. Thus he moves from predicaments we find ourselves in through our own mistakes, the trouble that comes upon us through bad luck and the misery we face because of the ill will of others; and moves on to lack of our most basic needs; then to adverse circumstances and violent attack; next come death and life; which are followed by those who are in charge of existence and those who oversee essence; then things present and things to come; and finally the powers – and 'anything else in all creation'. It turns out to be a list of the most gruesome of Jesus' experiences and challenges. Paul is saying there is nothing we can go through that Jesus has not first gone through. (And Paul has been through most of these things himself.) Thus suffering is transformed into participation: almost communion.

This turns out to be the only instance where 'for' is a good word. Not because it has momentarily displaced 'with'; but because here it is contrasted with 'against'. The only thing missing from Paul's list is any lingering sense that God is against us. Paul squashes any such suggestion: God is for us, not against us – Christ's incarnation and death prove it. God is with us at every step, Jesus has faced everything we might possibly face, we were with God in the very beginning of all things, we are now, and we always will be, and being with God in hardship is always better than being separate from God in comfort ever could be. It is a huge, and disputable, claim: but this is Paul's declaration about suffering.

Some suffering isolates, alienates and impoverishes every aspect of existence. Even this, as Paul indicates, may be a form of participation in Christ. Some suffering, however bonds, yields truth, discloses wisdom, brings new companions, even creates community. Suffering can be a time of being painfully without; but it can also be a season of being surprisingly with – with others, and with God. There can be moments of transfiguration in which the sufferer and those close to them can perceive a reality more intense than before, a gratitude more fulsome than ever known, an attention, delight, enjoyment more focused because moments are short, togetherness is precious, truth can be named. Transfiguration can be an instant of glory, when essence appears in the midst of existence, forever is glimpsed in the middle of now, and faces appear more splendid than the sun.

Conclusion

A Wondrous Story

The preceding treatment, perhaps particularly the final chapter, may leave the reader with lingering questions. In these closing words I offer some indication of how I sense these unresolved questions may land. The questions may be divided into two kinds. The first kind say, surely you have gone too far? The second say, what if you were to go further? Unsurprisingly most attention settles on the former; but my interest is mostly on the latter.

Among the first kind I am here going to address five. What becomes of the fall? What becomes of the language of salvation and atonement? What is to be done with the emphasis of much scripture and preaching that focuses on Christianity as bringing redemption through the cross? Does God suffer? And, If Jesus does not 'come to die', why then *does* Jesus die? The answers to these questions are all implied in the foregoing account, but I understand the need to be explicit here, to avoid misunderstanding.

I begin with the fall. My whole study is framed by the notion of story. The titles of each section of the book, together with those of the Introduction and of this Conclusion, nod to the unsubstitutable narrative character of experience and of revelation. In the Introduction and in Chapters 4, 5, 6, 8 and 10 I explained how a story in which the fall has a determinative role is incompatible with the repeated New Testament references to the election of Jesus before the foundation of the world – that is, before the fall. That is a statement about the status of the fall in the story. But there is also a statement to be made about the fall itself, which I addressed in Chapter 10. If sin is not fundamentally characterised as transgressing a code, but as inhabiting a false story (and meanwhile evil is portrayed as promoting a malign false god), then the fall is not so much an event in historical time as a potential construal of events inherent in the contingent character of creation. Sin is the misconstrual of a narrative such that a story of grace and abundance is distorted into one of resentment and scarcity. It is not so much the malign acts that result as the warped story that gives those acts false credibility. Events are interpreted, reported, imagined and conceived: any of these can be done faithfully and truthfully or partially and wantonly. If there is going to be revelation, there is going to be the possibility of a skewed account of the same material. The possibility of sin is intrinsic to the nature of historical existence. God did not 'create' or 'ordain' sin, nor turn sin to the divine purpose; God simply recognised that a beautiful story is always at risk of being distorted – yet is worth telling and indwelling nonetheless. Sin is not a personified or objective adversary; it is more like a poison that defiles even the good and undermines even the noble.

Moving to salvation and the atonement, I have made it abundantly clear in Chapters 1 and 3 of this book and in many other publications that I believe *being with* aptly characterises the purpose of God in incarnation and creation and the ultimate destiny of all things at the eschaton. The problem with notions of the 'work of Christ' (usually as distinct from the 'person of Christ') is that the whole configuration of the terminology presupposes the orientation of *for*. It thus incurs all the missteps of the assumptions of *for*. If one accepts that God's means and ends are congruent, it would be a distortion of God's character to take on a role of *for*, given that God's underlying purpose is always with. Jesus comes, lives and dies out of the Trinity's desire to be with us – with humankind and the whole creation. To revert from *with* to *for* at the moment of crucifixion would be to betray that purpose – however noble the enterprise may seem. So if atonement means an act in which Jesus steps up to do something on behalf of humanity that in some manner releases humanity from some curse or obligation arising from the fall, my argument rules out such a step. But if atonement means God becoming evermore at-one with us – evermore with us – then that is exactly congruent with my proposal.[1]

Likewise in regard to salvation, the term is conventionally associated with a verse like 'Christ Jesus came into the world to save sinners' (1 Tim 1:15). But salvation is not entirely outside the vision I describe in this book, for three reasons. First, if sin is a false story, to be brought into, grafted into, baptised into and formed into a true story is to be delivered from sin into eternal life. Salvation is the experience of inhabiting and being clothed by this true story. Second, salvation means safety. God's utter commitment to being with us is that safety. It does not preclude pain and suffering, as the discussion of Romans 8 in Chapter 10 demonstrated. But God being with us is the only reliable form of safety there is: anything else is a temporary measure.

Third, in the crisis of the cross, Jesus faces the defining test of the durability of being with. The fact that Jesus did not come to die to fix the sin problem does not make the cross less important: it makes it more important. God prepares to bring the world finally to an end and to be with us forever. The whole story is about being with, beginning, middle and end. God becomes incarnate in Jesus and dwells among us. Jesus meets us in our fragility, our folly and our fecklessness. He is Immanuel, God with us. Then suddenly he is surrounded, arrested, assaulted, condemned, crucified. If he escapes to the Father now – if he withdraws, flinches or bolts – he has then detonated, demolished

[1] In their *Mapping Atonement*, William G. Witt and Joel Scandrett articulate three evaluative criteria for models of atonement: (1) the narrative of scripture: models such as judgement, sacrifice, victory or ransom cannot simply be lifted out of the story and allowed to develop their own dynamic; (2) the history of Israel, Jesus and the church; and (3) the ontological reality of the Trinity, the incarnate Jesus, and the renewed creation. The economic Trinity discloses the immanent Trinity, and the Holy Spirit unites reconciled humanity and the risen Christ. Witt and Scandrett commend Thomas Aquinas, Karl Barth and T. F. Torrance as fulfilling these criteria. I maintain that my account offered in Chapter 10, which eschews the metaphorical models, stays close to the narrative, inhabits the history of Israel, Jesus and the church, and in particular explores the ontology of the Trinity, meets these evaluative criteria amply – even though I do not describe it as a theory of the atonement, as I explain above.

and discredited the whole story: the whole reason for creation, the whole destiny of eternity together, the whole purpose of the incarnation. If he cannot stay on the cross, even in the face of being abandoned by the Father, the whole initiative to be with us now and always is over. The cross is the ultimate test of whether God is serious about being with us. And what it shows in the face of agony, desertion, abandonment and isolation is that God is so serious about being with us that God is willing to jeopardise being with God. This is salvation, in the sense that it is the moment that opens out our eternal life with God. So in all three of these senses there is a place for salvation in the vocabulary of what it means to be a Christian. But it is not a word I have used in this book because it is generally intended to mean something I am suggesting is not in God's purpose. .

How then do I understand the emphasis of much scripture and preaching that focuses on Christianity as bringing redemption through the cross? This was the purpose of Chapter 2, which suggested covenant, community and communion as overarching themes that grounded being with in the narrative sweep of the Bible. These themes are both descriptive, in that they summarise the story, and teleological, in that they are the goal to which the story tends. There is no downplaying of the cross in my rendering of the story: the cross is the definitive expression of God's commitment to be with humankind and the creation. What does get less emphasis is an account of the cross that sees it as a device to secure a specific benefit for humankind. The cross is all about God, rather than achieving something for humankind. In that it definitively demonstrates God's commitment to be with us, it is a constitutive rather than illustrative statement.[2] But my treatment resists any account of the cross that detaches it from its narrative embedding in Jesus' being with us throughout his ministry and God's desire to be with us always. Take

[2] For constitutive and illustrative models of atonement, see White, *Atonement and Incarnation*, and Chapter 10 above.

that context away and you are left with a neo-gnosticism that makes the cross a special formula to escape the prospect of damnation.

Does God suffer? When they read what I have said about the rupture in the Trinity at the moment of Christ's cry of dereliction (Mk 15:34), some assume I am following the lead of such as Jürgen Moltmann and arguing that the Trinity itself experiences the pain of the crucifixion – and for some this contravenes the principle of divine apatheia on which they maintain God's sovereignty depends.[3] But this is to miss a point I make, perhaps too subtly, that the issue for the Trinity on Good Friday is not limitation, in other words the fragility of the human body and its exposure to agony and suffering – a suffering the Father may or may not also feel at the crucifixion; instead the issue is isolation.[4] The fundamental thing about the cross is not that Jesus experienced physical agony and thus shows how much God loves us – the gospels make almost no reference to physical pain; instead it is the separation from the Father and the isolation from those Jesus is profoundly seeking to be with – those who betray, deny, flee, scourge and mock. This does not impinge on apatheia. It addresses a deeper issue – what it means to be utterly adrift, either as a human being or as God; what it might mean for creation to come adrift from God or for one person of the Trinity to become adrift and isolated from another. The question is not how God's ability (or inability) to suffer impinges on God's capacity to save. The point is, the poignancy that the Trinity that is constituted by being with experiences the most profound form of being not-with, of being separated and isolated. It is not about inhibiting God's capacity to do; it is about God willingly undergoing a direct threat to what it means for God to be.

Why does Jesus die? Here an analogy is perhaps the best way to explain my case. The 2022 film *The Swimmers* portrays two teenage

[3] Hart, *The Beauty of the Infinite*, 155–67.

[4] For the fundamental divide between the human predicament as limitation and as isolation, see my *A Nazareth Manifesto*, 11–19.

sisters, Yusra and Sarah, who are living in Damascus during the Syrian civil war. They are serious swimmers, but see no future for themselves in Syria, where they are bound to be assaulted, impoverished or killed. So they escape to Turkey. Through a mixture of bribes, risks and luck, they get as far as a large dinghy to take them across the Aegean Sea to Europe. Here things go badly wrong. The boat has a couple of dozen people on it, which is evidently way too many. The owner hops off on departure, leaving the refugees to fend for themselves. They have no compass or navigation equipment, and the motor stalls after a few hours. It is night, and the waves are high, and everyone is terrified. The boat begins to sink, and all the luggage has to be thrown overboard. One passenger gets a signal on his phone and calls the coastguard – only for a voice to say, 'It's not our policy to rescue stranded boats.' The boat is too heavy and is leaking water, and it is inevitable that they are all going to drown. Sarah realises there is only one thing to do. She must jump into the water. She says goodbye to all the swimming medals she is wearing around her neck, and tosses them into the deep. Then she jumps in after them. The other passengers are bewildered and amazed. After a while her sister Yusra jumps in too. The boat lightens. After what seems like forever, the passengers spy land. It is a Greek island. It is Europe. Yusra and Sarah swim for the shore and drag the boat in. The story became famous because the sisters made their way to Germany, where Yusra found a swimming coach, and with her sister's encouragement ended up representing the tiny but courageous refugee team at the 2016 Rio Olympics.

The key moment is when Yusra and Sarah jump into the sea. They do not get on the boat intending to lay down their lives. They do not make the journey from Damascus expecting their lives and the lives of those around them to be in such deep danger. But they are swimmers. For them, when the deepest crisis arises, their most profound act of solidarity is to jump off the boat. They shuffle off their signs of glory – their medals – and dive into the abyss. They save two dozen lives. But fundamentally this is not something they are doing *for* others – they are doing it *with* them: it is a partnership. They are doing what they can do while others do what they can do. Like Sarah and Yusra, Jesus is not looking to die a martyr's death. He is looking to be in solidarity with us until the very end. But just as Yusra and Sarah are swimmers, Jesus is part of the Trinity. He cannot be anything other than what he is. Yusra and Sarah go into the water because they can be in solidarity with the people on the boat in a way particular to them. Jesus goes to the cross because he understands that facing death is the ultimate way to show solidarity with us. It is not that Yusra and Sarah had to die to save those on the boat. It is not that Jesus had to die to save us. It is that, at the defining point in their lives, they had to risk death because this was who they were: they could do no other.

So much for whether I have gone too far. I finish with some brief indications of where I could have gone further.

Studies of John Duns Scotus and his mostly Franciscan predecessors have mostly focused the question of whether, had there not been a fall, Jesus would still have come, and easily become distracted with scholastic questions of how God might act in other possible worlds – either this world with a different story or other worlds with unknown stories. I have tried in this book not to leave the question there or be waylaid into other possible worlds, but to take forward the broader implications of the New Testament's explicit statement that God loved Jesus before the foundation of the world – and therefore before any fall (Jn 17:24). A further study could bring the full analytical powers of the thirteenth-century theologians to bear on the constructive theological claims I make in Chapters 7–10.

Likewise while I explored in some detail the complexities around the Orthodox notion of deification, I was aware that few Orthodox theologians are troubled by Western concerns that the doctrine trespasses too close to eradicating the creator–creature distinction and to losing humankind's eschatological identity.

At several junctures, in Chapters 2, 3, 4 and 8, I highlighted the transfiguration as a theme laden with potential for further exploration. I ended my book *A Nazareth Manifesto* with a consideration of the significance of the transfiguration for intercessory prayer, and I ended Chapter 10 of this book with a similar treatment of transfiguration and suffering. Transfiguration transcends being with in helpful and challenging ways, depicting existence and essence simultaneously.

The distinction between essence and existence, while assumed and sustained throughout this study, is different from the way those terms are understood by Thomas Aquinas and others. While I find the distinction in the way I use it illuminating and helpful, I recognise it is not widely so understood or employed, and it might well take a full-length study to explore its dimensions and full ramifications.

Chapter 10 includes three significant theological proposals. One is that the cry of dereliction constitutes a rupture in the Trinity that comes about because of God's utter commitment in Christ to be with us.[5] The second is that the Holy Spirit remains with both the Father and the Son and in the resurrection binds the Trinity back together.[6] The third is that sin is more fundamentally a false story than a transgression, and this belongs more within a treatment of revelation than in one of theological anthropology. It goes without saying that all of these proposals could generate detailed exploration.

I take the principle, enunciated in Chapter 1 but pervasive in the book, that God's means and God's ends are identical to be not a limitation of God's freedom but a rendering of the trustworthiness and truthfulness of God. It presents the principal challenge to atonement theories. I recognise it is not a position universally held.

A fuller treatment that reached into the sphere of theological ethics would explore how God's desire to be with us, and the notions of covenant, community and communion, together with other gleanings such as conversation, could shape approaches to diverse and pressing topics such as artificial intelligence, social media and the

[5] This proposal is a significant expansion of the brief treatment of this theme in my *A Nazareth Manifesto*, 79–83 and 239–44.

[6] This echoes a proposal made by Eberhard Jüngel. See Chapter 10 above.

fostering of democratic practices in a divided political age – in addition to treatments I have offered elsewhere.

Andrew Louth's description of two arches, one, from fall to cross, representing Western theology, and the other, from creation to eschaton, representing Eastern theology, is a very helpful way to explicate how the Western, anthropocentric story is too short. I humbly suggest that the story I've been telling in this book is a third arch, bigger still than the Eastern arch: one that stretches from Trinity to eternity. And I humbly suggest that though the Eastern arch is commendably bigger than the Western arch, the Eastern arch is still rather too much of an anthropocentric story, and is still too much tied to a God of for, whereas the third arch I'm describing is a theocentric story about a God of with.

The last thing to say is that this book was conceived as an exploration of the true theological potential of the dimensions of being with, which I have hitherto extensively articulated in relation to ethics, public policy, missiology and pastoral studies. While this exploration has borne much fruit, I do not believe it is the end of the quest. The profound extent of the words 'God is with us' can never be fully encompassed, and their exploration is located where theology crosses over into doxology. Let angel minds enquire afresh.

Bibliography

Aquinas, Thomas, *Summa contra Gentiles: On the Truth of the Catholic Faith*, book 4, trans. Charles J. O'Neil (Garden City, NY: Doubleday, 1957).

Aquinas, Thomas, *Summa theologiae*, Latin/English Edition of the Works of St Thomas Aquinas, vols. 13–20, trans. Laurence Shapcote, ed. John Mortensen and Enrique Alarcón (Lander, WY: Aquinas Institute for the Study of Sacred Doctrine, 2012).

Athanasius, *On the Incarnation of the Word*, trans. Archibald Robertson, www.newadvent.org/fathers/2802.htm.

Augustine, *The City of God*, trans. Henry Bettenson (London: Penguin, 1984).

Augustine, *On Christian Doctrine*, www.ccel.org/a/augustine/doctrine.

Augustine, *On the Trinity*, trans. Edmund Hill (Hyde Park, NY: New City Press, 1991).

Aulén, Gustav, *The Faith of the Christian Church*, trans. Eric H. Wahlstrom (Philadelphia: Fortress, 1960).

Baillie, D. M., *God Was in Christ: An Essay on Incarnation and Atonement* (London and Boston: Faber and Faber, 1986).

Balthasar, Hans Urs von, *A Theology of History* (New York: Sheed and Ward, 1963).

Barth, Karl, *Church Dogmatics*, vol. I/1, trans. G. W. Bromiley, ed. G. W. Bromiley and T. F. Torrance, 2nd ed. (Edinburgh: T & T Clark, 1975).

Barth, Karl, *Church Dogmatics*, vol. II/2, trans. G. W. Bromiley et al., ed. G. W. Bromiley and T. F. Torrance (Edinburgh: T & T Clark, 1957).

Barth, Karl, *Church Dogmatics*, vol. III/1, trans. J. W. Edwards, O. Bussey and H. Knight, ed. G. W. Bromiley and T. F. Torrance (Edinburgh: T & T Clark, 1958).

Barth, Karl, *Church Dogmatics*, vol. III/2, trans. H. Knight et al., ed. G. W. Bromiley and T. F. Torrance (Edinburgh: T & T Clark, 1960).

Barth, Karl, *Church Dogmatics*, vol. III/3, trans. G. W. Bromiley and R. J. Ehrlich, ed. G. W. Bromiley and T. F. Torrance (Edinburgh: T & T Clark, 1961).

Barth, Karl, *Church Dogmatics*, vol. IV/1, trans. G. W. Bromiley, ed. G. W. Bromiley and T. F. Torrance (Edinburgh: T & T Clark, 1956).

Barth, Karl, *Church Dogmatics*,vol. IV/2, trans. G. W. Bromiley, ed. G. W. Bromiley and T. F. Torrance (Edinburgh: T & T Clark, 1958).

Basil of Caesarea, *On the Holy Spirit*, trans. Blomfield Jackson, www.newadvent.org/fathers/3203.htm.

Behr, John, 'From Adam to Christ: From Male and Female to Being Human', in Thomas Arentzen, Ashley M. Purpura and Aristotle Papanikolaou, eds., *Orthodox Tradition and Human Sexuality* (New York: Fordham University Press, 2022), 303–19.

Bonaventure, *Doctoris Seraphici S. Bonaventurae opera omnia*, ed. PP. Collegii S. Bonaventurae, 10 vols. (Quaracchi: Collegium S. Bonaventurae, 1882–1902).

Bonaventure, 'Sermon II on the Nativity of the Lord', in *What Manner of Man? Sermons on Christ by St. Bonaventure*, 2nd ed., trans. Zachary Hayes (Chicago: Franciscan Herald, 1989).

Bonhoeffer, Dietrich, *Sanctorum communio: A Theological Study of the Sociology of the Church*, Dietrich Bonhoeffer Works, vol. 1, trans. Reinhard Krauss and Nancy Lukens (Minneapolis, MN: Fortress, 1998).

Bonnefoy, Jean-François, *Christ and the Cosmos* (Paterson, NJ: St Anthony Guild Press, 1965).

Brown, Joanne Carlson, 'Divine Child Abuse', *Daughters of Sarah*, 18/3 (1992), 24–28.

Brueggemann, Walter, *First and Second Samuel* (Louisville, KY: John Knox, 1990).

Brueggemann, Walter, *Old Testament Theology: An Introduction* (Nashville, TN: Abingdon, 2007).

Brueggemann, Walter, *Theology of the Old Testament: Testimony, Dispute, Advocacy* (Minneapolis, MN: Fortress, 1997).

Bulgakov, Sergei, *Du verbe incarné* (Paris: Aubier, 1933).

Bulgakov, Sergei, *Kupina Neopalimaya* (Paris: YMCA Press, 1927).

Calvin, John, *Institutes of the Christian Religion*, 2 vols., ed. John T. McNeill, trans. Ford Lewis Battles (Philadelphia: Westminster, 1960).

Carol, Juniper B., *Why Jesus Christ? Thomistic, Scotistic and Conciliary. Perspectives* (Manassas, VA: Trinity Communications, 1986).

Case, Brendan, '"More Splendid than the Sun": Christ's Flesh among the Reasons for the Incarnation', *Modern Theology*, 36/4 (2020), 758–77.

Clendenin, Daniel B., 'Partakers of Divinity: The Orthodox Doctrine of Theosis', *Journal of the Evangelical Theological Society*, 37/3 (September 1994), 365–79.

Collins, Paul M., *Partaking in the Divine Nature: Deification and Communion* (London: T & T Clark, 2010).

Cotter, Jim, *Prayer at Night: A Book for the Darkness*, 3rd ed. (Exeter: Cairns, 1986).

Cross, Richard, *Duns Scotus* (New York: Oxford University Press, 1999).

Daniélou, Jean, *Christ and Us*, trans. Walter Roberts (New York: Sheed and Ward, 1961).

Darwall, Stephen, 'Being With', *Southern Journal of Philosophy*, 49 (2011), 4–24.

Darwall, Stephen, *The Second-Person Standpoint: Morality, Respect and Accountability* (Cambridge, MA: Harvard University Press, 2006).

Davis, Ellen F., *Proverbs, Ecclesiastes and the Song of Songs* (Louisville, KY: Westminster John Knox, 2000).

Davis, Ellen F., 'Reading the Song Iconographically', *Journal of Scriptural Reasoning*, 3/2 (August 2003), https://jsr.shanti.virginia.edu/back-issues/vol-3-no-2-august-2003-healing-words-the-song-of-songs-and-the-path-of-love/reading-the-song-iconographically/.

Davis, Ellen F., *Scripture, Culture and Agriculture: An Agrarian Reading of the Bible* (Cambridge: Cambridge University Press, 2009).

Dean, Maximilian Mary, *A Primer on the Absolute Primacy of Christ* (New Bedford, MA: Academy of the Immaculate, 2006).

Delio, Ilia, 'Revisiting the Franciscan Doctrine of Christ', *Theological Studies*, 64/1 (2003), 3–23.

Dorner, I. A., *History of the Development of the Doctrine of the Person of Christ*, vol. 3, trans. Patrick Fairbairn (Edinburgh: T & T Clark, 1878).

Edwards, Denis, *Jesus, the Wisdom of God: An Ecological Theology* (Maryknoll, NY: Orbis, 1995).

Eklund, Rebekah A., 'Community', in Robert L. Brawley, ed., *The Oxford Encyclopedia of the Bible and Ethics*, vol. 1 (New York: Oxford University Press, 2014), 107–11.

Finlan, Stephen, *Problems with Atonement: The Origins of, and Controversy about, the Atonement Doctrine* (Collegeville, MN: Liturgical Press, 2005).

Florovsky, Georges, 'Cur Deus homo? The Motive of the Incarnation', in *Evharisterion: Hamilcar Alivisatos* (Athens, 1957), 70–79.

Fukuyama, Francis, *Identity: Contemporary Identity Politics and the Struggle for Recognition* (London: Profile, 2018).

Gregory of Nazianzus, Epistle 101, 'The First Letter to Cledonius the Priest against Apollinarius', www.newadvent.org/fathers/3103a.htm, trans. Charles Gordon Brownes and James Edward Swallow, Nicenes and Post-Nicene Fathers, ser. 2, vol. 7, ed. Philip Schaff and Henry. Wace (Buffalo, NY: Christian Literature Publishing Co., 1894), rev. and ed. Kevin Knight.

Grosseteste, Robert, *De cessatione legalium*, ed. Richard Dales and Edward King, Auctores Britannici Medii Aevi, 7 (London: Oxford University Press, 1986).

Hanson, Paul D., *The People Called: The Growth of Community in the Bible* (San Francisco: Harper and Row, 1986).

Hart, David Bentley, *The Beauty of the Infinite: The Aesthetics of Christian Truth* (Grand Rapids, MI: Eerdmans, 2003).

Hart, David Bentley, *The Doors of the Sea: Where Was God in the Tsunami?* (Grand Rapids, MI: Eerdmans, 2005).

Hauerwas, Stanley, *Approaching the End: Eschatological Reflections on Church, Politics, and Life* (Grand Rapids, MI: Eerdmans, 2013).

Hauerwas, Stanley, *Matthew* (Grand Rapids, MI: Brazos, 2006).

Hauerwas, Stanley, '"Salvation Even in Sin": Learning to Speak Truthfully about Ourselves', in *Sanctify Them in the Truth: Holiness Exemplified* (Edinburgh: T & T Clark, 1997), 61–74.

Haught, John, *God after Einstein: What's Really Going On in the Universe?* (New Haven, CT: Yale University Press, 2022).

Hayes, Zachary, *The Hidden Center: Spirituality and Speculative Christology in St. Bonaventure* (New York: Franciscan Institute, 1992).

Hays, Richard, *The Moral Vision of the New Testament: Community, Cross, New Creation: A Contemporary Introduction to New Testament Ethics* (San Francisco: Harper, 1996).

Herion, Gary, 'Covenant', in David Noel Freedman, ed., *Eerdmans Dictionary of the Bible*(Grand Rapids, MI: Eerdmans, 2000), 288–92.

Heschel, Abraham Joshua, *The Sabbath* (New York: Farrar, Straus and Giroux, 1951).

Hitchcock, Nathan, *Karl Barth and the Resurrection of the Flesh: The Loss of the Body in Participatory Eschatology* (Eugene, OR: Pickwick Publications, 2013).

Hochmuth, Marie, 'Kenneth Burke and the "New Rhetoric"', *Quarterly Journal of Speech*, 38/2 (1952), 133–44.

Horan, Daniel P., 'How Original Was Scotus on the Incarnation? Reconsidering the History of the Absolute Predestination of Christ in Light of Robert Grosseteste', *Heythrop Journal*, 52 (2011), 374–91.

Hunter, Justus H., *If Adam Had Not Sinned: The Reason for the Incarnation from Anselm to Scotus* (Washington, DC: Catholic University of America Press, 2020).

Ingham, Mary Beth, *Scotus for Dunces: An Introduction to the Subtle Doctor* (St Bonaventure, NY: Franciscan Institute, 2003).

Irenaeus, *Adversus haereses*, trans. Alexander Roberts and William Rambaut, www.newadvent.org/fathers/0103.htm.

Alexander Roberts and William Rambaut, 'Selections from the Work against Heresies by Irenaeus, Bishop of Lyons: "The Refutation and Overthrow of the Knowledge Falsely So Called"', in Cyril C. Richardson, ed., *Early Christian Fathers* (New York: Touchstone, 1996), 387–91.

Jasper, Ronald C. D., *George Bell: Bishop of Chichester* (London: Oxford University Press, 1967).

Jennings, Willie, *Acts: A Theological Commentary on the Bible* (Louisville, KY: Westminster John Knox, 2017).

Jenson, Robert, *God after God: The God of the Past and the God of the Future, Seen in the Work of Karl Barth* (Indianapolis: Bobbs-Merrill, 1969).

Jenson, Robert, *Systematic Theology*, vol. 1: *The Triune God* (New York: Oxford University Press, 1997).

Jenson, Robert, *Systematic Theology*, vol. 2: *The Works of God* (New York: Oxford University Press, 1999).

Johnson, Keith L., *The Essential Karl Barth: A Reader and Commentary* (Grand Rapids, MI: Baker, 2019).

Johnson, Luke Timothy, *The Acts of the Apostles* (Collegeville, MN: Liturgical Press, 1992).

Jüngel, Eberhard, *God as the Mystery of the World: On the Foundation of the Theology of the Crucified One in the Dispute between Theism and Atheism*, trans. Darrell L. Guder (Grand Rapids, MI: Eerdmans, 1983).

Jüngel, Eberhard, *God's Being Is in Becoming: The Trinitarian Being of God in the Theology of Karl Barth*, trans. John Webster (London: Bloomsbury, 2004).

Kabasilas, Nicolas, *The Life in Christ*, trans. C. J. De Catanzaro (Crestwood, NY: St Vladimir's Seminary Press, 1974).

Kung, Hans, *Justification: The Doctrine of Karl Barth and a Catholic Reflection* (Philadelphia: Westminster, 1964).

Lash, Nicholas, *Believing Three Ways in One God: A Reading of the Apostles' Creed* (Notre Dame, IN: University of Notre Dame Press, 1993).

Levenson, Jon D., 'The Universal Horizon of Biblical Particularism', in Mark G. Brett, ed., *The Bible and Ethnicity* (Leiden: E. J. Brill, 1996), 143–69.

Lohfink, Gerhard, *Jesus and Community: The Social Dimension of Christian Faith*, trans. John P. Galvin (Philadelphia: Fortress, 1984).

Lossky, Vladimir, *In the Image and Likeness of God* (Crestwood, NY: St Vladimir's Seminary Press, 1985).

Louth, Andrew, *Maximus the Confessor* (London: Routledge, 1996).

Louth, Andrew, 'The Place of Theosis in Orthodox Theology', in Michael J. Christensen and Jeffrey A. Wittung, eds., *Partakers of the Divine Nature: The History and Development of Deification in the Christian Traditions* (Cranbury, NJ: Associated University Press, 2007), 32–44.

Lovejoy, Arthur, *The Great Chain of Being: A Study of the History of an Idea* (Cambridge, MA: Harvard University Press, 1971).

Maddox, Randy L., 'John Wesley and Eastern Orthodoxy: Influences, Convergences and Differences', *Asbury Theological Journal*, 45/2 (1990), 29–53.

Maloney, George A., *The Cosmic Christ: From Paul to Teilhard* (New York: Sheed and Ward, 1968).

Martensen, Hans, *Christian Dogmatics: Compendium of the Doctrines of Christianity*, trans. William Urwick (Edinburgh: T & T Clark, 1898).

Mauser, Ulrich, 'Image of God and Incarnation', *Interpretation*, 24/3 (July 1970), 336–56.

Maximus the Confessor, *Questions to Thalassius*, in *On the Cosmic Mystery of Jesus Christ: Selected Writings from St Maximus the Confessor*, ed. Paul M. Blowers and Robert Louis Wilken (Crestwood, NY: St Vladimir's Seminary Press, 2003).

McCabe, Herbert, *What Is Ethics All About?* (Washington, DC, and Cleveland, OH: Corpus Books, 1969).

McCormack, Bruce L., *The Humility of the Eternal Son: 'Reformed' Kenoticism and the Repair of Chalcedon* (Cambridge and New York: Cambridge University Press, 2021).

McEvoy, James, *Robert Grosseteste* (Oxford: Oxford University Press, 2000).

McFarland, Ian A., *The Word Made Flesh: A Theology of the Incarnation* (Louisville, KY: Westminster John Knox Press, 2019).

Mehrabian, Albert, *Nonverbal Communication* (New Brunswick, NJ: Aldine Transaction, 1972).

Meilach, Michael D., *The Primacy of Christ in Doctrine and Life* (Chicago: Franciscan Herald Press, 1964).

Milbank, John, *Being Reconciled: Ontology and Pardon* (London and New York: Routledge, 2003).

Minns, Denis, *Irenaeus* (Washington, DC: Georgetown University Press, 1994).

Moberly, R. W. L., *Old Testament Theology: Reading the Hebrew Bible as Christian Scripture* (Grand Rapids, MI: Baker Academic, 2013).

Moltmann, Jürgen, *The Crucified God: The Cross of Christ as the Foundation and Criticism of Christian Theology*, trans. R. A. Wilson and John Bowden (London: SCM, 1974).

Moltmann, Jürgen, *The Trinity and the Kingdom: The Doctrine of God*, trans. Margaret Kohl (London: SCM, 1981).

Nellas, Panayiotis, *Deification in Christ: Orthodox Perspectives on the Nature of the Human Person*, trans. Norman Russell (Crestwood, NY: St Vladimir's Seminary Press, 1987).

Nikodemos of the Holy Mountain and St Makarios of Corinth, *The Philokalia: The Complete Text*, trans. G. E. H. Palmer, Philip Sherrard and Kallistos Ware (London: Faber and Faber, 1979–84).

O'Donovan, Oliver, *The Problem of Self-Love in St Augustine* (Eugene, OR: Wipf and Stock, 2006).

Origen, *On First Principles*, trans. C. Butterworth (New York: Harper Torchbooks, 1966).

Osborn, Eric, *Irenaeus of Lyons* (Cambridge: Cambridge University Press, 2001).

Otto, Rudolf, *The Idea of the Holy: An Inquiry into the Non-Rational Factor in the Idea of the Divine and Its Relation to the Rational*, trans. John W. Harvey (London: Oxford University Press, 1928).

Pancheri, Francis Xavier, *The Universal Primacy of Christ*, trans. and adapted by Juniper B. Carol (Front Royal, VA: Christendom Publications, 1984).

Pannenberg, Wolhart, *Systematic Theology*, vol. 2, trans. Geoffrey Bromiley (Grand Rapids, MI: Eerdmans, 1994).

Papanikolaou, Aristotle, 'Orthodoxy, Postmodernity, and Ecumenism: The Difference That Divine–Human Communion Makes', *Journal of Ecumenical Studies*, 42/4 (Fall 2007), 527–46.

Pattison, George, *A Short Course in Christian Doctrine* (London: SCM, 2005).

Pease, Allan and Barbara, 'The Definitive Book of Body Language', *New York Times*, 24 September 2006, www.nytimes.com/2006/09/24/books/chapters/0924-1st-peas.html.

Pohier, Jacques, *God – in Fragments*, trans. John Bowden (London: SCM, 1985).

Pomplun, Trent, 'The Immaculate World: Predestination and Passibility in Contemporary Scotism', *Modern Theology*, 30/4 (October 2014), 525–51.

Pseudo-Dionysius the Areopagite, *Divine Names*, trans. John Parker, www.tertullian.org/fathers/areopagite_03_divine_names.htm.

Pseudo-Dionysius the Areopagite, *Ecclesiastical Hierarchy*, trans. John Parker, www.tertullian.org/fathers/areopagite_14_ecclesiastical_hierarchy.htm.

Rabi'a, 'Oh My Lord', trans. Jane Hirshfield, Poetry Foundation, www.poetryfoundation.org/poems/55267/o-my-lord-56d236a947ec8 (accessed 12 March 2024).

Rahner, Karl, *Mary, Mother of the Lord: Theological Meditations*, trans. W. J. O'Hara (New York: Herder and Herder, 1964).

Rahner, Karl, *Theological Investigations*, vol. 5, trans. Karl-H. Kruger (Baltimore: Helicon, 1966).

Reid, Duncan, 'A Reading of Westcott's Gospel of Creation: An Early Venture into Ecological Theology?', *Journal of Anglican Studies*, 12/2 (November 2014), 185–202.

Robson, Michael, 'Saint Bonaventure', in G. R. Evans, ed., *The Medieval Theologians* (Oxford: Blackwell 2001), 187–200.

Rowe, C. Kavin, *Christianity's Surprise: A Sure and Certain Hope* (Nashville, TN: Abingdon, 2020).

Rupert of Deutz, De gloria et honore Filii hominis super Mattheum, Corpus Christianorum continuatio mediaevalis, 29 (Turnhout, Belgium: Brepols, 1971).

Schleiermacher, Friedrich, *The Christian Faith*, trans. Donald M. Baillie, ed H. R. Mackintosh and J. S. Stewart (Edinburgh: T & T Clark, 1999).

Schmauss, Michael, *Dogma*, vol. 1: *God in Revelation* (New York: Sheed and Ward, 1968).

Scotus, John Duns, *B. Ioannis Duns Scoti opera omnia*, vol. 9 (Civitas Vaticana: Typis Vaticanis, 2006).

Scotus, John Duns, *Four Questions on Mary*, trans. Allan B. Walter (St Bonaventure, NY: Franciscan Institute, 2000).

Soulen, R. Kendall, *The God of Israel and Christian Theology* (Minneapolis, MN: Fortress, 1996).

Tanner, Kathryn, *Christ the Key* (Cambridge: Cambridge University Press, 2010).

Tanner, Kathryn, *Jesus, Humanity and the Trinity: A Brief Systematic Theology* (Minneapolis, MN: Fortress, 2001).

TeSelle, Eugene, *Christ in Context: Divine Purpose and Human Possibility* (Philadelphia: Fortress, 1975).

Thunberg, Lars, *Man and the Cosmos: The Vision of St. Maximus the Confessor* (New York: St Vladimir's Seminary Press, 1985).

Thurman, Howard, *Jesus and the Disinherited* (Nashville, TN: Abingdon, 1949; repr. Boston: Beacon, 1996).

Tollefsen, Torstein, 'The Metaphysics of Maximus: Becoming One with God', in Daniel Haynes, ed., *A Saint for East and West: Maximus the Confessor's Contribution to Eastern and Western Christian Theology* (Eugene, OR: Cascade, 2019), 223–30.

Tollinton, R. B., *Clement of Alexandria*, vol. 2 (London: Williams and Norgate, 1914).

Torrance, T. F., *Atonement: The Person and Work of Christ* (Downers Grove, IL: IVP Academic, 2009).

Traherne, Thomas, *Centuries*, in *Selected Poems and Prose*, ed. Alan Bradford (London: Penguin, 1991).

Turner, Denys, *Julian of Norwich, Theologian* (New Haven, CT: Yale University Press, 2011).

Turner, Dominic, 'Robert Grosseteste, Bishop of Lincoln (1235–1253) on the Reasons for the Incarnation', *Franciscan Studies*, 16/1 (1956), 26–54.

Unger, Dominic J., 'The Love of God the Primary Reason for the Incarnation According to Isaac of Nineveh', *Franciscan Studies*, 9/2 (June 1949), 146–55.

van Driel, Edwin Chr., 'Climax of the Covenant vs Apocalyptic Invasion: A Theological Analysis of a Contemporary Debate in Pauline Exegesis', *International Journal of Systematic Theology*, 17/1 (January 2015), 6–25.

van Driel, Edwin Chr., 'God and God's Beloved: A Constructive Re-Reading of Scotus's Supralapsarian Christological Argument', *Heythrop Journal*, 63 (2022), 995–1006.

van Driel, Edwin Chr., 'Incarnation and Israel: A Supralapsarian Account of Israel's Chosenness', *Modern Theology*, 39/1 (January 2023), 3–18.

van Driel, Edwin Chr., *Incarnation Anyway: Arguments for Supralapsarian Theology* (New York: Oxford University Press, 2008).

van Driel, Edwin Chr., 'Sharing in Nature or Encountering a Person: A Tale of Two Different Supralapsarian Strategies', *Scottish Journal of Theology*, 75 (2022), 193–206,

van Driel, Edwin Chr., '"What Is Jesus Doing?" – Christological Thoughts for an Anxious Church and Tired Pastors', in Edwin Chr. van Driel, ed., *What Is Jesus Doing? God's Activity in the Life and Work of the Church* (Downers Grove, IL: IVP Academic, 2020), 1–23.

Van Engen, John H., *Rupert of Deutz* (Berkeley: University of California Press, 1983).

Wainwright, Geoffrey, *Doxology: The Praise of God in Worship, Doctrine and Life: A Systematic Theology* (New York: Oxford University Press, 1980).

Ware, Kallistos, *The Orthodox Way* (Oxford: Mowbray, 1979).

Weil, Simone, 'Reflections on the Right Use of School Studies with a View to the Love of God', 1942, www.christclassical.com/wp-content/uploads/2016/09/Right-Use-of-School-Studies-Simone-Weil.pdf.

Wells, Samuel, *A Cross in the Heart of God: Reflections on the Death of Jesus* (Norwich: Canterbury, 2020).

Wells, Samuel, *Hanging by a Thread: The Questions of the Cross* (Norwich: Canterbury, 2016).

Wells, Samuel, *How Then Shall We Live? Christian Engagement with Contemporary Issues* (Norwich: Canterbury, 2016); US ed. (New York: Church Publishing, 2017).

Wells, Samuel, *Humbler Faith, Bigger God: Finding a Faith to Live By* (Grand Rapids, MI: Eerdmans, and Norwich: Canterbury, 2022).

Wells, Samuel, *Incarnational Ministry: Being with the Church* (Grand Rapids, MI: Eerdmans, and Norwich: Canterbury, 2017).

Wells, Samuel, *Incarnational Mission: Being with the World* (Grand Rapids, MI: Eerdmans, and Norwich: Canterbury, 2018).

Wells, Samuel, *A Nazareth Manifesto: Being with God* (Oxford: Wiley-Blackwell, 2015).

Wells, Samuel, and Marcia A. Owen, *Living without Enemies: Being Present in the Midst of Violence* (Downers Grove, IL: IVP, 2011).

Wells, Samuel, Russell Rook and David Barclay, *For Good: The Church and the Future of Welfare* (Norwich: Canterbury, 2017).

Westcott, B. F., 'The Gospel of Creation', in *The Epistles of St John: The Greek Text with Notes and Essays*, 2nd ed. (London: Macmillan, 1886), 285–328.

Westminster Shorter Catechism, 1647, www.westminsterconfession.org/resources/confessional-standards/the-westminster-shorter-catechism.

White, Vernon, *Atonement and Incarnation: An Essay in Universalism and Particularity* (Cambridge: Cambridge University Press, 1991).

Williams, David, *Vinculum amoris: A Theology of the Holy Spirit* (Bloomington, IN: iUniverse, 2004).

Williams, Robert R., 'Sin and Evil', in Peter Hodgson and Robert King, eds., *Christian Theology: An Introduction to its Traditions and Tasks* (London: SPCK, 1982), 168–95.

Williams, Rowan, *On Christian Theology* (Oxford and Malden, MA: Blackwell, 2000).

Wirzba, Norman, *Agrarian Spirit: Cultivating Faith, Community and the Land* (Notre Dame, IN: University of Notre Dame Press, 2022).

Witt, William G., and Joel Scandrett, *Mapping Atonement: The Doctrine of Reconciliation in Christian History and Theology* (Grand Rapids, MI: Baker, 2022).

Wolter, Allan, 'John Duns Scotus on the Primacy and Personality of Christ', in Damian McElrath, ed., *Franciscan Christology: Selected Texts, Translations and Introductory Essays* (New York: Franciscan Institute of St Bonaventure, 1980), 139–82.

Wright, Christopher J. H., 'Ethics', in Willem A. VanGemeren, ed., *New International Dictionary of Old Testament Theology and Exegesis* (Grand Rapids, MI: Zondervan, 1997), 585–95.

Wright, Christopher J. H., *The Mission of God: Unlocking the Bible's Grand Narrative* (Downers Grove, IL: IVP Academic, 2006).

Wright, N. T., *Paul and the Righteousness of God* (London: SPCK, 2013).

Wyschogrod, Michael, *The Body of Faith: God in the People Israel* (Lanham, MD: Rowman and Littlefield, 1983).

Zaretsky, Robert, 'Simone Weil's Radical Conception of Attention'. *Literary Hub*, 9 March 2021, lithub.com/simone-weils-radical-conception-of-attention.

Zaretsky, Robert, *The Subversive Simone Weil: A Life in Five Ideas* (Chicago: University of Chicago Press, 2021).

Zizioulas, John D., *Being as Communion: Studies in Personhood and the Church* (Crestwood, NY: St Vladimir's Seminary Press, 1985).

Index

Page numbers in italics indicate references in footnotes.

Scripture Index

Notes:

• Codes are given as [Page number. Line number]

• References to the notes are given as [Page number. n Line number] where "n" indicates "Notes" and "Line Number" indicates the line number in the notes section on that page.

• Note that references to the notes in the subject index are in italics. You could alter the notation here so that it's consistent.

www.ingramcontent.com/pod-product-compliance
Ingram Content Group UK Ltd.
Pitfield, Milton Keynes, MK11 3LW, UK
UKHW031333260525
458877UK00001B/2

* 9 7 8 1 0 0 9 4 9 2 7 0 6 *